JEWISH FORCED LABOR
IN ROMANIA, 1940-1944

JEWISH FORCED LABOR IN ROMANIA, 1940–1944

Dallas Michelbacher

Indiana University Press

This book is a publication of

Indiana University Press
Office of Scholarly Publishing
Herman B Wells Library 350
1320 East 10th Street
Bloomington, Indiana 47405 USA

iupress.indiana.edu

© 2020 by Dallas Michelbacher

All rights reserved
No part of this book may be reproduced or utilized in any form or by any means, electronic or mechanical, including photocopying and recording, or by any information storage and retrieval system, without permission in writing from the publisher. The paper used in this publication meets the minimum requirements of the American National Standard for Information Sciences—Permanence of Paper for Printed Library Materials, ANSI Z39.48-1992.

Manufactured in the United States of America

Library of Congress Cataloging-in-Publication Data

Names: Michelbacher, Dallas, author.
Title: Jewish forced labor in Romania, 1940-1944 / Dallas Michelbacher.
Description: Bloomington, Indiana : Indiana University Press, [2020] | Includes bibliographical references and index.
Identifiers: LCCN 2019052306 (print) | LCCN 2019052307 (ebook) | ISBN 9780253047380 (hardback) | ISBN 9780253047434 (paperback) | ISBN 9780253047458 (ebook)
Subjects: LCSH: Forced labor—Romania—History—20th century. | Jews—Romania—History—20th century. | World War, 1939-1945—Jews—Romania.
Classification: LCC HD4875.R6 M53 2020 (print) | LCC HD4875.R6 (ebook) | DDC 940.53/1813409498—dc23
LC record available at https://lccn.loc.gov/2019052306
LC ebook record available at https://lccn.loc.gov/2019052307

1 2 3 4 5   26 24 23 22 21 20

For my parents, Leonard and Kathie

Contents

	Acknowledgments	ix
	Introduction	1
1	"Work in the Community Interest"	11
2	Trial and Error	26
3	The "Review of the Working Jews"	58
4	In the Shadow of Belzec	75
5	The Apogee	100
6	Travails Ended, Justice Averted	133
	Conclusion	151
	Bibliography	157
	Index	161

Acknowledgments

I owe debts of gratitude to several people and organizations for this book. First, I would like to thank my mentor, Eric A. Johnson, for his guidance during my research, as well as Doina Harsanyi, Tim O'Neil, Joachim von Puttkamer, and Vladimir Solonari, who provided important feedback on my work. I also wish to express my appreciation to the Conference on Jewish Material Claims against Nazi Germany, which provided funding that was essential for the completion of this project. I also must thank the reference staff of the United States Holocaust Memorial Museum for its assistance in my research process. In addition, I would like to thank Steve Feldman for his assistance with the publication process. And last, but certainly not least, I would like to thank my parents, Leonard and Kathie, and my wife, Michelle, for their invaluable support at every stage of this project.

JEWISH FORCED LABOR
IN ROMANIA, 1940-1944

Introduction

"Everybody was—the wives, the mothers [were] crying," William Farkas recalled of the day in the summer of 1941 when he was called up for work in a labor battalion. "'What will happen with my husband? What will happen with my child? What with . . .' or something like this. So everybody was crying, crying. [It] was a terrible situation." Farkas was sent to work on a railway tunnel in the Carpathian Mountains more than three hundred kilometers from his home. The work was very dangerous, with untrained men using dynamite to blast through the rocky terrain. "My best friend [died] there," Farkas remembered, "because when [the dynamite] was exploding . . . one rock [hit him] in his head, and he [died] immediately there. One of my best friends, he [died] there, yes."[1]

Between August 1941 and August 1944, more than seventy-five thousand Romanian Jews like William Farkas were conscripted into forced labor by the Romanian military. Most worked in labor camps and detachments on projects related to the war effort, including construction and repair of roads, railroads, fortifications, and waterways; mining and quarrying; and agriculture. Others worked on jobs of local significance, such as repairing government buildings and city streets. During the winter, they were assigned to menial tasks like clearing snow from streets and railroad tracks. Jews with academic qualifications or specialized skills were "requisitioned" for use in private businesses and industry. The forced labor system was both poorly managed, leading to tragedies like the death of Farkas's friend, and rife with corruption. Those who could pay the requisite bribes could purchase an "exemption" from forced labor that allowed them to continue working in their regular jobs. Despite several reorganizations of the system and revisions of the regulations on the use of forced labor, problems such as poor management and supervision of workers; inadequate housing, food, and medical supplies; laborers' inaptitude for the tasks they were asked to perform; and rampant corruption were never solved, leading to frustration for the military and civilian leadership and hardship for the Jewish laborers. Nonetheless, forced labor continued until Ion Antonescu's government collapsed and the new government invalidated his regime's antisemitic legislation.

The historical literature on forced labor in Romania is not well developed. However, there is a much larger body of research on forced labor in Nazi Germany and Hungary. In the popular imagination, Jewish forced labor is often associated with the idea of "extermination through labor," mitigated only by heroic figures like Oskar Schindler, who used forced labor as a ruse to rescue Jews. However, recent works, particularly those on Germany, have challenged the rather simplistic paradigm of extermination through labor and provided a more nuanced analysis of forced labor that reflects the complicated economic and political considerations that determined its course. This improved analytical framework better describes the decision-making process regarding the use of Jewish labor and its role in the progression from legal persecution to mass murder and enables a more complete understanding of how forced labor fits within the broader narrative of the Holocaust.

As Wolf Gruner notes in his seminal work on Jewish forced labor in Nazi Germany, many early historians of the Holocaust treated forced labor as an intermediate step between early discriminatory measures and the Final Solution to the Jewish Question (the Nazi euphemism for the extermination of the Jews of Europe) or simply as an early stage of the extermination process. He argues, however, that forced labor was a separate component of Nazi policy that originated independently from the Final Solution, observing that Jews began to be used as forced laborers prior to the start of the Second World War. The first form of Jewish forced labor, which began in 1938, was what Gruner termed the "segregated labor deployment" system (*geschlossene Arbeitseinsatz*), in which Jews—initially only those who were unemployed or on public assistance but later most Jewish men—were recruited into labor units to perform work such as street cleaning, construction, and harvesting crops. By April 1939, twenty thousand Jews were working in this system, and at its peak, in the spring of 1941, it employed more than fifty thousand men.[2]

After the Second World War began, Germany faced substantial labor shortages. Even as early as 1938, the recovery of the German economy had begun to tighten the labor market, and the mobilization of large numbers of men for war led to a widespread lack of manpower in important industries. German leaders responsible for economic affairs, such as Hermann Göring, saw the Jews of Germany and the occupied territories as an ideal source of cheap labor.[3] In occupied Poland, both the Reich Labor Office and the SS established labor camps for Jews, while thousands more were recruited to work in war-related industrial concerns operated by the Wehrmacht. These policies were based on both the desire to force Jews left unemployed by discriminatory legislation to contribute to the economy and to fill the ever-increasing need for labor to fuel the German war machine. Gruner argues that, as a result, forced labor was a "key element" in Nazi Jewish policy from 1939 onward, rather than an interim solution.[4]

However, as Christopher Browning has noted, there was no general consensus among the Nazi leadership regarding Jewish forced labor despite the economic utility it provided. In fact, he argues, some within the Nazi bureaucracy, foremost among them Heinrich Himmler, were outright hostile to the idea of widespread exploitation of Jewish labor, fearing that it would impede the Final Solution.[5] While some administrators in occupied Poland—such as Friedrich-Wilhelm Krüger, the higher SS and police leader in the General Government—recognized the irrationality of simply deporting the Jews without exploiting their labor fully, officials in Berlin, like Reinhard Heydrich, saw forced labor as an opportunity for employers to protect Jews from deportation by claiming that they were of vital economic importance. Although Himmler allowed some Jewish concentration camp prisoners to be used as laborers for the Wehrmacht, Browning argues that this was a temporary concession designed to placate the Wehrmacht rather than a long-term strategic plan.[6]

Because of the primacy given to the extermination process after the Final Solution began, German officials had only limited leeway to carry out policies they viewed as rational, such as the use of Jewish laborers who were slated for deportation. Ulrich Herbert frames the balancing act between economic needs and racial policy as a "search for compromises that could reconcile long-term perspectives and short-term demands in keeping with the current military and political situation."[7] Browning concluded that the German authorities acted rationally at times regarding Jewish labor but that such rational decision-making was only permissible within the limits of the extermination process. However, as he notes, these temporary reprieves were the difference between life and death for many Jews.[8]

In Hungary, by contrast, forced labor was directly connected to the military from its inception. The Hungarian labor service was implemented in 1938 by Law No. II, which declared that all Hungarians twenty-one or older who were deemed "unfit" for military service could be conscripted into "public labor service" (*közérdekű munkaszolgálat*) for periods of no more than three months. Jews were considered inherently "unreliable" for military service due to the popular association of Jews with Soviet communism by antisemitic politicians (a belief that was also common in Romania at the time). In his groundbreaking work on the Hungarian labor service system, Randolph Braham observed that while the intent and scope of forced labor in Hungary was not immediately apparent, the "public labor service" facilitated the exclusion of political enemies and ethnic minorities from the military, as part of a larger push to remove Jews from the social and economic life of the country.[9] In the Hungarian system, Jews were conscripted into labor battalions through army recruitment centers and worked under the jurisdiction of army corps commanders. They were used as manual laborers, building roads, harvesting crops, and clearing forests, as well as in military-related industries. Initially, Jews worked alongside other Hungarians in the labor detachments and did not face serious discrimination, as they received the same pay, food, and housing as the other laborers and were allowed to wear military uniforms.[10]

However, after Hungary entered the war in 1941, the character of Jewish forced labor changed dramatically. When the Hungarian Second Army was deployed to the eastern front in 1942, large numbers of Jewish laborers—estimates range from thirty-nine thousand to as many as fifty thousand—were sent along with them. By this time, the laborers had been stripped of many of their rights, including their military uniforms. They performed the most dangerous tasks, including digging trenches and clearing minefields, as well as other backbreaking jobs such as building roads and man-hauling goods in order to spare the horses. Others were sent to hard and hazardous labor in the copper mines at Bor, in the Hungarian-occupied portion of Serbia. In January 1943, the Red Army launched Operation Little Saturn, following up on its devastating counterattack at Stalingrad. During this offensive, the Hungarian Second Army was encircled at Ostrogozhsk and almost completely destroyed. Thousands of Jewish laborers were abandoned to die in the Russian winter or were murdered by the retreating Hungarian troops. Robert Rozett estimates that at least thirty-three thousand Hungarian Jewish laborers died on the eastern front, although the true number could have been higher.[11]

Somewhat paradoxically, after Germany occupied Hungary in March 1944 and the deportation of Hungarian Jews to Auschwitz began, the labor service system became a "refuge for thousands of Hungarian Jewish men threatened with deportation and almost certain extermination."[12] After the Arrow Cross regime took power in October of that year, thousands of laborers who had escaped deportation to Auschwitz were instead sent to Germany to work, where many of them perished in concentration camps such as Mauthausen. In light of the deliberate murder or abandonment of so many Jewish laborers on the eastern front, Rozett argues that in Hungary, forced labor was a means for solving the "Jewish question."[13] Braham agrees, remarking that forced labor was "used primarily as one of the components of the Hungarian 'solution to the Jewish question'" and that deaths of the laborers were the purpose of Hungarian policy rather than a side effect.[14]

The lack of a detailed study of the Romanian forced labor system deprives the field of another valuable point of comparison. To understand how the forced labor system in Romania fits within the larger phenomenon of Jewish forced labor during the Holocaust in Europe, it is necessary to understand why forced labor was introduced in Romania, how it was organized, what its role was within the Antonescu regime's Jewish policy, and how it was connected to the "solution to the Jewish question" in Romania. These questions cannot be divorced from their Romanian context, and they must be viewed with an eye to the historical debates on the Holocaust in Romania as well.

The persecution of the Jews in Romania was uneven and Antonescu's statements and actions were often contradictory. While Romania was responsible for the deaths of more Jews than any country other than Nazi Germany—between 250,000 and 350,000 according to the Wiesel Commission report on the Holocaust in Romania—the vast majority of Jews within the prewar borders of Romania survived. Antonescu initially consented to Romania's participation in the Nazi Final Solution in the summer of 1942, but he later reneged and refused repeated German entreaties to reconsider. Because Romania was never under direct German occupation, Antonescu was able to take an independent line in his Jewish policy (albeit under heavy German influence), and the idiosyncratic nature of his policies has produced a variety of historical interpretations.

Scholars have generally viewed Antonescu's attitudes toward the Jews and the policies his government pursued prior to Romania's entry into the Second World War as a continuation of those of previous antisemitic politicians and governments. As Jean Ancel noted, Antonescu's policies were heavily influenced by his predecessors, including the former prime minister Octavian Goga and Goga's partner in government, Alexandru C. Cuza. Some of the writings of Cuza and other antisemitic intellectuals of his time found their way almost verbatim into Antonescu's antisemitic laws.[15] However, unlike previous regimes, Antonescu was not constrained by the monarch or democratic political processes and was able to implement his antisemitic policies at will. At the heart of Antonescu's prewar Jewish policy was a program known as "Romanianization" (*românizare*), the goal of which was to remove Jews from Romania's social and economic life and replace them with non-Jewish Romanians. This process relied on policies including the expropriation of Jewish property and businesses, the expulsion of Jews from the civil service, and the exclusion of Jews from the workforce and the military. Radu Ioanid summed up the nature of Romanianization succinctly, describing it as the "economic expression of state antisemitism."[16] The endgame of Romanianization was the complete physical removal of Jews from Romania, although the means for achieving this goal were still not precisely defined.[17]

In the spring of 1941, as war with the Soviet Union became imminent, Antonescu's ideas and plans relating to the Jewish question became more radical. Ancel attributes this radicalization to the increasing influence of Nazi Germany over Romanian policy and Antonescu's desire to maintain his good image with Hitler. He argues that this radical turn "made it possible for [Antonescu's government] to adopt the Nazi Final Solution and actively participate in its implementation."[18] Hildrun Glass has supported this interpretation, noting that ascendant German influence—economic, political, and military—in southeastern Europe enabled the practice of Nazi-style antisemitism in Romania.[19] On the eve of the Axis invasion of the Soviet Union, Antonescu ordered the Romanian forces to "cleanse the land" in the territories they occupied. Tens of thousands of Jews were massacred by the Romanian soldiers, gendarmes, and police in the opening weeks of the war. In the following months, tens of thousands more were deported to the Transnistria Governorate—the part of Ukraine between the Dniester and Bug Rivers which was occupied by Romania—where they were left in an "ethnic dumping ground" along with local Ukrainian Jews. Hundreds of thousands of local Ukrainian Jews and deported Romanian Jews died in Transnistria as a result of massacres, starvation, and disease.[20]

Ancel argues that Antonescu had a concrete plan to deport the Jews living within the prewar borders of Romania as early as the fall of 1941.[21] However, other historians have disputed the existence of such a plan. Vladimir Solonari, for example, notes that the idea of an escalating grand plan conflicts with the situation on the ground in Transnistria, where the worst incidents of violence occurred in the winter of 1941–1942 and de-escalated after the spring of 1942.[22] Armin Heinen argues that the weakness of Antonescu's control in Bessarabia, Bukovina, and Transnistria and the disorganization of the Romanian administration precludes the idea that Romania was carrying out a "systematic extermination" of the Jews analogous to that which was being perpetrated by Nazi Germany.[23] Nonetheless, the broad contours of Antonescu's Jewish policy at that point in the war were clear: the Jews were to be systematically robbed and excluded from the economy through legislation, and later removed from the country, even if the means for the latter had not yet been planned in detail.

The turning point in the Holocaust in Romania was Antonescu's decision in the fall of 1942 to reject the German plans for the Final Solution in Romania, preventing the deportation of the Jews living within the prewar borders of Romania. Negotiations between the Germans and the Romanians regarding Romanian participation in the Final Solution began shortly after it was codified at the Wannsee Conference in January 1942. The primary German representative in Bucharest was SS-Hauptsturmführer Gustav Richter, who met directly with both Antonescu and his deputy prime minister, Mihai Antonescu. In July 1942, Richter believed he had secured Ion Antonescu's agreement to deport the Jews living within the prewar borders of Romania (the Old Kingdom and southern Transylvania) to the Belzec extermination camp in occupied Poland. However, the established starting date for the deportations came and passed without event, and in October 1942, Mihai Antonescu informed Richter that Ion Antonescu had decided not to deport Romania's Jews.[24]

After the fall of 1942, Antonescu's Jewish policy underwent what Jean Ancel termed a "sea change," and its focus shifted from removal by deportation and extermination to removal via emigration to Palestine (a change that, due to the logistical and political difficulty of moving people to Palestine under wartime conditions, virtually guaranteed the continued presence of Jews in Romania in the short term).[25] Paradoxically, Romania's Jewish policy de-escalated while the Nazi Final Solution was at its peak. However, discriminatory policies such as forced labor and extensive financial levies against the Jewish community continued until Antonescu's government collapsed in August 1944.[26] The end result of the decision not to deport the remaining Jews in Romania was a geographic divide between the Jewish populations of the territories of Bessarabia, Bukovina, and Transnistria, which were largely destroyed, and the Jewish population of the Old Kingdom and southern Transylvania, which remained mostly intact.

Historians have not written extensively on the role forced labor played within the Antonescu regime's Jewish policy. Ioanid described it as a "key component of the fascists' antisemitic legislation."[27] Ancel viewed forced labor as a continuation of Romanianization policies focused on excluding Jews from the Romanian workforce. He argued that it "satisfied the ideological side of Romanianization" by providing a way for Jews who had been removed from their jobs to contribute to the Romanian economy but that it could not break Romania's need for skilled Jewish laborers and professionals. However, Ancel considered forced labor mainly a means to humiliate the Jews and extort money from them rather than a rational policy designed to obtain an economic benefit from Jewish labor.[28]

More recent scholarship by Romanian historians, including Ana Bărbulescu and Mihai Chioveanu, has challenged this interpretation. Bărbulescu has argued that forced labor was intended to confer at least some economic benefit and that Antonescu and the military leadership had both ideological and economic motivations for the introduction of forced labor.[29] Mihai Chioveanu agreed, noting that the Romanians were not "totally indifferent" to the idea of increasing efficiency and rationalizing the forced labor system while continuing to pursue the larger ideological objective of "ethnic purification" of Romanian society through the exclusion of Jews from economic and public life.[30] He also argues that forced labor in Romania was neither as violent nor as extensive as it was in other countries, such as Nazi Germany, noting that "in the Romanian case, one cannot speak of the existence of 'slave masters,'" primarily due to the corruption that allowed many Jews to escape forced labor but also because, in most cases, the Romanian perpetrators were not directly trying to kill the Jewish laborers. He noted that while thousands were killed or injured during forced labor because of the "inhumane conditions," it could not be considered mass murder—suggesting that the paradigm of extermination through labor is not applicable to the Romanian case.[31]

The lack of detailed documentation and analysis of the forced labor system is a significant gap in the literature on the Holocaust in Romania. It leaves one of the major facets of the Antonescu regime's persecution of the Jews largely unexplored and its place within Romania's larger antisemitic program unexplained. To understand the role of forced labor within Antonescu's Jewish policy, it is necessary to examine his purpose for introducing forced labor, how his government balanced economic needs and racial ideology in policy decisions related to forced labor, how the organization of the forced labor system developed and changed, why forced labor failed to deliver the anticipated results, and how Antonescu's approach to the Final Solution affected forced labor. The answers to these questions in turn inform the larger historiographic debates on the underlying rationale of Antonescu's Jewish policy and its evolution during the war. In addition to answering these questions, it is vital to document the experiences of the Jewish laborers themselves. Forced labor affected almost a quarter of the Jews living in the Romanian Old Kingdom and southern Transylvania during the Antonescu era, and including these voices is essential to creating a complete historical narrative of the Holocaust in Romania.

The source base for this work consists of both official documentation and published and oral testimony from survivors of forced labor. The relatively small number of available survivor testimonies means that this work must rely heavily on official documents, primarily those produced by or sent to the Supreme General Staff (usually referred to as the General Staff) of the Romanian army, as well as reports from labor camp and detachment commanders and inspectors, transcripts of the meetings of the Council of Ministers and other governmental bodies, and the writings and memoirs of government officials. The availability and quality of reports from individual labor detachments varied over time. In June 1942, the General Staff introduced requirements for detachment commanders to keep more detailed records; however, before that time, records from the detachments are inconsistent, and the earlier chapters of this book are forced to rely more heavily on documents created by the General Staff and Supreme General Headquarters.

These perpetrator sources cannot, of course, be taken verbatim. Reports from the top levels of command often blamed problems on detachment commanders and other lower-level officials, while detachment commanders often protested that their hands were tied by poor logistics and lack of support from higher ranks. Both also tended to blame the workers for low productivity while tacitly (and occasionally explicitly) acknowledging the institutional failings of the forced labor system. Where possible, perpetrator sources have been corroborated or disputed through witness testimony, particularly in the case of reports about conditions in the labor camps and detachments and the deaths of laborers. Where sources conflict, precedence is given to the statements of Jewish witnesses in order to amplify Jewish voices above those of the perpetrators and provide a balanced picture of the forced labor system.

Notes

1. Interview with William Farkas, United States Holocaust Memorial Museum Archives (USHMMA), RG-50.030*0026, USHMM Oral History Collection.
2. Wolf Gruner, *Jewish Forced Labor under the Nazis: Economic Needs and Racial Aims, 1938-1944* (Cambridge: Cambridge University Press, 2006), xiv-xvii.
3. Dieter Maier, *Arbeitseinsatz und Deportation: Die Mitwirkung der Arbeitsverwaltung bei der nationalsozialistischen Judenverfolgung in den Jahren 1938-1945* (Berlin: Edition Hentrich, 1994), 19-23.
4. Gruner, *Jewish Forced Labor*, 277.
5. Christopher Browning, *Nazi Policy, Jewish Workers, German Killers* (Cambridge: Cambridge University Press, 2000), 59.
6. Ibid., 80.
7. Ulrich Herbert, *Hitler's Foreign Workers: Enforced Labor in Germany under the Third Reich* (Cambridge: Cambridge University Press, 1997), 137.
8. Browning, *Nazi Policy*, 59-60.
9. Randolph Braham, *The Hungarian Labor Service System, 1939-1945* (Boulder, CO: Eastern European Monographs, 1977), 5.
10. Ibid., 10-11.
11. Robert Rozett, *Conscripted Slaves: Hungarian Jewish Forced Laborers on the Eastern Front during the Second World War* (Jerusalem: Yad Vashem, 2013), 60-62.
12. Braham, *Hungarian Labor Service System*, ix.
13. Rozett, *Conscripted Slaves*, 15.
14. Braham, *Hungarian Labor Service System*, vii.
15. Jean Ancel, *The Economic Destruction of Romanian Jewry* (Jerusalem: Yad Vashem, 2007), 13.
16. Radu Ioanid, *The Holocaust in Romania: The Destruction of the Jews and Gypsies under the Antonescu Regime, 1940-1944* (Chicago: Ivan R. Dee, 2000), 24.
17. Jean Ancel, *The History of the Holocaust in Romania* (Jerusalem: Yad Vashem, 2011), 181.
18. Ibid., 204.
19. Hildrun Glass, *Deutschland und die Verfolgung der Juden im rumänischen Machtbereich 1940-1944* (Munich: R. Oldenbourg, 2014), 18.
20. Mihai Chioveanu, "Death Delivered, Death Postponed: Romania and the Continent-Wide Holocaust," *Studia Hebraica* 8 (2008): 151.
21. Ancel, *History of the Holocaust in Romania*, 2.
22. Vladimir Solonari, "A Conspiracy to Murder: Explaining the Dynamics of Romanian 'Policy' toward Jews in Transnistria," *Journal of Genocide Research* 19, no. 1 (2017): 3.
23. Armin Heinen, *Rumänien, der Holocaust und die Logik der Gewalt* (Munich: R. Oldenbourg, 2007), 95.
24. Ancel, *History of the Holocaust in Romania*, 484.
25. Ibid., 508.
26. Lya Benjamin, "Politica antievreiască a regimului Antonescu 1940-1944 (Cu referire la evreii din Vechiul Regat și sudul Transilvaniei)," *Holocaust: Studii și cercetări* 2, no. 1/3 (2010): 28.
27. Ioanid, *Holocaust in Romania*, 26.

28. Ancel, *Economic Destruction*, 166.

29. Ana Bărbulescu, "Muncă obligatorie în România anului 1941: Ideologie vs. randament economic," *Holocaust: Studii și cercetări* 1, no. 2 (2009): 59–70.

30. Mihai Chioveanu, "Muncă forțata în holocaustul din România," *Sfera Politicii* 20, no. 5 (2012): 91.

31. Ibid., 90.

1 "Work in the Community Interest"

Ion Antonescu's government introduced forced labor for Romanian Jews on December 5, 1940, through the Law on the Military Status of the Jews, which barred Jews from serving in the armed forces and replaced their compulsory military service with a requirement to perform "work in the community interest" (*muncă în folos obștesc*). This law was part of a succession of antisemitic legislation that was designed to remove Jews from every facet of the Romanian economy and public life and replace them with non-Jewish Romanians. This process, known as Romanianization, was the culmination of several decades of antisemitic politics that preceded Antonescu's dictatorship. Romanianization was the central focus of Antonescu's Jewish policy prior to Romania's entry into the Second World War.

Forced labor had an important role in Romanianization as a solution to the problems created by the exclusion of Jews from the labor force and the military. Jews who had been removed from their jobs would no longer be able to make an economic contribution to the state by paying taxes, and the prohibition on Jewish military service prevented them from directly participating in a potential future war (which, by late 1940, seemed increasingly likely). By performing forced labor, Jews could provide economic utility to Romanian state institutions and businesses and support any war effort by working on projects of military importance, such as improving Romania's road and railway network or building fortifications and other defensive works. Forced labor thus met both the ideological requirements of Romanianization and the needs of the Romanian economy and military, making it a logical extension of Antonescu's Romanianization program.

The concept of Romanianization did not originate with Antonescu, nor were his anti-Jewish policies sui generis. Antisemitism rooted in economic resentment had a long history in Romania prior to his accession to power. Laws excluding Jews from certain parts of the Romanian economy had existed even before Romania formally gained independence in 1878; for example, an 1874 law prohibited Jews from serving as chief doctors in Romanian hospitals.[1] However, it was not until after the First World War that the conception of Romanianization as it was later implemented by Antonescu began to take shape. One of the main promoters of antisemitic legislation during the early twentieth century was Alexandru C. Cuza, a jurist and professor from Iași, a city in the historic region of

Moldavia that had a large Jewish population (more than one-third of the city's population, as of the 1930 census). In 1922, Cuza founded an antisemitic political party, the National Christian Union, which was renamed the National Christian Defense League the following year. The league's platform called for the exclusion of Jews from the Romanian economy, followed by their physical removal from the country. To remedy alleged Jewish "domination" of Romanian society, Cuza proposed to restrict Jewish representation in industry, business, education, and government to Jews' proportion of the national population—around 4 percent in 1930—which he referred to as the "principle of proportionality."[2]

In 1927, Corneliu Zelea Codreanu, the leader of the party's student wing, split with Cuza and founded the ultranationalistic and antisemitic Legion of the Archangel Michael, later known as the Iron Guard (after the name of its paramilitary wing).[3] The Iron Guard gained notoriety through acts of antisemitic and political violence, including the assassination of Prime Minister Ion Duca—who had attempted to suppress the Iron Guard—on December 29, 1933.[4] Fear of Iron Guard violence and a potential revolt was omnipresent in Romanian politics during the 1930s, and the organization was one of King Carol II's primary domestic policy concerns.

The National Christian Defense League remained a marginal political force and never entered into government as an independent party. However, by the early 1930s, the ideology of Romanianization had begun to make inroads with the mainstream democratic parties, and both of the major political parties of the interwar period—the National Liberal Party and the National Peasant Party—made attempts at excluding Jews from the Romanian economy. Iuliu Maniu's National Peasant government passed legislation to restrict minority participation in the workforce in 1930. A similar law, known as the Law for the Use of Romanian Personnel in Enterprises, was passed by Gheorghe Tătărescu's National Liberal government in 1934. The 1934 law required that ethnic minorities comprise no more than 20 percent of the workforce of any firm. However, both of these measures failed, primarily because business owners were uninterested in terminating their Jewish employees and replacing them with unknown and potentially less qualified workers. Less than 1 percent of the labor force was Romanianized under the 1934 law.[5] A third law, passed by the Tătărescu government in 1937, required factories seeking military contracts to have a payroll that was at least 95 percent ethnic Romanian. This law failed for similar reasons as the previous two. Wilhelm Filderman, president of the country's largest Jewish organization, the Union of Romanian Jews, derided the 1937 law as "the country cutting off its nose to spite its face" because of the harm it would have caused to the Romanian economy.[6]

In 1935, the National Christian Defense League merged with the right-wing National Agrarian Party, led by the poet Octavian Goga, to form the National

Christian Party. The new party combined Goga's agrarian ideology with Cuza's antisemitism and Romanianization policies.[7] The first election the National Christian Party contested, in December 1937, was a decisive one for the future of Romanian politics and the Romanian Jews. The National Christian Party achieved only modest success, finishing in fourth place with just over 9 percent of the vote and winning thirty-nine seats. However, for the first time since Romania's independence, the party the king had chosen to form the government, the National Liberals, failed to win a majority of the votes or even achieve the 40 percent threshold that would have granted it a parliamentary majority under the constitution. In the past, the party chosen by the king had always managed to secure itself a strong majority because it controlled the conduct of the elections through the county prefects, which it appointed.[8]

The shock result in the 1937 election was largely due to an alliance between the National Peasant Party and the Iron Guard's All for the Fatherland Party, which finished as the second and third parties, respectively, and won a total of 152 seats, equal to the number won by the National Liberals.[9] Because no party had obtained a sufficient mandate, the king was entitled to select a new prime minister to form a government. Carol feared the ascendant Iron Guard, but he was unwilling to reward the cynical strategy of the National Peasants (whose leader, Maniu, he personally disliked) and was dissatisfied with Dinu Brătianu's National Liberals. Thus, he chose Goga and the National Christian Party to lead the new cabinet. On December 28, Goga was proclaimed prime minister.[10]

The Goga-Cuza government, as it is often known, remained in power for only forty-four days, but during that time it introduced a radical measure—the Law for the Review of Jewish Citizenship—which resulted in the denaturalization of almost one-third of the country's Jewish population.[11] However, the new government's plans for additional antisemitic legislation, including a new law for the Romanianization of labor, did not come to fruition. While Nazi Germany had approved of the ascent of the Goga-Cuza government, the Western Allies strongly opposed its behavior toward the Jews and made their displeasure known to Carol.[12] On February 10, the king dismissed Goga and suspended constitutional rule. Romanian Orthodox patriarch Miron Cristea was named prime minister and a new constitution that granted Carol immense power and created what was effectively a royal dictatorship was announced on February 20. It was ratified eight days later in a sham referendum in which over 99 percent of the electorate allegedly voted in its favor.[13] During the following months, Carol moved against his primary domestic enemy, the Iron Guard, imprisoning a number of its leaders. Many of them, including Codreanu, were shot by gendarmes on the night of November 29–30, 1938. In retaliation, members of the Iron Guard assassinated Cristea's successor as prime minister, Armand Călinescu, on September

21, 1939. The domestic stability Carol had sought to create by concentrating political power in his own hands proved illusory.[14]

However, the primary agent in Carol's downfall and Antonescu's rise to power was the deteriorating situation outside Romania's borders, not the political tensions within them. The Munich Agreement of September 30, 1938, concerned Carol, who feared German expansionism in eastern Europe and doubted the feasibility of maintaining Romania's territorial integrity against its irredentist neighbors, Hungary, Bulgaria, and the Soviet Union. The policy of appeasement embraced by the Western Allies diminished Carol's confidence in France and Britain as potential guarantors of Romanian sovereignty. The Molotov-Ribbentrop Pact of August 1939 was an even more devastating blow. One of the secret provisions of the pact was German recognition of the Soviet Union's territorial "interests" in Bessarabia and an understanding that Germany would not intervene militarily to oppose Soviet actions to recover this territory from Romania. On June 26, 1940, the Soviet Union presented Romania with an ultimatum to withdraw from Bessarabia and northern Bukovina (the latter of which had not been included in the terms of the pact) within forty-eight hours or face an invasion. Carol was initially hesitant to comply with such odious demands and attempted to negotiate with the Soviets; however, a second ultimatum forced his hand, and he ordered the withdrawal of Romanian troops and the evacuation of civilians from the two territories on June 30.[15]

After the loss of Bessarabia and northern Bukovina and the rapid German defeat of France, Carol believed Nazi Germany was the only country that could protect Romania against further Soviet aggression and Hungarian and Bulgarian revanchism. To curry Hitler's favor, he dismissed Prime Minister Gheorghe Tătărescu and replaced him with his firmly pro-German foreign minister, Ion Gigurtu, on July 4. Gigurtu was palatable to Hitler both because of his Germanophile orientation and because he was a wealthy industrialist with close ties to German businessmen. Gigurtu enabled increased German economic penetration of Romania and invited Germany to station troops in Romania. While the appointment of Gigurtu prolonged Carol's reign by only two more months, it was a watershed moment for Romania's Jews. In keeping with his and Carol's desire to promote closer relations with Nazi Germany, Gigurtu carried out a miniature *Gleichschaltung* in Romania, bringing the country's domestic and foreign policy in line with Germany's. This realignment of policy included the introduction of restrictive measures against the country's Jews, such as the expulsion of Jews from the civil service on July 9.[16]

On August 8, 1940, Gigurtu issued the Decree-Law Concerning the Legal Status of the Jewish Residents of Romania, commonly referred to simply as the Jewish Statute, which laid the foundation for the Romanianization policies that Antonescu enacted after he came into power. Like the Nazi Nuremberg Laws, the Jewish Statute created a new legal definition of Jewishness based on racial criteria. In addition to practicing Jews, secular Jews and unbaptized converts to Christianity with at least one Jewish parent were considered "Jews by blood" (*evrei de sânge*).[17] Those considered Jews by this definition were divided into three categories based on when they had arrived in Romania or gained Romanian citizenship. Category I consisted of Jews who arrived in Romania after December 30, 1918, which included Jews born in Bessarabia and Bukovina before those territories were incorporated into Romania after the First World War. Category II comprised Jews who had been individually naturalized by parliamentary decree (the only way Jews could obtain Romanian citizenship before the First World War); Jews from Dobruja, who were naturalized under a series of laws in the early twentieth century; and Jews who had served in combat in the Second Balkan War and First World War, except those who had been prisoners of war. Only a few thousand Jews in total qualified for inclusion in Category II. All other Jews were placed into Category III.

These categories determined the degree of discrimination an individual would face, with the harshest restrictions imposed on those Categories I and III. Jews in these categories were no longer permitted to

   (a) occupy public functions;
   (b) participate directly in public services;
   (c) be members in professions which have . . . direct contact with the public authorities . . . such as lawyers and notaries public . . . ;
   (d) be members of the administrations of enterprises of any nature; be vendors in rural communities;
   (e) be vendors of alcoholic beverages and holders of [state] monopolies [on certain goods];
   (f) be guardians or caretakers of [Christian] invalids;
   (g) be soldiers;
   (h) be operators . . . of cinemas . . . editors of Romanian books, newspapers, or magazines . . . ;
   (i) be leaders, members, or players in national sporting associations;
   (j) own rural property [this provision also applied to Jews in Category II];
   (k) work as service personnel at public institutions;
   (l) or exercise parental authority [i.e. adoption or legal guardianship] over Christian children.[18]

The Jewish Statute also barred Jews in Categories I and III from serving in the military, while Jews in Category II could no longer be career officers. Compulsory military service was to be replaced for the Jews in Categories I and III by a financial obligation "according to the material means of each Jew" or an obligation to work "according to the needs of the state and public institutions." The Ministry of National Defense had the authority to define the terms of the labor performed under this provision.¹⁹ No such instructions were published prior to the collapse of the Gigurtu government, but the Jewish Statute nonetheless established the precedent for the Law on the Military Status of the Jews four months later.

Despite Carol's overtures to Nazi Germany, including a trade pact that would have made the Reich the sole destination for Romanian oil exports and surplus grain, the Hungarian and Bulgarian governments had already ingratiated themselves to Hitler more effectively, and their territorial interests were given priority. On August 30, 1940, Germany and Italy announced the result of their "mediation" of territorial disputes between Romania and Hungary over Transylvania. Hungary was awarded over forty thousand square kilometers of northern Transylvania, an area with a population of approximately 2.5 million people, about half of whom were ethnic Romanians. Again, Romania was left with little choice but to cede the territory and withdraw. Romania was also forced to surrender part of southern Dobruja to Bulgaria by the Treaty of Craiova, signed on September 7.[20]

These additional territorial losses destroyed what little legitimacy and public support Carol's dictatorship had left. By September 1, widespread protests calling for his abdication had broken out across Romania. On September 4, 1940, Carol dismissed Gigurtu and appointed Ion Antonescu as the new prime minister. Carol believed that Antonescu would be acceptable both to the traditional elite (because of his military background) and to the Iron Guard (because of his antisemitism and friendship with Codreanu). However, the installation of Antonescu did not appease the public. Protests continued, and even Carol's closest advisors urged him to step down. Carol was initially defiant, but he eventually relented and announced his abdication on September 6, turning the throne over to his eighteen-year-old son, Mihai.[21]

However, Mihai was to be little more than a figurehead, as Carol had granted the dictatorial powers he had wielded under the 1938 constitution to Antonescu rather than to the new king. Mihai was compelled to declare Antonescu the head of state and bestow on him Carol's previous title of *conducător* ("leader"); after Romania entered the war in July 1940, Antonescu received the additional title of marshal of Romania. Antonescu concluded a political alliance with Horia Sima, Codreanu's successor as leader of the Iron Guard, in which power was shared between the two parties and the cabinet was composed of both military personnel loyal to Antonescu and Iron Guard members. The resulting regime was known as the National Legionary State, with Antonescu acting as the ceremonial head of the Iron Guard, and the new government was publicly declared in a ceremony on September 14.[22]

Antonescu, a career officer in the Romanian army, had distinguished himself in the suppression of the Peasant Revolt of 1907 and served as General Constantin

Prezan's chief of staff during the First World War, attaining the rank of lieutenant colonel by the end of the war. In the postwar period, he was affiliated with General Alexandru Averescu's populist People's Party and was later posted to Paris and London as a military attaché during the 1920s.[23] For this reason, as well as his wife's longtime residency in France, Antonescu had a much stronger affinity for France and Britain than he did for Germany. He was briefly chief of the General Staff from 1933 to 1934, and was minister of national defense in the Goga-Cuza cabinet. Antonescu held a strong hatred of Jews and associated with prominent antisemites, including Goga, Cuza, and Codreanu.[24] However, Antonescu had also been a military school classmate of prominent Jewish community leader Wilhelm Filderman, which would afford Filderman a level of access to his country's leader that was unparalleled in Nazi-aligned Europe.[25]

Antonescu's views on Jewish affairs were similar to and influenced by those of Cuza and other antisemitic intellectuals of the interwar period. Antonescu saw the Jews as "parasites" and believed that it was necessary to ethnically "purify" Romania by eliminating them from society.[26] Because Carol's dictatorship had removed the constraints of constitutional government, Antonescu's regime was subject to neither electoral politics nor popular opinion, and he had a free hand to implement antisemitic policy in a way that his predecessors had not. Like Cuza, he supported the Romanianization of the economy followed by the removal of the Jews from the country. While the Iron Guard also approved of such measures, Antonescu and Sima differed in their methods. In contrast to the Iron Guard's long tradition of antisemitic violence and robbery, Antonescu preferred to expropriate the Jews gradually and through legal means. Although his belief in the outsized influence of Romania's Jews on the economy was conditioned by antisemitic propaganda, it was nonetheless true that skilled Jewish workers were important to Romanian businesses and many communities depended on the services of Jewish professionals.[27]

Antonescu laid out his philosophy regarding Romanianization in an interview with the Italian newspaper *La Stampa* (The press) on September 30, 1940. He told the Italian correspondent that he intended to "solve the Jewish problem in the course of reorganizing the State, replacing Jews with Romanians step by step."[28] This incremental approach did not sit well with Sima. In a September 27 meeting of the Council of Ministers, he complained to Antonescu about the public perception that the National Legionary government had not yet acted decisively against the Jews. Antonescu rebuffed his complaint, noting that none of the other fascist regimes in Europe, including Nazi Germany, had expropriated the Jews right away and that a gradual process was necessary to avoid damaging the economy.[29]

Nonetheless, Antonescu granted the Iron Guard broad power in the Romanianization process. On October 4, a new law created Romanianization commissions, which were responsible for the expropriation of Jewish property and mostly composed of Iron Guard members. The results were predictable. The Iron Guard began a campaign of legally sanctioned robbery, seizing property from Jews by force and infuriating Antonescu. His ire was further aroused by the fact that this property was not turned over to the state but was instead looted or sold for personal profit. Antonescu's plan for an organized, systematic expropriation of the Jews quickly devolved into chaos.[30]

The National Legionary State also resumed the Romanianization of labor. Several laws in October and early November placed restrictions on Jewish economic activity beyond those already imposed by the Jewish Statute; for example, the government banned the sale of pharmacies to Jews and revoked the licenses of Jewish tavern owners. However, Antonescu envisioned a larger project to Romanianize the entire labor force, much as Cuza had wished to do in the 1930s.[31] On November 16, 1940, the National Legionary government issued the Decree-Law for the Romanianization of Personnel in Enterprises. This new decree went much further than the failed Romanianization laws of the 1930s, requiring that Romanian companies eliminate all Jewish employees by December 31, 1941. The only exceptions granted were for Jews who were direct descendants of veterans of the War of Independence (1877–1878) who had converted to Christianity, Jewish veterans who were wounded in the First World War, and orphans whose fathers were killed in action during the First World War.[32]

The thirteen-month period before the deadline was intended to allow businesses to prepare for the loss of their Jewish workers. During this time, Jewish employees would be "doubled" by a non-Jew who would learn the skills required for the job; in essence, the Jews were responsible for training their replacements. These "doubles" (*dublanți*) would earn 50 percent of what their Jewish mentors made for the first year and 75 percent of their salaries thereafter until they took over the jobs themselves. If the doubles had not adequately learned the necessary skills by December 31, 1941, companies could petition the Ministry of Labor for a six-month extension of the Jewish employee's term. Jews terminated under this law would "have the right" to labor in "works of public interest." The conditions under which such work would be carried out were to be established by the Council of Ministers rather than the Ministry of National Defense, as had been stipulated in the Jewish Statute.[33]

On November 23, 1940, Romania signed the Tripartite Pact and joined the Axis powers. Despite his personal sympathies toward France and Britain, Antonescu decided, as Carol had, that only Germany was capable of protecting Romania's sovereignty against Soviet aggression. Though Antonescu was unaware at the time of Hitler's plan to invade the Soviet Union, he had his own concerns about Romania's eastern neighbor. Because of the Soviet Union's hostile annexation of Bessarabia and northern Bukovina, Antonescu feared further Soviet territorial demands or even a potential invasion. As a result, he coordinated with German officials to create a plan for the defense of Romania in the event of a Soviet attack. The ground operations would be conducted primarily by Romanian troops, with air support provided by the Luftwaffe. During this time, German troops were gradually moved into Romania; by June 1941, more than 600,000 Wehrmacht and Luftwaffe personnel were stationed in the country. Germany took primary responsibility for the defense of sensitive areas in Romania, particularly the oil fields and refineries of Ploiești, which were protected by German antiaircraft guns and both German and Romanian fighter planes.[34]

Antonescu's concerns about a potential conflict with the Soviet Union made it necessary to clarify the military obligations of the Jews in wartime. While the Jewish Statute excluded Jews in Categories I and III from the military and replaced their compulsory military service with taxes and forced labor, the exact nature of those requirements was unclear because the anticipated instructions from the Ministry of National Defense had never been issued. On December 5, 1940, Decree-Law No. 3984, the Law on the Military Status of the Jews, was published. Unlike the Jewish Statute, the new law banned all Jews, regardless of category, from serving in the Romanian armed forces. All Jewish men eighteen to fifty years old were instead "obligated to pay military taxes . . . and to perform work in the community interest according to the needs of the state."[35]

Although only Jews who were physically fit for manual labor would be required to work, even Jews who were considered unfit for military service would be required to pay the new taxes. The rates of taxation were to be established by the Ministry of Finance, which would also be responsible for the assessment of the taxes using the lists of Jews of military age created by the local recruitment centers (*cercurile de recrutare*). During periods of mobilization or in wartime, the tax and labor obligations would exist as long as other Romanians were subject to conscription, meaning that Jews could be required to perform forced labor indefinitely.[36]

The new law declared that "work in the community interest will be done in the service of the Ministry of National Defense or in service of other departments or public institutions in agreement with the Ministry of National Defense."[37] The recruitment centers would be responsible for the conscription of Jewish laborers in their local areas. The sole exception to the ban on Jews in the armed forces applied to Jews with specialized skills and academic degrees (such as doctors, pharmacists, veterinarians, engineers, and architects) who could be integrated into military units and assigned the appropriate rank and corresponding pay. Jews who were working in businesses or industries that were part of the army's mobilization plan (i.e., those engaged in war-related production) would be eligible for exemption from forced labor and would be considered "requisitioned" (*rechiziționat*) by their employers; however, they would still be obligated to pay the military tax.[38]

The Law on the Military Status of the Jews satisfied the long-standing desire of Romanian antisemites to Romanianize the military. The decision to introduce forced labor alongside the exclusion of Jews from the military reflected both economic and ideological needs. From an economic standpoint, it provided the military and other state institutions with a source of inexpensive labor, which was valuable enough in peacetime but even more so in the event of a war, when large numbers of men of working age would be mobilized and labor shortages would be widespread. Improving Romania's transportation infrastructure and military installations was a major concern for the General Staff and the conscription of Jewish men of military age would provide tens of thousands of laborers who could work on essential projects, such as the expansion of Romania's road and rail networks, the reinforcement of existing fortifications and defensive works, and construction of new ones. From an ideological standpoint, the new law removed a group of people Antonescu considered politically unreliable from the military while still requiring them to participate in a future war effort. Thus, forced labor was a logical extension of the Romanianization of labor and the military, and it would remain connected with those processes throughout the war.

A little over a month after the Law on the Military Status of the Jews was issued, the Iron Guard staged a rebellion in an attempt to overthrow Antonescu and seize complete control of the government in response to his efforts to curtail the Iron Guard's power and his dismissal of several Iron Guard ministers. Between January 21 and 23, a violent uprising took place in Bucharest, along with additional demonstrations by Iron Guard members—many of which were also violent—in other cities throughout Romania. The uprising in Bucharest was accompanied by atrocities against the city's Jewish community in which 125 people were killed. On January 23, Antonescu ordered the army to crush the rebellion in Bucharest. After only a few hours of fighting, the rebellion had been suppressed. Most of the Iron Guard's leaders were either imprisoned or fled into exile. After the rebellion, Antonescu quickly consolidated his power as the sole leader of Romania. On January 27, he installed a new cabinet that consisted mostly of officers, effectively creating a military dictatorship.[39]

Immediately before and after the rebellion, two new laws were issued clarifying the provisions of the Law on the Military Status of the Jews. The first, concerning the special military taxes to be paid by Jews, was issued on January 21. It established four levels of taxation, based on the age of the taxpayer. Jews between eighteen and twenty-one years old would pay a fixed tax of 6,000 lei per year, the estimated value of the premilitary service from which they were excluded. Jews who were between twenty-one and twenty-four years of age would pay 5,000 lei plus 30 percent of their incomes combined with that of their parents and wives. Jews from twenty-four to forty-one years old were required to pay 3,000 lei per year plus 20 percent of their incomes, and Jews between forty-one and fifty would pay 15 percent of their annual income without an additional fixed amount. When the army was mobilized, these rates would increase by 50 percent, and during wartime, they would double.[40]

The rates for these taxes would be adjusted each year by the Ministry of Finance. Every Jewish man of military age (or, in the case of Jews under twenty-four years old, their parents) would be required to make an annual declaration of his income and assets through the local recruitment center. Those who failed to make this declaration or avoided the payment of taxes were to be subject to punishment at the will of the local officials, which could include a financial penalty of up to five times the amount of their tax debt or imprisonment of up to three months. Those who could not pay the tax would be sent to forced labor if they were fit to work.[41]

Six days later, the new minister of national defense, General Iosif Iacobici, issued Ministerial Decree No. 23325 regarding the requisition of Jewish medical professionals and other specialists. This decree permitted the armed forces to draft Jewish doctors, pharmacists, veterinarians, engineers, and architects, exempting them from the ban on Jewish military service imposed by the Law on the Military Status of the Jews. They would be assimilated into the army at the appropriate rank for their level of qualification (or the rank they had attained during previous military service). Medical personnel would wear the standard medic's uniform with a color-coded rod of Asclepius (red for doctors, green for pharmacists, blue for veterinarians). Engineers and architects would wear regular uniforms bearing a compass symbol with a letter *I* (*inginer*) circumscribed within for engineers and an *A* (*arhitect*) for architects. Medical personnel who were assimilated at officer ranks would hold the title "medic," while those who were assimilated as noncommissioned officers would be "assistant medic" (*medic ajutor*). The same naming convention would apply for engineers (*inginer/inginer ajutor*) and architects (*arhitect/arhitect ajutor*).[42]

While they would be allowed to wear the standard uniform and insignia for their specialization (and, in theory, were not to face racial or religious discrimination), Jewish specialists would nonetheless be required to wear symbols that identified them as Jews. Assistant medics would wear a cross with the color that corresponded to their specialization. Medics would be required to wear one-centimeter six-pointed stars on their epaulets. The color and number of stars varied according to rank: one white star for ranks below second lieutenant, one yellow star for second lieutenants, two for first lieutenants, and three for captains. This grading was repeated for higher ranks: one for majors, two for lieutenant colonels, and three for colonels. Assistant engineers and architects would wear only the compass symbol, while full engineers and architects would also wear six-pointed stars, following the above pattern according to rank.[43]

In his January 14 meeting with Hitler, Antonescu had been informed, in very general terms, of the plan to invade the Soviet Union. While he, like the leaders of Germany's other allies, was not told the exact date of the attack until less than two weeks before it commenced, he knew nonetheless that his country would soon be involved in the war. War on such a massive scale would inevitably cause a shortage of manpower for public works projects well beyond what could be filled by the conscription of Jews for forced labor. On May 15, 1941, the Decree-Law for the Organization of National Labor was issued, creating a national civilian labor service. The new law required all Romanian men and women between the ages of twenty and fifty-seven who did not have regular employment, as well as students sixteen and older, youths who were not regularly attending school, and men in the premilitary service (those between eighteen and twenty-five years old), to work on projects of public interest.[44]

The obligation to work, as the law stated, was incumbent on all Romanians, and those who did not work would not be entitled to receive state benefits. Men and women conscripted into the labor service could be sent to work for various state institutions on a variety of projects, including road and railroad construction, the excavation of dams and waterways, the improvement of defensive works and fortifications, and agricultural labor.[45] The work of the civilian labor service would be governed by the newly created National Labor Council, made up of delegates from the Ministry of Labor and other government ministries, as well as the General Staff.[46] After the war began, tens of thousands of Soviet prisoners of war were also pressed into labor, as were members of national minority groups. The Jewish military labor service and the civilian labor service operated in parallel throughout the war, though Jews and civilian laborers were always kept separate from one another.

On June 22, 1941, Nazi Germany invaded the Soviet Union. Romania joined in the fighting ten days later, as the Romanian Third and Fourth Armies moved into Bessarabia and Bukovina alongside the German Eleventh Army and Einsatzgruppe D. The Axis forces achieved their objectives rapidly. The capital of Bukovina, Cernăuți (Czernowitz; now Chernivtsi, Ukraine), was recaptured by the Third Army on July 5, and the Eleventh Army took the capital of Bessarabia, Chișinău (Kishinev), on July 16. Three days later, the Fourth Army and Eleventh Army reached the Dniester, completing the recovery of all Romanian territory lost the previous summer.[47] The invasion of the Soviet Union was accompanied by widespread massacres of Jews in Bessarabia and Bukovina by Romanian soldiers and gendarmes, acting under Antonescu's order to "cleanse the land" in the occupied territories.[48]

One month after Romania entered the war, the systematic mobilization of Jewish men for forced labor began. In preparation for this process, new regulations were issued on July 14. While some labor battalions had already been formed (for example, in the Cotroceni neighborhood of Bucharest, where a new shooting range was to be built) and other Jews were working in camps like Doaga, most Jews eligible for the labor service had not yet been called up. Under the Law on the Military Status of the Jews, the local recruitment centers were responsible for issuing conscription notices, registering Jewish workers, and conducting medical screenings. According to the new regulations, on receiving their conscription notices, Jews were required to report to the nearest recruitment center, where the commander would record their name, marital status, ethnic origin, and profession. They would then undergo a physical examination conducted by the commander and an army medic. Only those Jews who passed this examination could be assigned to forced labor; however, those who were declared unfit would still have to pay the military tax.[49]

All Jews between eighteen and fifty who met the fitness requirements were eligible to be sent to work in camps, in small groups, or in larger labor detachments, for the use of the army or other state institutions. These detachments could be deployed locally (referred to as "local detachments") or to other parts of the country (referred to as "external detachments") depending on need. While any state institution could make a request to use Jewish laborers, the General Staff theoretically had sole responsibility for issuing work assignments. The external detachments would be staffed and supervised by reserve officers and regular soldiers, while local detachments would be under the command of soldiers from the local garrisons. Jewish workers had the right to the same food, shelter, and pay as regular soldiers. However, they would not receive army uniforms and would instead wear their civilian clothes with a yellow ten-centimeter armband identifying them as members of the Jewish labor service. While Jews assigned to the external detachments would be quartered near their work sites, Jews in the local detachments (usually made up of men under twenty-one or over forty years old) could sleep at home but were required to provide their own food. Jews working for institutions other than the military, as well as those requisitioned by private enterprises, would receive their pay, food, and shelter from their employers rather than from the military.[50]

All Jews were required to report to their recruitment centers within sixty days of the publication of the July 14 regulations to receive a military identification card. Jews who had previously served in the military and already had an identification card would have their cards stamped with the word *evreu* (Jew) in red text. Inside these cards, the recruitment center would print the periods during which the bearer had been assigned to forced labor, so that he could prove he had performed his labor obligation. The recruitment center would keep records of the time each man spent in the labor service.[51]

The July 14 regulations were the final piece of the Antonescu government's initial forced labor policy. However, the implementation of this policy over the following weeks did not create the productive Jewish labor service the military leadership had planned. The problems that plagued the system throughout its existence became apparent within the first days after the mobilization of workers began. The disastrous 1941 labor campaign caused Antonescu to question the value of the forced labor system to the war effort, as well as its place within his Jewish policy.

Notes

1. Carol Iancu, *Evreii din România (1866–1919): De la excludere la emancipare*, 2nd ed. (Bucharest: Editura Hasefer, 2006), 208.
2. Horia Bozdorghină, *Antisemitismul lui A. C. Cuza în politică românească* (Bucharest: Editura institutul național pentru studierea holocaustului din România "Elie Wiesel," 2012), 153–159.
3. Roland Clark, *Holy Legionary Youth: Fascist Activism in Interwar Romania* (Ithaca, NY: Cornell University Press, 2015), 63–64.
4. Ancel, *History of the Holocaust in Romania*, 42.
5. Ștefan Cristian Ionescu, *Jewish Resistance to "Romanianization," 1940–1944* (London: Palgrave Macmillan, 2015), 34–35.
6. Wilhelm Filderman, *Memoirs and Diaries*, ed. Jean Ancel, vol. 1 (Jerusalem: Yad Vashem, 2004), 486.
7. Ancel, *History of the Holocaust in Romania*, 23–24.
8. Keith Hitchins, *Rumania 1866–1947* (Oxford: Oxford University Press, 1994), 417.
9. Ibid., 419.
10. Ancel, *History of the Holocaust in Romania*, 25.
11. Henry Eaton, *The Origins and Onset of the Romanian Holocaust* (Detroit: Wayne State University Press, 2013), 6.
12. Ancel, *History of the Holocaust in Romania*, 38.
13. Hitchins, *Rumania*, 421.
14. Ancel, *History of the Holocaust in Romania*, 42–43.
15. Dennis Deletant, *Hitler's Forgotten Ally: Ion Antonescu and His Regime, Romania 1940–1944* (London: Palgrave Macmillan, 2006), 15.
16. Hitchins, *Rumania*, 483.
17. Lya Benjamin, *Evreii din România între anii 1940–1944*, vol. 1, *Legislația antievreiască* (Bucharest: Editura Hasefer, 1993), document 3, 46.
18. Ibid., document 3, 46–47.
19. Ibid., document 3, 48.
20. Deletant, *Hitler's Forgotten Ally*, 23–25.
21. Ibid., 49–50.

22. Tuvia Friling et al., *Final Report of the International Commission on the Holocaust in Romania* (Iași: Polirom, 2005), 109.
23. Ancel, *History of the Holocaust in Romania*, 138.
24. Deletant, *Hitler's Forgotten Ally*, 44.
25. Ancel, *History of the Holocaust in Romania*, 138–142.
26. Chioveanu, "Death Delivered," 141.
27. Friling et al., *Final Report*, 182.
28. Benjamin, *Evreii din România între anii 1940–1944*, vol. 2, *Problema evreiască* (Bucharest: Editura Hasefer, 1993), document 47, 135.
29. Ibid., document 46, 133.
30. Ancel, *History of the Holocaust in Romania*, 106.
31. Ancel, *Economic Destruction*, 76–82.
32. Friling et al., *Final Report*, 193.
33. Benjamin, *Legislația antievreiască*, document 16, 76.
34. Deletant, *Hitler's Forgotten Ally*, 76.
35. Benjamin, *Legislația antievreiască*, document 25, 95.
36. Ana Bărbulescu et al., *Munca obligatorie a evreilor din România: Documente* (Bucharest: Editura institutul național pentru studierea holocaustului din România "Elie Wiesel," 2013), document 2, 62.
37. Benjamin, *Legislația antievreiască*, document 25, 95.
38. Ibid., document 25, 95.
39. Deletant, *Hitler's Forgotten Ally*, 69.
40. Bărbulescu et al., *Munca obligatorie*, document 3, 66.
41. Ibid., document 3, 67.
42. USHMMA, RG-25.003M, selected records from the Romanian Ministry of Defense, 1940–1945, reel 134, file 1977, 278.
43. Ibid.
44. Bărbulescu et al., *Munca obligatorie*, document 6, 74–75.
45. Ibid., document 6, 74.
46. Ibid., document 6, 75–76.
47. Mark W. Axworthy, Cristian Crăciunoiu, and Cornel Scafeș, *Third Axis, Fourth Ally: Romanian Armed Forces in the European War, 1941–1945* (London: Arms and Armour, 1995), 46–47.
48. Friling et al., *Final Report*, 131.
49. Bărbulescu et al., *Munca obligatorie*, document 7, 79.
50. Ibid., document 7, 81–83.
51. Ibid., document 7, 84.

2 Trial and Error

More than six months passed between the publication of the Law on the Military Status of the Jews and the Axis invasion of the Soviet Union. During this time, forced labor was used sporadically in several contexts, most of which were not connected to the military labor service. These included the internment camps, like the one at Târgu Jiu, operated by the Ministry of Internal Affairs; the Doaga labor camp; and the Iron Guard's ad hoc labor groups. A small number of Jewish labor units were operating under the Romanian military during this time, but they only comprised a few thousand men, a fraction of the number who would be employed during the war. It was only after the Axis invasion of the Soviet Union that the military labor service was mobilized and the 1941 labor campaign began in earnest. In the summer and fall of 1941, forced labor took place in three main venues: the internment camps; the labor camps and detachments established by the army; and factories, businesses, and state institutions where Jews were either "requisitioned" for work or had been exempted from forced labor and allowed to remain in their prewar jobs.

Despite previous plans for the General Staff to handle mobilization, the Ministry of Internal Affairs was initially responsible for the mobilization of Jewish laborers for nonmilitary projects, coordinating with the army recruitment centers to distribute them to places in need of labor. The mobilization, which began on August 2, was disastrously disorganized. Civilian and military authorities issued conflicting instructions, which confused lower-level officials. Many Jews were able to escape forced labor by bribing local officials for medical exemptions, while others simply did not respond to their conscription notices and were never tracked down. Others who were legitimately medically unfit for physical labor were sent to work anyway after apathetic officials gave them only cursory examinations or ignored letters from their doctors declaring them unfit for forced labor. After a week of this chaos, Ion Antonescu ordered that the conscription of laborers would thereafter be solely the responsibility of the General Staff. The chief of staff quickly issued new instructions that were intended to streamline the mobilization of laborers and fix the problems that the Ministry of Internal Affairs had created. These instructions were only partially successful, due to both the severity of the problems the General Staff inherited and the incompetence and corruption of its own officials. As a result, forced labor in 1941 was much less productive than the military officials had anticipated, and Jewish laborers suffered because of the officials' negligence and disorganization, as well as, in some cases, the cruelty of the officers and soldiers with whom they interacted.

While Antonescu left most of the policymaking to the General Staff and government ministries involved in forced labor, he did not hesitate to express his feelings about the forced labor system. He was harshly critical of the system in a November 1941 cabinet meeting and proposed to end it altogether and replace it with additional taxes.[1] Antonescu's frustrations resulted from both the disorganization and corruption that had plagued the system and the fact that forced labor was not giving the expected economic benefit. He was dissuaded from canceling the entire endeavor by his advisers, but he demanded significant reforms before the resumption of forced labor in 1942.

While the Law on the Military Status of the Jews introduced the system of state-sanctioned forced labor under military control, it did not introduce the practice of conscripting Jews into compulsory labor. Under the Iron Guard, police and city officials had frequently compelled groups of Jews to work on their behalf, humiliating them in front of their neighbors, who would mock and spit on them. For example, on the night of November 21, 1940, the Iron Guard–aligned prefect of Prahova County, Marin Stănescu, ordered the Jews of Ploiești to clean up the rubble of a synagogue and Jewish school that had been destroyed by the Iron Guard after the November 10 earthquake that devastated much of southern and eastern Romania. Local engineers had advised against the demolition of these buildings after determining that they were still structurally sound, but the Iron Guard destroyed them anyway. The practice of rounding up Jews for ad hoc forced labor groups continued after the Law on the Military Status of the Jews was issued. On December 12, Jews (including an elderly rabbi) were forced to sweep the streets of Târgoviște, about seventy-four kilometers northwest of Bucharest. Jews were frequently forced to clear streets and rail lines of snow in Romanian cities during the winter months of 1940 and 1941, a practice that would continue in the following years, after the military took over forced labor.[2]

The Iron Guard also conscripted Jewish laborers for other tasks. Jewish writer Mihail Sebastian was among the Jews who was compelled to work in a labor detachment by the Iron Guard. He described his experience in his journal months afterward. He and a group of other Jews were taken from Bucharest by train to perform agricultural work in Lugoj by the Iron Guard in the fall of 1940, following a roundabout route to get there and enduring difficult working conditions.[3] These incidents of Iron Guard terror bothered Antonescu, who considered the imposition of forced labor without respect to age or sex to be "inhuman."[4] However, Antonescu did not object to the use of prisoner labor at the Târgu Jiu internment camp, operated by the Ministry of Internal Affairs, which opened in 1939,[5] or at the labor camp at Doaga, which was under the control of the Fifth Pioneers Regiment and established in late 1940.[6]

Forced labor was also imposed on Jews both during and after the episode of mass antisemitic violence that became known as the Iași pogrom. On June 27, Antonescu ordered the evacuation of the forty-five thousand Jews living in Iași to the Târgu Jiu camp and added that any Jew who attacked Romanian soldiers should be shot. A detachment of the Romanian Special Intelligence Service (Siguranța) had been dispatched to Iași the week before to counteract any potential acts of sabotage—Jews were frequently depicted in Romanian propaganda as agents of the Soviet Union who would eagerly sabotage the Romanian war effort. After the war began, antisemitic agitation in the city ramped up. After two Soviet bombing raids on the city—a minor one on June 24, followed by a larger one on June 26—unfounded rumors spread through the city that Jews had signaled to the Soviet aircraft to help them find their targets.[7] The escalation toward mass violence in the days leading up to the massacre was evident, as young Jews were forced to dig large ditches in the Jewish cemetery and Christian homes were marked with crosses. On June 28, mobs led by Romanian police and gendarmes broke into Jewish homes, robbed the inhabitants, and then killed them or dragged them to police headquarters, where they were held hostage. The Special Intelligence Service armed civilians and encouraged them to participate in the robberies and murders.[8]

On June 29, Ion Antonescu and his deputy prime minister, Mihai Antonescu, ordered the evacuation of the remaining Jews from Iași. The survivors of the initial massacre were taken to the train station, where they were loaded onto trains that traveled slowly across the countryside for several days in the extreme summer heat. Most of the passengers of these trains died due to the heat or dehydration, and as a result, these trains became known as the "death trains." The first death train, which left Iași on June 30, was sent to Călărași, in southern Romania. Between 2,430 and 2,590 Jews were loaded onto this train, of whom approximately 1,400 died.[9] Those who did survive were either imprisoned in a large internment camp near the city or forced to work in labor units—separate from the military labor system—in the surrounding area. Twenty-five-year-old Aristide Rauch survived the first death train and was subsequently pressed into forced labor. He and a small group of other deportees were taken to a Jewish cemetery in Călărași, where they were required to clean and maintain grave sites. During the four months they spent in Călărași, Rauch and the other deportees slept on the floor of an abandoned house and were supplied with basic needs, such as food and blankets, by the city's Jewish community.[10] In October 1941, the surviving deportees were allowed to return to Iași, where many of them would be conscripted into forced labor by the military in the winter of 1941 or spring of 1942.

The second death train traveled only twenty kilometers to the town of Podu Iloaiei, northwest of Iași along the Bahlui River. When the train reached its destination after a journey of over eight hours, the 708 survivors (out of 1,902 original passengers) were sent to the village of Scobâlțeni, about six kilometers from the town center, where they were to perform agricultural labor for an indefinite period that was as short as three weeks for some men and as long as five months for others.[11] Eighteen-year-old Iancu Țucărman was 1 of 8 survivors from among the 137 men in his car on the second death train. On his arrival, he was sent to live with a local family in Scobâlțeni, a living arrangement that was theoretically forbidden (but sometimes still used) in the military labor system. He and the other Jews there worked from sunrise to sunset with a half-hour lunch break six days a week, harvesting sunflowers and threshing wheat.[12]

Although the journey to Podu Iloaiei had been brutal, Țucărman recalled that his time spent living with the local family was tolerable and that he was treated decently there. In the morning, he was fed *mămăligă* (a Romanian dish of corn meal, similar to polenta) and tea, sometimes including a bit of honey, which supplemented the diet of mămăligă and thin soup they were fed by the soldiers at their work site. Țucărman did not recall any deaths among the laborers at Podu Iloaiei, though he recognized that his time there was intended as an extension of the persecution he had already experienced.[13] On November 27, 1941, Țucărman and his fellow workers were returned to Iași by train. Between the massacres in Iași and the death trains, the pogrom claimed the lives of between 13,266 (according to government statistics) and 14,850 lives (according to Jewish community statistics).[14] Many of the Jewish survivors who returned to Iași were sent to forced labor detachments in the following years.

The creation of internment camps for Jews began well before the introduction of forced labor. Some of the largest camps, like the one at Târgu Jiu—which held interned Polish military personnel and political prisoners, in addition to Jews—had been open for almost two years by the summer of 1941. Jews had been sent to the internment and labor camp at Doaga since 1940, which was greatly expanded after the start of the forced labor campaign and became one of the largest camps in Romania.[15] Many smaller internment camps had been created by Ministry of Internal Affairs Order No. 4147 on June 21, 1941, the day before the invasion of the Soviet Union. This order provided legal cover for the "evacuation" of the Jews living between the Siret and Prut Rivers in northeastern Romania, near the border with the Soviet Union, which had begun three days earlier on Antonescu's orders. The purpose of the evacuation was to remove Jews from areas near the front lines, a reflection of Antonescu's paranoia about alleged Jewish collaboration with the Soviets.[16]

The Jews evacuated from these areas were taken to internment camps in southern Romania, located at Călărași, Caracal, Craiova, Giurgiu, Ialomița, Lugoj, Romanați, and Turnu Severin. Others, mainly men of military age, were taken to the Târgu Jiu camp, commanded by Colonel Gheorghe Zlătescu.[17] Another internment camp, also operated by the Ministry of Internal Affairs, was

Table 2.1. Populations of internment camps as of August 7, 1941.

Camp	Number of Prisoners	Women and Children	Origin of Prisoners
Calafat	780	500	Rădăuți
Craiova	1,053	700	Rădăuți
Giurgiu	800	0	Bessarabia
Ialomița	1,100	0	Iași
Lugoj	500	500	Dorohoi
Romanați	1,500	0	Dorohoi
Târgu Jiu	1,846	0	Dorohoi
Teiș-Târgoviște	1,188	Unknown	Ploiești
Turnu Severin	600	600	Dorohoi
Vlașca	800	500	Bessarabia
TOTAL	10,167	2,800	

built at Teiș-Târgoviște for Jews and Communists from the strategically sensitive oil-producing region of Prahova County and the city of Ploiești in August 1941.[18] This camp was commanded by Lieutenant Colonel Augustin Ionescu and had a staff of 5 officers, 4 noncommissioned officers, and 150 soldiers.[19] By August 7, there were 10,167 men, women, and children in the major internment camps in southern Romania.[20] Smaller internment camps were created throughout Romania to hold Jews deported from areas that were considered sensitive from a national security perspective. For example, camps were established in the villages of Osmancea, Mereni, and Ciobănița for Jews from the important Black Sea port of Constanța and the surrounding area.

On July 18, 1941, the deputy minister of Internal Affairs, General Ion "Jack" Popescu, ordered on behalf of Antonescu that all Jews in the internment camps be put to hard labor, either in workshops within the camps or in groups outside the camp under close supervision. If anyone escaped, one of every ten prisoners in the camp was to be shot in retribution. Prisoners who refused to work would not be given food, nor would they be allowed to buy food.[21] While these warnings were ominous, it is uncertain whether the prescribed punishments were ever actually carried out. There is no documentation of such executions, and the General Headquarters reported in an internal memorandum on October 15, 1941, that none had taken place.[22] It is possible that executions occurred and were simply not reported or that the General Headquarters memorandum deliberately obscured them; however, none of the available witness testimony attests to such executions either.

Problems arose almost immediately in the internment camps. Corruption was already commonplace, as some Jews had brought money and valuables into the camps with them and bribed the guards to obtain their release.²³ The situation of those who could not do so, however, was often dire. Because of the indiscriminate nature of the internment camps, many of the Jews who were sent there were not suited to physical labor. The prefect's reports from Constanța reveal that people were taken to the camps with very little notice and that most only had the clothing they were wearing at the time of their arrest. Since most of these people had been interned in June 1941, very few of them had winter clothing. Some were elderly or suffering from serious illnesses.²⁴

As a result, county prefects received barrages of requests from interned persons and their relatives to have them freed from the internment camps. The prefect of Constanța fielded dozens of requests for release of Jewish internees in September 1941 alone.²⁵ For example, a prisoner named Lazar Sulimovici wrote to the prefect in September to petition for his release from the Osmancea camp because he was a decorated veteran of the First World War and therefore exempt from internment and forced labor. Sulimovici's letter indicated that he was born in 1877, and was therefore either sixty-three or sixty-four years old at the time.²⁶ Another internee, Solomon Simca, wrote to the prefect in September to request a temporary release from Osmancea so that he could receive medical treatment for tuberculosis and chronic rheumatism in both legs.²⁷ The number of people who were held in the internment camps in spite of old age and poor health, as well as the terrible conditions in the camps, led Wilhelm Filderman to write to the prefect of Constanța to suggest the release of all interned Jews in the county.²⁸

The requests sent to the prefect of Constanța reveal the haphazard nature of the internment and the improbability of productive labor in these camps. The wholesale internment of entire Jewish populations was also problematic for Romanian firms that relied on Jewish workers, often prompting angry reactions from business owners who demanded their employees' release. For example, a representative from the Uzinelor Române (Romanian Factories) group in Ploiești wrote to the Prahova County recruitment center to request the release of a Jewish employee named M. Rath from the Teiș-Târgoviște camp, expressing frustration at the interruption to business caused by his internment.²⁹ The problems encountered in the internment camps foreshadowed those that would later develop in the military labor detachments.

In addition to separating labor camps (*tabere de muncă*) from labor detachments (*detașamente de muncă*), military terminology made a distinction between two types of army labor detachments: "local" and "external." The local detachments worked in and around the cities in which they were organized. Generally, the Jews in these detachments were either youths under twenty-one years old or older men who were more than forty years old, as well as men with children. They were allowed to live and eat at home as long as they showed up for work on time every day. The external detachments were deployed outside their cities of origin, generally in rural areas. These detachments were usually composed of men between twenty-one and forty and did the hardest work, including road and railroad construction, mining and quarrying, building and repairing fortifications, and agricultural labor. In practice, the difference between labor camps and external detachments was minimal and the use of the word *camp* to refer to army labor units was later discontinued.

A few army labor camps and detachments were organized by the General Staff in late June, just after the war began, and a smaller number had been in operation for months before the war began. However, only a few thousand Jews were at work for the military prior to August 2, 1941, a fraction of the number that would eventually be mobilized. One of the earliest military projects on which Jewish laborers were employed by the military was the construction of a shooting and artillery range in the Bucharest neighborhood of Cotroceni (Poligonul Cotroceni). This project dated back to the fall of 1940 at the latest, before the Law on the Military Status of the Jews was issued.[30] Cotroceni was the model for the local detachments—the laborers were residents of Bucharest and lived in their own homes rather than at the shooting range.[31]

On August 2, the General Headquarters issued Order No. 207, activating all eligible Jewish men for labor service.[32] The same day, Ministry of Internal Affairs Order No. 492 instructed all local recruitment centers to create rosters of Jews to be conscripted for labor service. During the next four days, the Ministry of Internal Affairs sent additional orders to specific recruitment centers to order the creation of detachments; for example, on August 3, it requested that the recruitment center in Neamţ County, in east-central Romania, create a detachment of one thousand Jews for construction and maintenance work on the county's highways.[33]

Most of the detachments established at this time were assigned to the state railway agency, Căile Ferate Române (CFR); the General Directorate of Roads; and the Ministry of Agriculture. Common tasks included laying rail or track ballast, loading and unloading train wagons, laying gravel or paving roads, and harvesting the autumn crops. Some of these jobs were directly related to military interests, including the construction of road and rail connections between major cities in Romania or in the direction of the front. Tasks such as harvesting crops or unloading goods were not of immediate relevance to the war effort but were nonetheless important to the economy. During the first week of mobilization, 5,876 Jews were conscripted in Bucharest and 11,124 more were called up in the rest of Romania.[34]

The implementation of the orders of the General Headquarters and Ministry of Internal Affairs at the local level was thoroughly disorganized. Conscription notices were sent to Jews with no records made at the recruitment center. Many of these notices went unanswered—the addressee never reported to the recruitment center and his absence was never investigated. Other recruits bribed corrupt local officials to secure medical exemptions or were granted exemptions after a cursory physical examination. However, others were declared healthy enough for manual labor when they were in fact suffering from illness or disability. In addition, many Jews were not told to bring warm clothing and other supplies with them to the recruitment center and were thus deployed without them.[35] CFR complained multiple times to the General Staff because recruitment centers had sent men who were unfit for physical labor to its detachments or had sent men considered fit for only light manual work. The head of CFR detachments, Lieutenant Colonel Traian Panaitescu, remarked that there was no "light work" in a railroad construction detachment.[36]

In his memoirs, Fred Gerbel described the condition of some of the men who were sent to work with him in an excavation detachment near Pașcani, in northeastern Romania, in the fall of 1941: "We had a hunchback in our ranks, and his hunch was considerably bad. Another 'volunteer' was missing four fingers on his right hand. A third had a leg which was too short (or perhaps the other was too long). A fourth had a mutilated arm. One had tuberculosis, another was a diabetic. We also had an insane man who had previously been confined in an asylum, and the gallery was completed with an epileptic." Gerbel noted that the medical examination his detachment received was very cursory: a single doctor spent no more than ten minutes examining a group of 260 men. After the men in his unit had gathered and undergone this brief inspection, Gerbel said sarcastically, "with everyone together, we were ready to begin."[37] As Gerbel's recollections indicate, many recruiters and medical examiners put no effort into their jobs, sending people to forced labor despite the fact that they had severe physical disabilities that would have prevented them from working effectively, leaving detachment commanders and laborers alike in a difficult position.

The problems with the implementation of forced labor drew the attention of both the government and the General Staff. On August 5, Deputy Prime Minister Mihai Antonescu gave an extensive report to the Council of Ministers on the mobilization of laborers. He informed them that "it has come to my attention that our police, in some places, repeating old, sad, and stupid habits as before, have created systems of favoritism, and have even released some people from the camps if they paid money for it."[38] While he "[did] not want to ... take measures which would benefit the Jews," he wanted the government to address the issues with forced labor in a "serious, effective, and efficient" way and not to "paralyze ... economic activity and ... provoke a disturbance of the public order."[39]

Following his speech, Mihai Antonescu had a lengthy discussion with the undersecretary of state for the army, General Constantin Pantazi; the minister of national defense, General Iosif Iacobici; and the minister of finance, General Nicolae Stoenescu. Iacobici and Stoenescu agreed that the exemption of certain

Figure 2.1. Romanian Jews chosen for forced labor assemble near the work site. United States Holocaust Memorial Museum, courtesy of Federation of Jewish Communities.

Jews was necessary to maintain the economic stability of the country and that the Ministry of Finance and Ministry of the National Economy should have a substantial say in this matter. However, the council also concluded that control over the recruitment of workers should be turned over to the military authorities and that the work performed by the Jews should be under a "military regime" to solve what Ion Antonescu believed was fundamentally a "moral problem."[40]

Representatives of the General Staff, Ministry of Internal Affairs, and Ministry of Labor met the following day to discuss the reorganization of the recruitment process. In this meeting, it was decided that the Ministry of Internal Affairs would cede authority over the conscription of workers through the recruitment centers and the organization of labor detachments and coordinate with Ministry of Labor to determine where those detachments should be deployed (on August 20, the General Staff decided that the Ministry of Internal Affairs would retain control over labor in the Dolj, Ialomița, Romanați, Vlașca, Târgu Jiu, and Teiș-Târgoviște internment camps). Furthermore, new procedures would be established to improve oversight of the mobilization process and prevent the many lapses that had occurred under the Ministry of Internal Affairs.[41] These procedures were published on August 8 as General Staff Order No. 31.200, the General Instructions on the Application of the Regulations on the Law on the Military Status of the Jews, commonly referred to simply as the General Instructions.

The General Instructions served three major purposes: clarifying the procedures for the recruitment of Jews and their assignment to the labor detachments, establishing an "order of urgency" for the deployment of Jewish laborers, and delineating the responsibilities of each echelon of the military chain of command, as well as their relationships with the other ministries responsible for forced labor (mainly the Ministry of Labor and the Ministry of the National Economy). The recruitment centers were instructed to prioritize the recruitment of unemployed Jews, particularly those "who hang around in the streets or waste time in clubs and cafés."[42] Jews were to be assigned to work according to whatever skills or training they possessed, a principle that had been established by the Law on the Military Status of the Jews but had been largely ignored in the initial mobilizations. Only those Jews who failed their medical examinations or who were "indispensable" to their employers and had been working for them prior to June 21, 1941, were to be exempted. All approvals of "indispensable" workers would be issued by the General Staff on the employer's request.[43]

Each camp or detachment with more than 250 workers would have a reserve officer to maintain "order and discipline" and ensure productivity. Every camp or detachment with more than 500 workers was to have a Jewish medic. Jews working in camps or external detachments who had family living nearby, as well as Jews in local detachments, would still be allowed to eat and sleep at home or at the homes of their relatives. This rather lenient provision was based on previous experience with the Cotroceni detachment. Since the Jews working there had all been recruited from the city of Bucharest, the army decided to allow the men to sleep at home to improve morale; only those who did not appear for work would be forced to live in the barracks at the shooting range. General Pantazi reported to the Council of Ministers that both productivity and attendance had been improved by this measure, leading the General Staff to adopt it for all detachments where it was possible; in practice, however, few Jews were assigned to work close enough to their own homes to permit such an arrangement, aside from those in the local detachments.[44]

The "order of urgency" established in the General Instructions reflected the original purpose of the labor service: to provide laborers for the military and other state institutions, with other interests of secondary concern. Requests from the military were to be filled first, followed by requests from other agencies, such as the Ministry of Public Works and Communications, CFR, and General Directorate of Roads. Any workers remaining after all these needs were fulfilled could be sent to work in agriculture, industry, and commerce. Workers sent to private employers for such needs were classified as "requisitioned." The Ministry of Labor and Ministry of the National Economy would advise the General Staff on the needs of private enterprises and how their requests should be prioritized. A later memorandum stated that all requests for Jewish labor by the German military authorities in Romania would be given top priority and handled directly by the General Staff.[45] Despite the disdain that German officials would later express toward the Jewish labor system,[46] they had no qualms about taking advantage of it and frequently requested the services of Jewish specialists and professionals. Requests from the Germans were always given the highest priority by the General Staff, even above the needs of the Romanian military.[47]

The responsibilities for recruiting workers and determining where they should be deployed, as well as handling requests from both state and private employers, were divided among the three levels of the domestic military chain of command: the recruitment centers, the seven army Territorial Commands, and the General Staff. The recruitment centers were expected to maintain updated lists of all eligible Jewish workers in their area, organized by age and skill. They were also required to keep records of all Jews deployed to and exempted from the labor detachments and requests for workers. The Territorial Commands were to collect records from the recruitment centers in their area and maintain a centralized list of working Jews. In the short term, they were also required to provide the General Staff with records of all Jews sent to forced labor and all Jews requisitioned by private employers in their areas by September 1. The General Staff would keep records of recruitment and deployment from each Territorial Command and supervise the lower-level authorities' application of their instructions. The General Staff was also ultimately responsible, along with the Ministry of Labor, for the productivity of the labor service.[48] The General Staff ordered a ten-day moratorium on the recruitment of workers from August 11 to 21 to allow time for the lower command echelons to implement the new instructions before resuming the mobilization process.[49]

On August 25, the General Staff issued a clarification regarding the exemption of workers considered "indispensable" by their employers. Commissions were to be established in each county capital to create lists of Jews to be exempted and propose them to the respective Territorial Commands. These commissions were to consist of the prefect of that county (who would act as president) and a delegate each from the Ministry of Labor, Ministry of the National Economy, Chamber of Commerce, and the local recruitment center. The commission in Bucharest would be headed by Minister of Labor Petre Tomescu and include delegates from the Second (Bucharest) Territorial Command and the Chamber of Labor. Requests for exemption that came from businesses that were part of the mobilization plan or held military contracts would still be handled directly by the General Staff. Only those determined to be "absolutely, strictly necessary" were to be exempted and exempted Jews could not comprise more than 50 percent of the employees of a firm. These commissions would begin work on September 15, except for the Bucharest commission, which would start on September 30.[50]

The General Staff and other state institutions responsible for forced labor made additional attempts to rationalize and streamline the organization of the labor system and the recruitment of workers during the last weeks of the summer of 1941. From September 2 to 5, a conference was convened in Bucharest with representatives of the General Staff, Ministry of Labor, Ministry of the National Economy, and the Chamber of Labor. At this conference, several new proposals were made regarding the organization of forced labor and the recruitment and exemption of workers. The unifying feature of these proposals was an increased emphasis on cooperation between the military and civilian authorities, both at the national and local levels.[51]

The organization of labor camps and detachments remained the responsibility of the General Staff, but changes were made to the camps' administrative structures. Because large camps and detachments had proven to be the most effective, Jews were to be organized in this manner whenever possible. Additional officers were proposed to ensure proper supervision of larger groups of Jews: one officer for every 250 Jews, one company commander for every 500, and one battalion commander for every 1,000. The Ministry of Labor would now set the "programs of work" for labor detachments, which would determine the projects they worked on and how they were to be approached. Its representatives proposed that craftsmen and laborers in camps be employed in workshops within the camps and laborers in detachments be organized into work groups (*echipe*), where they could be more easily supervised. A liaison was to be created to facilitate cooperation between the General Staff and Ministry of Labor in organizational matters. However, no timetable for the establishment of this liaison was set, and it would be more than two months before the legislation to create it was issued.[52]

The General Staff also made changes to the process of requesting exemptions. All requests for fewer than one hundred Jews were to be handled by the recruitment centers, in coordination with the local commissions created on August 25. Requests for more than one hundred laborers were to be addressed to the General Staff, which would respond to them with input from Ministry of Labor. All such requests, whether they were made to the recruitment centers or the General Staff, were to be made for a certain number of workers, rather than for individual workers by name, to prevent abuse of the system; nonetheless, some employers ignored this requirement and exploited the exemption system to help individual Jews escape forced labor.[53]

Some institutions that employed Jews also created their own regulations for the responsibilities and rights of the laborers in addition to the regulations imposed by the General Staff. For example, on September 3, 1941, CFR published its instructions for the use of Jewish laborers. Jews working for CFR would be paid forty-five lei per day: thirty-five for food, five for "upkeep," and five for tobacco. In return, they would be expected to excavate 1.5 cubic meters of earth (an increase to 2.5 cubic meters was discussed, but it is unclear whether it was implemented) or have their unit lay between 20.0 and 50.0 meters of track during a ten-hour workday. Workers who did not meet their quotas would have their pay reduced accordingly.

Arrangements would be made with the county prefects for the procurement and transport of food and the workers would be given cookware, but they were expected to acquire fuel on their own and bring their own utensils from home. They would be housed in wooden barracks or, if wood was unavailable, quartered in villages at the expense of CFR. This decision contradicted Antonescu's explicit orders that Jews were not to be quartered in villages, because of his fear of the detrimental effect interactions with Jewish laborers could have on civilian morale, but the General Staff ultimately did not intervene to stop it. Medications and medical supplies would be provided by CFR. The workers' periods of leave were greatly reduced, but they would be allowed a day of rest on Sunday, when they would have the opportunity to bathe and wash their clothes. These regulations would, in theory, create better living conditions than the minimum standards established by the General Staff; however, workers' statements reveal that in practice, their situation did not improve as a result of these policy changes.[54]

On September 29, the General Staff published a report from the adjutant to the chief of staff, General Nicolae Mazarini, that reviewed the regulations that had been enacted since August 6. While noting that the initial mobilization of laborers had caused problems, which he blamed on the chaos of the war and other "exceptional events," Mazarini concluded that since the military took control, the recruitment of laborers had conformed to the regulations in force.[55] This claim was dubious at best but reflected the General Staff's desire to convey to Antonescu that the forced labor system had been successfully reformed in order to convince him that it should be maintained. Mazarini ordered that forced labor would continue through December 15, when the labor camps and detachments would be dissolved for the winter and the Jews allowed to return home until the spring of 1942.[56]

The labor performed by internment camp inmates was generally organized in one of two ways: in workshops within the camp or in external labor groups. For example, at Târgu Jiu, some prisoners worked at the camp workshop producing clothing and other goods for the army. Others who were less fortunate were sent to work in agriculture, on the Bumbești-Livezeni rail line, or in the mines of the Jiu Valley, where the work was very hard and dangerous. The officer commanding the Jews working in the Jiu Valley, Lieutenant Trepaduș, was tried and convicted as a war criminal in 1946.[57] Labor in other camps, including Ialomița and Giurgiu, was organized in a similar manner. Most of the prisoners in those camps worked as agricultural laborers in the surrounding area.[58] In most cases,

Figure 2.2. Jewish forced laborers farm a field. United States Holocaust Memorial Museum, courtesy of Federation of Jewish Communities.

work that took place in a fixed area, such as agricultural labor, was done by Jews in internment camps or the General Staff's labor camps rather than by mobile labor detachments, which were used for projects such as road and railroad construction, which would require the laborers to travel as work progressed.

The internment camps experienced problems in addition to those caused by the initial mobilization. One of the first to emerge was food shortages. Neither the Ministry of Internal Affairs nor the General Staff had adequate logistics in place to supply food to the Jews in the camps. This problem was compounded by the fact that the Jews were explicitly forbidden to leave the camp under any circumstances except to go to work, preventing them from going to buy food on their own. Even when sufficient food was available, the food offered was relatively simple and there was little variety. The staple of the prisoners' diets was mămăligă, most often supplemented by bread and cabbage or potato soup, with meat and other vegetables only rarely available.[59]

As winter approached, shortages of winter clothing became acute, as almost none of the prisoners had blankets or winter coats. Exposure to the elements exacerbated existing health problems among the prisoners and facilitated the spread of disease. This problem was noted by inspectors who visited a labor camp in the village of Mintia, Hunedoara County, in southern Transylvania, who reported that productivity in the camp was "almost nil" because few of the workers had warm clothing and many of them were sick. Furthermore, due to a shortage of available Jewish doctors (many of whom had been requisitioned by the army for service in combat units and hospitals), medical care in the camps was substandard, if any was provided at all.[60]

A clear dichotomy exists in the official reports on the productivity in the internment camps. The work done in the workshops, which was supervised by camp personnel and often done by skilled workers, was often productive; agricultural, railroad, mining, and other heavy manual labor done outside the camps generally was not. The General Staff attributed this disparity to the difference in supervision of workers within the camp versus those outside of it. This attitude was reinforced by positive reports on productivity. On September 22, the commander of the Dâmbovița Gendarmerie Legion, Lieutenant Colonel Gheorghe Cartianu, reported that the 1,190 Jews in the Teiș-Târgoviște camp were repairing and cleaning the streets in Târgoviște. He noted that the Jews worked well "out of fear of being shot," though Cartianu did not report any instances of such executions occurring. Nonetheless, the workers must have been aware that the policy was in place.[61] Such reports would greatly influence the General Staff's thinking on how to improve the productivity of Jewish labor during the overhaul of the forced labor system in 1942.

Life in the army camps and detachments was likewise difficult and, in many cases, worse than in the internment camps, since the external detachments were generally farther away from cities and their supply lines therefore longer and less reliable. The daily routine in the camps and external detachments followed a similar pattern: the men were marched from their quarters to the work site, performed eight to ten hours of hard labor, and were then marched back to their quarters. They were fed their meals before and after these marches and during a thirty- to sixty-minute break in the middle of the day. Medical care was, in theory, provided within the camp or detachment quarters. The men were supervised at work by officers and soldiers, generally older reservists or, in the local detachments, members of the city garrison, who were responsible for ensuring the productivity of their labor as well as their presence at work and the safety and organization of the work site.

However, in practice, there were shortcomings in almost every area of logistics and the supply chain. The workers were supposed to be housed in barracks located a "safe" distance away from populated areas. Antonescu feared that if the Jews were quartered in or near Romanian towns and villages, they would wander about and spread "odious propaganda" and "discourage the populace."[62] However, many Jews, particularly those who were sent to the external detachments, arrived at their work sites to find that no housing existed for them at all and that they were expected to build their own barracks. In many cases, the workers arrived before the building materials for their housing did, either due to logistical failures or shortages of materials. Thus, in the early days of the 1941 labor campaign, many Jews were forced to sleep under the open sky. This problem was not exclusive to the labor detachments; it also affected the Doaga labor camp, which was undergoing rapid expansion at this time to accommodate not only additional Jewish laborers but also Soviet prisoners of war. Allen Feig, a Jewish laborer from Deva, said that when he first arrived at Doaga in the fall of 1941, he and his comrades slept in a trench with a straw roof while they built their own barracks.[63] Bica Bercovici, an eighteen-year-old Jew from Bucharest, also recalled poor conditions in Doaga, noting that his barrack only had three walls.[64] Paul Rosenfeld, a nineteen-year-old Jew who was assigned to a road construction detachment in Turda in the fall of 1941, remembered that his barrack had no heating and the men had no blankets, so they never undressed at night. Rosenfeld said that the living conditions in the detachment were more difficult for the workers to endure than the work itself.[65]

In other detachments, workers were quartered in abandoned buildings. William Farkas recalled that his detachment, which was deployed near Sighișoara, was housed in a deserted, unfinished school building. The building had neither windows nor doors, so the men had little protection from the elements. In addition, it was infested with vermin: one morning, a mouse jumped into his cup of ersatz coffee.[66] Haskal Brociner, a nineteen-year-old Jew from Bucharest, was sent to a labor camp at Dadilov, located in south-central Romania, about halfway between Bucharest and Giurgiu. He and the other two hundred Jews in the camp were housed in farm buildings, where they slept on the straw-covered floor. They were also forced to dig their own latrines.[67]

Road and railroad construction detachments faced another problem with housing: as construction progressed, the work site moved farther and farther away from the laborers' quarters. As a result, the distance they had to march to work each day increased to the point where it detracted from productivity. The commander of railroad detachment working near the city of Făgăraș, in central Romania, noted that because of frequent delays in acquiring building materials, it was almost impossible to construct housing for the Jews because by the time the barracks were completed, they were too far away from the work site to be viable. He proposed housing Jews near the edges of villages, in direct contravention of Antonescu's orders, but the General Staff never approved this proposal. However, in some cases, the detachment commanders or their supervising agencies did it anyway out of necessity.[68]

The quality of the workers' diets and the quantity of food available in the camps and detachments varied from location to location, depending on ease of access to food suppliers, the quality of transportation networks, and the financial means to procure enough food for all the men. They were usually responsible for preparing their own food and providing their own utensils; sometimes they were also sent to nearby towns and villages to purchase their own food, despite the General Staff's requirement that the Jews' employers supply them with food. Aurel Lupovici, who worked on a strategic highway for Romanian infantry near Dudești, recalled that the men in his detachment were expected to bring food from home or receive food through food packages. Many poor families could not send food to their relatives, so the better-off Jews helped those who were less fortunate. Eventually, the commander of the detachment, Captain Tomașuiu, had to take workers into Dudești to obtain sufficient food to feed the entire detachment.[69]

In some cases, local suppliers refused to sell food to the labor detachments because they did not want to give food to Jews. For example, workers from CFR Detachment 66 were sent to Turda to buy flour and bread but were turned away by a baker named Sfârlea, who had been ridiculed by the locals for providing food to the Jews.[70] Jewish laborers were easily identifiable both by their disheveled appearance and their armbands, allowing the store owners in the villages to charge the hungry men high prices for basic goods like bread and flour or refuse to sell them food at all. In addition, villagers frequently protested the presence of Jews coming to buy food. A General Staff report recorded complaints that Jews were "inundating" the villages and that their purchases of large amounts of food supplies drove up the cost of living for the residents, though no evidence for this complaint was provided.[71]

Some detachment commanders were forced to turn to the local Jewish communities for help with food supplies. Endre Altmann, who worked in a detachment repairing the rail line between Făgăraș and Sibiu, recalled that his detachment was supplied with food from the Jewish community in Arad—the city from which it had been dispatched—although Arad is nearly three hundred kilometers west of Făgăraș, halfway across the country. One or two Jews from his detachment made weekly trips to Arad to secure food supplies for the workers.[72] Most workers stated that they received enough food to avoid malnutrition, but little more. In a November 12 report, the head of CFR, Colonel (later General) T. C. Orezeanu, informed the General Staff that food shortages were a widespread problem in the railroad detachments, delivery of food had been irregular, and productivity had suffered as a result.[73]

Medical care in the labor detachments was often poor or nonexistent. In theory, there was to be one Jewish medic for every five hundred men in a camp or detachment. However, because of the shortage of doctors, this standard was rarely met. For example, an agricultural labor detachment in Latinu-Vădeni requested additional medical personnel in October 1941 because they had only one doctor for fifteen hundred laborers.[74] Most detachments had no trained medical personnel and treatment for injuries and illnesses was very rudimentary. Martin Schottek, who worked in a labor detachment cutting wood in the forest near the

Lișavă River, in southwestern Romania, recalled that there was no medic in his detachment and that he and his fellow laborers were lucky that there were no serious outbreaks of disease.[75] Stores of drugs and other medical supplies were also generally insufficient, even in camps and detachments with adequate numbers of medical personnel. In many cases, the only way the laborers could obtain even basic medications was through the intervention of the local Jewish community. As with food, assistance from the Jewish community leadership became a more or less official workaround to the problems created by the incompetent military and civilian administrators.

Due to the shortage of both doctors and medications, as well as the close quarters and generally poor living conditions, infections and illnesses were common among the workers. Vermin were a frequent problem as well. Haskal Brociner recalled that his sleeping quarters in the Dadilov labor camp, nothing more than a patch of straw on the floor of a farm building, were full of lice. He and the other men in Dadilov were deloused and had their heads shaved as a precaution against typhus.[76] Malaria and infected wounds were common maladies. Nonetheless, detachment commanders and military officials were eager to scapegoat sick Jews rather than accept responsibility for their pathetic condition. They were accused of injecting themselves (or having the Jewish medics inject them) with "harmful substances" to get out of work, an implausible but nonetheless convenient cover story for the inadequate provision of medical services.[77]

Rates of desertion from forced labor detachments were very high, much to the frustration of the military authorities. The General Headquarters complained that Jews had "sought through all means to escape from work" in a November 9 report on the progress of forced labor, which they attributed to a lack of "national spirit" and the "infernal character of the Jewish race."[78] Survivors who fled cited the poor conditions in the detachments and a desire to return to their families as the motivating factors in their decision. In practice, desertion was one of the only means of resistance available to the laborers. Harsh punishments were meted out to deserters. Andrei Văleanu was court-martialed and sent to Văcărești prison on a twenty-five-year sentence after deserting from Cotroceni shooting range; however, he was released in 1944, after the Antonescu government collapsed.[79]

It is unclear whether or how often prisoners were shot for attempting to escape or in reprisal for escapes as Antonescu had ordered in July 1941. Baruch Cohen, a twenty-two-year-old Jew working at the Cotroceni detachment, reported that one man was shot while attempting to escape from the detachment (although he did not say whether the man was killed).[80] Max Goldberger, who was at the Cotroceni detachment at roughly the same time, did not mention this shooting, although he did recall a Romanian officer threatening the men with decimation if anyone escaped.[81] Official reports, such as the one issued by the General

Headquarters, downplayed the use of such punishments; however, it is possible that these statements were a deliberate attempt to cover up shootings of laborers. Other survivors did not specifically mention shootings of escapees, but it is possible that they were carried out and neither witnessed nor reported. In any event, the threat of such punishments does not seem to have been an effective deterrent against desertion in most cases. The search for a solution to the high desertion rate was one of the primary reasons for the reorganization of the detachment structure in the early summer of 1942, as the military authorities believed poor supervision by the guards to be responsible for both the frequent desertions and the poor productivity of Jewish labor.[82]

In addition to the awful living conditions, the work the Jews were required to do was physically exhausting and, in many cases, dangerous. Injuries were common, particularly in the road and railway construction detachments and among those sent to work in stone quarries. Fatalities were not as common, but they were reported. In mid-September 1941, Jewish laborer Marcel Moise, who was working in a quarry near Mehedinți, was killed when a retaining wall on the side of the pit collapsed on him. His death was officially reported as an accident and no one was held responsible.[83] Haim Leizerovici, who worked in a quarry in Dobruja, recalled that several men in his detachment were killed while transporting heavy stones down a hill in late fall 1941. He also noted that while he did not feel that he and his fellow laborers were being deliberately worked to death, he did believe that the Romanian soldiers purposefully made their working conditions harder than they needed to be.[84] Other men died from health problems brought on or exacerbated by the stress of hard labor and inadequate medical attention. As Louis Beno Nedeleanu recalled, his detachment in Dobruja had no doctor, and disease was common; he stated that some sick prisoners may have died as a result.[85]

Some laborers also suffered from deliberate mistreatment and humiliation by the Romanian officers and soldiers guarding their detachments. While such behavior was theoretically not permitted—officially, the Jews were to be treated like soldiers in regular units—it was not uncommon. Many soldiers used the isolated labor camps and detachments as venues to express their hatred of Jews through both verbal and physical abuse. Beatings were meted out for tardiness, working too slowly, or any perceived slight committed by a Jewish laborer; ten to twenty-five lashes was the standard punishment.

Andrei Voinea recalled that his first commanding officer, at a road detachment in Vârciorog, was "a brute" and that the sergeant in charge of his second detachment, a CFR battalion near Cânepiști, was "an indoctrinated Legionnaire" who lectured him on his innate character deficiencies as a Jew, according to Iron Guard propaganda (while its leadership was purged from the government, former Iron Guard members were still present at the lower levels, including rank-and-file soldiers and local police).[86] Mihail Theodoru, who worked in a CFR detachment near Craiova, was berated by the Romanian soldiers there and told that the Jews were responsible for Romania's territorial losses in 1940, a common theme in the Antonescu regime's antisemitic propaganda. Theodoru said that the workers in his detachment were beaten when they did not meet their unrealistic daily work quotas.[87] Leon Herscovici, who was sent to a CFR detachment outside of Bucharest, reported that the workers there were beaten for working too slowly and that Romanian soldiers passing by on the rail lines often fired potshots at them (although no one was actually hit, according to Herscovici).[88] Paul Costin (born Paul Cohn) said that tardiness was punished by ten lashes in his detachment. Such punishments were carried out at the end of the week during Sunday roll call, in full view of the other laborers. According to Costin, the workers were careful only to talk about work around the officers, and there were some who were to be avoided at all costs (including one physically imposing man whom he estimated was about two meters tall).[89]

However, such experiences were not universal. Other survivors reported that they were treated with respect by their guards and that they were not subjected to antisemitic abuse. Endre Altmann recalled that his commander, a Transylvanian Saxon, was "a very nice person" who treated Altmann as an equal because of his qualifications as an engineer. Furthermore, the German engineer overseeing the technical aspects of the detachment's work met with the prefect to demand better treatment of the workers. Altmann noted that such a bold action could have been taken only by a German.[90] The most important determinants of an individual Jew's experience during his time in the forced labor system were the attitudes and behavior of the Romanian military personnel with whom he interacted. Their attitudes determined not only whether the laborers were treated decently but also the attempts they made (or did not make) to protect the laborers from dangers at the work site and the diligence (or lack thereof) of their efforts to procure sufficient supplies and ensure decent living conditions.

Along with the Jews in Ministry of Internal Affairs' internment camps and those working in the military camps and detachments, there was a third category of forced laborers: the requisitioned workers. This group included both men whose labor was requested by government agencies and private firms and those who were given exemptions to remain in their prewar jobs while they trained their ethnic Romanian "doubles." Most of these men were skilled laborers or university-educated professionals who were needed for war-related production or official business. The legally established process of requisition was similar for both types of workers. A request was made to the local commissions, formed after the September 1941 interministerial meeting (or, in Bucharest, directly to the General Staff) and, if the need for the workers in question was deemed valid, an exemption from service in the labor detachments was granted and the workers were assigned to their new employer. In theory, these requests were to be made for a certain number of workers, rather than for individual persons by name, to minimize abuse of the system. In practice, however, the system worked somewhat differently. The local commissions, either inundated with requests or uncertain how to handle them, sent many of the petitions they received to the General Staff's Recruitment Office for evaluation. While the government agencies that utilized Jewish labor generally followed the procedure correctly, private employers often did not, frequently requesting workers by name rather than number, to the General Staff's frustration.

In many cases, the needs of private interests included the release of Jewish personnel who had already been deployed to camps or detachments. On November 13, twenty-three Jews were released from the Teiş internment camp to work at the Senior War College in Bucharest.[91] Three weeks earlier, a Jew named Victor Zisserman had been granted a transfer from CFR Detachment 59 to CFR Detachment 58 and allowed a temporary reprieve from work so he could liquidate the accounts of his business in Bucharest, which he had been forced to sell to an ethnic Romanian.[92] Furthermore, companies that requested Jewish workers often ignored regulations on their use. Requisitioned Jews were officially forbidden from working in the offices of businesses. However, on October 9, the General Staff received a report that a Jewish technical advisor and two Jewish accountants were working in the office of the Laromet firm in Bucharest, constituting "a danger to security." In addition, the thirty-two Jews working at the firm had been requested by name, rather than by number, demonstrating that the General Staff was inconsistent in the application of its own rules regarding requisitions and that the system was open to abuse.[93]

While requests for workers from private firms were sometimes declined, whether due to lack of available personnel or a determination that the workers requested were unnecessary, requests from government agencies were usually granted. The needs of Romanian state institutions were prioritized according to their importance to the war effort. The state road and railway agencies received first consideration. However, Jews were often sent to work at relatively trivial tasks while the needs of CFR were frequently not met. In one such case, a Jew was sent to work at the Tudor Muşetescu Theater in Bucharest while a shortage of railroad construction workers continued.[94] They were only turned down on rare occasions, such as a request for one hundred Jewish workers at the port of Constanţa, declined due to inadequate numbers of available laborers.

Requests from the Wehrmacht, which often used Jewish labor to work on defensive installations or in factories with which they had contracted to supply war materiel, superseded even those from Romanian state institutions. For example, the German head quartermaster in Romania (Oberquartiermeister Rumänien) requested thirteen workers for the La Filip factory in Bucharest, which was producing goods for the Wehrmacht.[95] Another Jew named Arthur Storper was granted an exemption because he was working for the German Military Mission (Deutsche Heeresmission) in Bucharest.[96] Other foreign entities were also able to obtain exemptions for Romanian Jews. For example, on September 23, 1941, the Peruvian legation in Bucharest requested the exemption of Constantin Ruleta, a fluent Spanish speaker who had worked for them as an interpreter for two years.[97]

The enormous number of requests fielded by the local commissions and the General Staff underscored a major problem facing both the military and civilian authorities concerned with forced labor: Romania's continued dependence on the skilled labor of its Jewish population. While the November 16, 1940, Romanianization law required that all Jews be replaced with ethnic Romanians by December 31, 1941, an evaluation of the Jewish workforce on May 15 of that year revealed that there were 51,475 Jewish professionals and 22,765 Jewish craftsmen in Romania, a total of 74,240 skilled workers the country did not have the capacity to replace.[98] Furthermore, as the Ministry of National Defense noted in its October 1941 report on forced labor, over 75 percent of the senior administrative personnel and over 67 percent of the junior administrative personnel in Romanian industrial concerns with more than 100 employees were "foreigners" (i.e., nonethnic Romanians), most of whom were Jews.[99]

While there was only partial overlap between these Jews and the portion of the Jewish population that was eligible for conscription into forced labor, the requisition of skilled workers nonetheless removed a substantial portion of eligible workers from the labor pool. According to the General Headquarters, by November 1941, 9,365 Jews had been given exemptions, more than 11 percent of the available men.[100] Although the deadline for the removal of Jewish employees from Romanian businesses and industry was still over a month away, this large figure indicates the extent to which the Romanian economy was still reliant on Jewish skilled labor and the great difficulty Antonescu's government would have in its attempts to Romanianize the labor force.

The disorganization and poor productivity of the detachments, combined with the high number of exemptions given to Jewish workers, were a source of frustration for Antonescu. It was clear that forced labor was not providing the expected benefits and that those within the government to whom he had entrusted its administration had often proven incapable or corrupt. Antonescu discussed the results of forced labor in 1941 and debated its future with the members of his Council of Ministers in a meeting on November 19:

MIHAI ANTONESCU: Minister [of the National Economy Ion] Marinescu wishes to discuss the problem of Jewish labor.

ION ANTONESCU: The problem has been studied and [the study] is near completion. [The Jews] should be subject to a financial contribution [to the state].

COLONEL RADU DAVIDESCU, CHIEF OF THE MILITARY CABINET: The question was researched by the General Staff.

GENERAL NICOLAE STOENESCU, MINISTER OF FINANCE: It said that all Jews should be subjected to a fixed tax of 30,000 lei plus 3 percent of their income.

ION ANTONESCU: Do not fix it at 30,000 lei, because not all of them can pay that sum. The fixed contribution should be set in accordance with their income . . .

STOENESCU: Because of the fact that some have small incomes, we have set the fixed tax at 30,000 lei, to which we will add three percent of the income for the rich.

ION ANTONESCU: How can a poor Jew pay 30,000 lei?

STOENESCU: Then they will be sent to community labor.

ION ANTONESCU: I no longer want them to do this work. I want every Jew to pay.

MIHAI ANTONESCU: We can find a solution: a principal contribution, with exceptions . . .

ION ANTONESCU: It must be a proper solution, because each should pay in accordance with his ability and his income. What is the right way to apply this just principle . . . in which the Yids will pay in accordance with what they can?

MIHAI ANTONESCU: I believe that the minister of finance has the right idea when he says that for them to play only a fiscal role is not sufficient. That would benefit the Jews, especially those who have reduced incomes. It is possible to fix an amount, a minimum individual tax, aside from the portion of income as the minister of finance has suggested, and for exceptional cases, this amount can be decreased if it is justified.

ION ANTONESCU: No. [That would] enable abuses [of the system]. We should create a solution which does not allow a dishonest functionary to extort the Jews.

MIRCEA VULCĂNESCU, UNDERSECRETARY OF STATE FOR FINANCE: The problem can be solved like this: there are Jews who have money who are important in the economy. They can pay. But there are others who are excluded from economic life, who can no longer pay. They should be organized for labor . . .

ION ANTONESCU: Those who cannot pay will do work in the community interest. And, if they cannot work, the [Jewish] community will pay for them. Those who cannot work because they are sick, the community will pay for them.

VULCĂNESCU: The Germans have created a very well-organized system: they put [the Jews] in the ghetto and they work as cobblers, tailors, etc., to satisfy the needs of the German [people].

ION ANTONESCU: And they work like that here, they work as tailors or other things. At Târgu Jiu, they have produced two million [lei] in goods.

VULCĂNESCU: This work will be paid for with the money we collect from them.

ION ANTONESCU: But we have gotten away from the question. Here, "work in the community interest" has not gotten results, because the Yids have cheated and our crooks have enabled them. The Yids were put to unskilled labor, work which was not in accordance with their abilities and training. I do not want this situation to continue. I want them to make a contribution to the Romanian nation. The Jews do not shed blood for this country, but they use its highways, and they contribute very little to its struggles. Therefore, we should impose a tax upon them. This problem should be studied, because we [have seen] how they subvert the requirements and how they evade the crooks, and because the imposition should be just, it should be in accordance with the ability of every Jew to pay. Those who were excluded from the economy will perform forced labor. If they cannot work, they will pay. For those who cannot pay, the community will pay. If not, they will be expelled from the country, because we do not keep parasites in the country. They will be . . . expelled from the country, if the community does not pay.[101]

Antonescu's statements in this meeting indicate that his patience with the unproductive forced labor system was rapidly running out. He also revealed his desire that the Jews continue to make sacrifices for the country, lest they become "parasites," and the connection of forced labor with both their contribution to the economy and their participation in the nation's struggle demonstrates that he viewed forced labor as a tool for achieving both economic and ideological goals. The ideas that Antonescu proposed in the November 19 cabinet meeting were very similar to the guidelines he would provide for the General Staff as it began the process of reforming the forced labor system in the spring of 1941.

The military authorities carried out their own evaluation of the forced labor system in the fall of 1941. On November 9, the General Headquarters issued a report on the progress of forced labor. It was highly critical of both the General Staff and civilian administration, as well as the laborers themselves. Jews were accused of feigning injuries and illnesses to avoid work, as well as deserting and putting forth minimal effort—claims that were true in many cases, although the report is also laden with antisemitic stereotypes and racist propaganda. However, the administration of the forced labor system was criticized more heavily because of its initial failures in the recruitment and organization of laborers, poor supervision of the detachments, lax enforcement of discipline by the detachment commanders, permissiveness in granting exemptions, and other forms of corruption. The General Headquarters' report was self-exculpatory and the author praised his office's own efforts to enforce the labor regulations. However, despite their deliberate oversight of their own failings, the report is otherwise an accurate depiction of the problems that existed in the first three months of the labor campaign, as the reports from the detachments and testimonies of survivors indicate. As a result of the failures of the 1941 labor campaign, the General Headquarters proposed a massive reorganization of the entire system both to "obtain maximum productivity" and "improve public opinion of forced labor."[102]

Two important decisions were made based on this report. The first was that there should be a systematic review of the status of the Jews who were still working in private businesses and industry to determine who was "absolutely necessary" to the economy and who could be replaced with a non-Jew and conscripted into forced labor. This review was initially planned for the winter months, while the labor camps and detachments would be demobilized. However, in reality, it took place slightly later, in the spring of 1942, after many laborers had been remobilized. The second decision was an affirmation of the previous proposal that there should be a liaison office between the General Staff and the Ministry of Labor to coordinate the administration of the labor camps and detachments.[103]

This office, the General Inspectorate of Labor Camps and Detachments (Inspectoratul general al taberilor și coloanelor de muncă obligatorie)—commonly referred to as the General Inspectorate—was created by Decree-Law No. 1003, issued on November 15, 1941. The General Inspectorate was intended to work alongside the undersecretary of state for labor. It would be responsible for the establishment, organization, and administration of individual camps and detachments, as well as monitoring the progress of work in the camps and detachments. The inspectorate would also collect proposals from various government agencies regarding forced labor and communicate their needs to the General Staff, supervise the examination of workers and the coordination of their work assignments, and manage the budgets for the individual camps and detachments. The camps and detachments would still be staffed by army personnel and the laborers would still be subject to the military legal code, but the General Inspectorate would have substantial leeway to interpret the General Staff's instructions as it saw fit. Its personnel would be appointed by the undersecretary of state for labor with the approval of the General Staff.[104]

The General Staff ordered the demobilization of all Jewish laborers conscripted under the military system on December 15, 1941, due to inclement weather, with the expectation that forced labor would resume sometime in March 1942.[105] Despite this order, some workers remained at work as late as December 22. Rather than being allowed to return to their homes, Jewish laborers were required to remain in their respective counties' capitals, where they were forced to sweep snow from the streets and railways. Jews sent to work in government agencies and private firms were not granted release and had to continue working through the winter. Of the 84,042 Jews who were eligible for conscription into forced labor in 1941, 47,345 had been sent to work as of November 3, 9,365 had been exempted for various reasons, 11,933 remained available (most of whom were listed as "intellectuals" unfit for heavy labor), and the situation of the remaining 15,399 was unknown, demonstrating how disorganized the administration of the forced labor system was. In total, about one hundred labor camps and detachments had been created in 1941, excluding the internment camps operated by the Ministry of Internal Affairs.[106]

Although the General Staff and Ministry of Labor had attempted to "rationalize" the forced labor system by increasing the productivity of Jewish labor and allowing the exemption of workers deemed "necessary" to the economy, their efforts had largely been in vain. The ineffective recruitment, deployment, and supervision of workers, as well as the inefficiency of supply chains and poor living and working conditions, had doomed the first labor campaign. The failures of 1941 necessitated major improvements to the forced labor system, focused on better organization in the labor camps and detachments themselves as well as a more efficient process for determining which Jews were still "necessary" to their employers and granting exemptions.

A memo circulated by General Eugen Popescu, a member of the General Staff, on November 29 recognized the need for better organization and staffing of the labor detachments but also alluded to the eventual direction of the regime's Jewish policy and the fate of the forced laborers:

> [Forced labor] constitutes only a temporary solution—a reprieve—in the total solution of the problem, which can be nothing short of the deportation of all Jews from the country without exception, even if it must be done in multiple stages. The Jews have harmed us greatly through their capacity for exploitation and corruption, as well as through the ideas they propagate, but it is also true that they have had and still have an important role in Romanian industry and commerce. Hundreds of requests, directed by Romanians to the General Staff, show that Jews [have not been] replaced in many areas of industry and commerce, leading one to the conclusion that their departure would have serious consequences, which could greatly harm our commerce and industry. Their disorganized departure will therefore cause very important losses, which should be anticipated. But nothing can be done without sacrifices, and as the Jews in our country have proven to be a danger from every point of view, regardless of what losses we may suffer, we should not renounce the radical solution of the [Jewish] problem.[107]

The "radical solution" Popescu alluded to was already well underway in the recaptured territories of Bessarabia and Bukovina. On June 12, 1941, ten days before Operation Barbarossa began, Hitler informed Antonescu of the general Nazi plan to deport the Jews of occupied eastern Europe "to the east." In that same meeting, Antonescu revealed his goal of "cleansing the land" of Jews in Bessarabia and Bukovina. This "cleansing" was carried out by the Romanian army, police, and gendarmes, in cooperation with the German Eleventh Army and the accompanying Einsatzgruppe D, led by SS-Gruppenführer Otto Ohlendorf. Despite the presence of the German forces, the Romanians took the leading role in executing Antonescu's order, with German troops supporting them. General Constantin "Piki" Vasiliu, commander in chief of the Romanian Gendarmerie, explained "cleansing the land" as a three-step process. First, all rural Jews would be "liquidated." Second, all Jews in urban areas would be forced into ghettos. Finally, a standing order to arrest anyone suspected of collaborating with the Soviets would be put in place.[108]

Massacres in the reoccupied territories of Bessarabia and Bukovina commenced as soon as Romanian and the southernmost German forces began their phase of the invasion (Operation München) on July 2. One of the first such massacres occurred in the town of Ciudei, where Romanian forces murdered as many as 572 Jews.[109] On the same day, 200 Jews were killed in the city of Storojineț. During the following weeks, the massacres continued in almost every town and village captured by the Romanians: 880 were killed at Noua Suliță on July 6 and 1,000 died at Edineți that same day; 311 more Jews perished at the hands of Romanian troops in Sculeni; 185 were murdered by their peasant neighbors at Banila; 2,000 Jews were killed by the Romanians in Cernăuți on July 5 and a further 400 locked inside a synagogue that was burned to the ground by the Germans on July 9.[110]

However, the most lethal phase of the Holocaust in Romania was the deportation of Jews from the occupied territories to Transnistria, where the deportees, as well as native Ukrainian Jews, were confined to squalid, hastily prepared camps and ghettos. In late July, the Jews in Chișinău were concentrated into a ghetto in the city, from which they were subsequently deported to Transnistria in October 1941.[111] By the end of 1941, 135,000 Jews had been deported (some by train but in many cases on foot) across the Dniester and thrown into the "human dumping ground" of Transnistria, often without food or winter clothing.[112] Starvation, disease, and exposure, as well as massacres by Romanian soldiers and gendarmes, would claim tens of thousands of lives in the fall and winter of 1941. By the end of October, Romanian forces had already murdered between 45,000 and 60,000 Jews in Bessarabia and Bukovina.[113]

In late October 1941, violence against the Jews in Transnistria escalated further. After a monthlong siege by the Fourth Army in which the Romanian forces suffered nearly forty thousand casualties, Odessa finally fell on October 16.[114] Six days later, a delayed-fuse bomb left by the Soviets exploded at the Romanian army headquarters in Odessa, killing sixty-seven people, including the commander, General Ioan Glogojeanu. In retaliation, as many as twenty-five thousand Jews were killed in or near the city on the following three days.[115] The presence of typhus and other diseases in the camps, as well as the regime's fear of the Jews of the formerly Soviet-occupied territories as agents of "Judeo-Bolshevism," led to further massacres. For example, at Bogdanovca, forty-eight thousand Jews were massacred in December 1941 after a small outbreak of typhus in the camp. Other such massacres took place at the nearby Domanovca and Acmecetca camps.[116]

Unlike the Jews of Bessarabia, Bukovina, and Transnistria, the Jews of the Old Kingdom and southern Transylvania had thus far been spared the worst. They had been subjected to internal deportation, deprivation of property, and forced labor, but had not been subjected to mass killings (aside from the pogroms in Bucharest and Iași). However, a representative of the Reich Main Security Office, SS-Hauptsturmführer Gustav Richter, was already in Bucharest working to influence Romanian Jewish policy. After the Wannsee Conference in January 1942, his task was to persuade Antonescu to participate in what would soon be known as the Final Solution to the Jewish Question, the systematic mass murder of Europe's Jews in the Nazi extermination camps.[117]

The General Staff would introduce wide-ranging reforms to the forced labor system in 1942. These reforms included major changes to the organization of the labor detachments and the process for granting exemptions, some of which were beneficial from the government's perspective and some of which led to unintended and undesirable consequences. However, these reforms were made with the understanding that forced labor was only an intermediate phase in Antonescu's Jewish policy, which would continue until the "radical solution" Antonescu desired could be completed.

Notes

1. USHMMA, RG-25.002M, reel 18, file 483-41, 58–62.
2. Ancel, *History of the Holocaust in Romania*, 127.
3. Mihail Sebastian, *Journal 1935–1944: The Fascist Years* (Chicago: Ivan R. Dee, 2000), 302.
4. Ancel, *History of the Holocaust in Romania*, 127.
5. Ovidiu Creangă, "Târgu Jiu," in *The United States Holocaust Memorial Museum Encyclopedia of Camps and Ghettos*, ed. Geoffrey P. Megargee, Joseph R. White, and Mel Hecker (Bloomington: Indiana University Press, 2018), 3:781.
6. Ovidiu Creangă, "Doaga," in Megargee, White, and Hecker, *United States Holocaust Memorial Museum Encyclopedia*, 3:668–669.

7. Radu Ioanid, *The Iași Pogrom, June–July 1941: A Photo Documentary from the Holocaust in Romania* (Bloomington: Indiana University Press, 2017), 2.
8. Friling et al., *Final Report*, 120–124.
9. Ioanid, *Iași Pogrom*, 8–10.
10. Aristide Rauch, interview 28763, *Visual History Archive*, USC Shoah Foundation, 2011, accessed online at the United States Holocaust Memorial Museum on February 6, 2015, http://vhaonline.usc.edu/viewingPage?testimonyID=30973&returnIndex=0.
11. Ancel, *History of the Holocaust in Romania*, 142.
12. Iancu Ț., interview from Projekt Zwangsarbeit 1939–1945, za280, audio interview.
13. Ibid.
14. Friling et al., *Final Report*, 126.
15. Creangă, "Doaga," 3:668–669.
16. USHMMA, RG-25.003M, reel 144, file 2410, 370–371.
17. Ibid., 219.
18. Ovidiu Creangă, "Teiș-Târgoviște," in Megargee, White, and Hecker, *United States Holocaust Memorial Museum Encyclopedia*, 3:789.
19. USHMMA, RG-25.002M, Romanian State Archives Records, reel 10, Dosar Special, 61.
20. USHMMA, RG-25.003M, reel 144, file 2410, 218–219. The camps at Giurgiu and Vlașca are poorly documented, and no specific information regarding the origin of their deportees (beyond simply "Bessarabia") is available in the archival records. These Jews were likely deported in a second wave of deportations after hostilities began, although no date for their departure or arrival at the camps is available.
21. Bărbulescu et al., *Munca obligatorie*, document 8, 86.
22. USHMMA, RG-25.003M, reel 140, file 2370, 930.
23. USHMMA, RG-25.003M, reel 144, file 2410, 220.
24. USHMMA, RG-25.003M, reel 144, file 2413, 237–238.
25. Ibid., 242–264.
26. Ibid., 246.
27. Ibid., 252.
28. USHMMA, RG-25.003M, reel 140, file 2370, 314–315.
29. USHMMA, RG-25.003M, reel 144, file 2413, 328–329.
30. Sebastian, *Journal*, 479. Sebastian references a "Poligon detachment" in operation in October 1940.
31. USHMMA, RG-25.003M, reel 141, file 2371, 400–401.
32. USHMMA, RG-25.003M, reel 144, file 2410, 370.
33. USHMMA, RG-25.003M, reel 141, file 2371, 589.
34. Bărbulescu et al., *Munca obligatorie*, document 43, 178.
35. USHMMA, RG-25.003M, reel 141, file 2371, 287.
36. Bărbulescu et al., *Munca obligatorie*, document 43, 180.
37. Fred Gerbel, *Sâmbătă se deportează: Reportagii din vremea prigoanei* (Bucharest: Holicom, 1946), 22.
38. USHMMA, RG-25.003M, reel 144, file 2410, 220.
39. Ibid., 222.
40. Ibid., 238.
41. USHMMA, RG-25.003M, reel 144, file 2413, 246.
42. USHMMA, RG-25.003M, reel 138, file 2367, 109.

43. USHMMA, RG-25.003M, reel 144, file 2410, 222.
44. Ibid., 224.
45. Bărbulescu et al., *Munca obligatorie*, document 11, 93.
46. Glass, *Deutschland und die Verfolgung der Juden*, 194.
47. Bărbulescu et al., *Munca obligatorie*, document 11, 93.
48. Ibid., document 11, 93–94.
49. Ibid., document 11, 94.
50. Ibid., document 14, 97.
51. USHMMA, RG-25.003M, reel 144, file 2410, 40–50.
52. Ibid., 43.
53. Ibid., 47.
54. Bărbulescu et al., *Munca obligatorie*, document 19, 104–109.
55. USHMMA, RG-25.003M, reel 144, file 2410, 346.
56. Ibid., 347.
57. Interview with Ion Butnaru, USHMMA, RG-50.030*0049, USHMM Oral History Collection.
58. USHMMA, RG-25.003M, reel 144, file 2410, 368.
59. Bărbulescu et al., *Munca obligatorie*, document 22, 112.
60. USHMMA, RG-25.003M, reel 140, file 2370, 681.
61. USHMMA, RG-25.002M, reel 10, Dosar Special, 61.
62. Benjamin, *Problema evreiască*, document 112, 322–323.
63. Allen Feig, interview 16852, Visual History Archive, USC Shoah Foundation, accessed online at the United States Holocaust Memorial Museum on February 5, 2015, http://vhaonline.usc.edu/viewingPage?testimonyID=17520&returnIndex=0.
64. Bica Bercovici, interview 50196, Visual History Archive, USC Shoah Foundation, accessed online at the United States Holocaust Memorial Museum on February 5, 2015, http://vhaonline.usc.edu/viewingPage?testimonyID=53091&returnIndex=0.
65. Paul Rosenfeld, interview 12572, Visual History Archive, USC Shoah Foundation, accessed online at the United States Holocaust Memorial Museum on February 5, 2015, http://vhaonline.usc.edu/viewingPage?testimonyID=13530&returnIndex=0.
66. Interview with William Farkas, USHMMA, RG-50.030*0026, USHMM Museum Oral History Collection.
67. Haskal Brociner, interview 21836, Visual History Archive, USC Shoah Foundation, accessed online at the United States Holocaust Memorial Museum on February 6, 2015, http://vhaonline.usc.edu/viewingPage?testimonyID=22813&returnIndex=0.
68. Bărbulescu et al., *Munca obligatorie*, document 41, 173–174.
69. Aurel Lupovici, interview 25432, Visual History Archive, USC Shoah Foundation, accessed online at the United States Holocaust Memorial Museum on March 7, 2015, http://vhaonline.usc.edu/viewingPage?testimonyID=27075&returnIndex=0.
70. Bărbulescu et al., *Munca obligatorie*, document 42, 175.
71. USHMMA, RG-25.003M, reel 141, file 2371, 396.
72. Endre Altmann, interview 11613, Visual History Archive, USC Shoah Foundation, accessed online at the United States Holocaust Memorial Museum on March 7, 2015, http://vhaonline.usc.edu/viewingPage?testimonyID=10931&returnIndex=0.
73. USHMMA, RG-25.003M, reel 141, file 2371, 345.
74. Ibid., 115.

75. Martin Schottek, interview 49548, Visual History Archive, USC Shoah Foundation, accessed online at the United States Holocaust Memorial Museum on February 6, 2015, http://vhaonline.usc.edu/viewingPage?testimonyID=52393&returnIndex=0.
76. Brociner, interview 21836.
77. USHMMA, RG-25.013M, Preşidinţia Consiliului de Miniştri—Cabinetul Militar (Fond 764), reel 21, file 566, 3–4.
78. Bărbulescu et al., *Munca obligatorie*, document 43, 179.
79. Andrei V., interview from Projekt Zwangsarbeit 1939–1945, za279, audio interview.
80. Baruch Cohen, interview 27946, Visual History Archive, USC Shoah Foundation, accessed online at the United States Holocaust Memorial Museum on February 5, 2015, http://vhaonline.usc.edu/viewingPage?testimonyID=30014&returnIndex=0.
81. Max Goldberger, interview 25547, Visual History Archive, USC Shoah Foundation, accessed online at the United States Holocaust Memorial Museum on March 6, 2015, http://vhaonline.usc.edu/viewingPage?testimonyID=27260&returnIndex=0.
82. Bărbulescu et al., *Munca obligatorie*, document 43, 179–180.
83. USHMMA, RG-25.003M, reel 141, file 2371, 22.
84. Haim Leizerovici, interview 12250, Visual History Archive, USC Shoah Foundation, accessed online at the United States Holocaust Memorial Museum on February 7, 2015, http://vhaonline.usc.edu/viewingPage?testimonyID=11381&returnIndex=0.
85. Louis Beno N., interview from Projekt Zwangsarbeit 1939–1945, za279, video interview.
86. Andrei V., interview from Projekt Zwangsarbeit 1939–1945, za280, audio interview.
87. Mihail Theodoru, interview 49504, Visual History Archive, USC Shoah Foundation, accessed online at the United States Holocaust Memorial Museum on February 8, 2015, http://vhaonline.usc.edu/viewingPage?testimonyID=52408&returnIndex=0.
88. Leon Herscovici, interview 50436, Visual History Archive, USC Shoah Foundation, accessed online at the United States Holocaust Memorial Museum on February 7, 2015, http://vhaonline.usc.edu/viewingPage?testimonyID=53271&returnIndex=0.
89. Paul C., interview from Projekt Zwangsarbeit 1939–1945, za270, audio interview.
90. Altmann, interview 11613.
91. USHMMA, RG-25.003M, reel 141, file 2371, 518.
92. Ibid., 36–37.
93. Ibid., 13.
94. Ibid., 44.
95. USHMMA, RG-25.003M, reel 144, file 2410, 418.
96. USHMMA, RG-25.003M, reel 141, file 2371, 28.
97. Ibid., 336.
98. USHMMA, RG-25.003M, reel 144, file 2410, 15.
99. Bărbulescu et al., *Munca obligatorie*, document 37, 149.
100. Ibid., document 39, 170–171.
101. USHMMA, RG-25.002M, reel 18, file 483-41, 58–62.
102. Bărbulescu et al., *Munca obligatorie*, document 43, 182.
103. Ibid., document 43, 182–185.
104. Ibid., document 48, 193–195.
105. Ibid., document 48, 166–167.
106. Ibid., document 39, 170–171.
107. USHMMA, RG-25.003M, reel 144, file 2410, 12–13.

108. Ancel, *History of the Holocaust in Romania*, 224–225.
109. Ioanid, *Holocaust in Romania*, 97–108.
110. Ancel, *History of the Holocaust in Romania*, 222–223; Ioanid, *Holocaust in Romania*, 94–101.
111. Paul Shapiro, *The Kishinev Ghetto, 1941–1942: A Documentary History of the Holocaust in Romania's Contested Borderlands* (Tuscaloosa: University of Alabama Press, 2015), 24 and 69.
112. Sebastian Balta, *Rumänien und die Großmächte in der Ära Antonescu (1940–1944)* (Stuttgart: Franz Steiner, 2005), 217.
113. Heinen, *Rumänien*, 65.
114. Axworthy, Crăciunoiu, and Scafeș, *Third Axis, Fourth Ally*, 56.
115. Friling et al., *Final Report*, 150.
116. Ibid., 148–150.
117. Ancel, *History of the Holocaust in Romania*, 463–464.

3 The "Review of the Working Jews"

AFTER THE FAILURES of the 1941 forced labor campaign, Antonescu and the General Staff both recognized the need for substantial reforms to the labor system to ensure the same mistakes would not be repeated in 1942 and to increase the productivity of Jewish labor. This process began with a collaborative effort between the General Staff and the Ministry of Labor through a new policymaking body, the General Inspectorate of Labor Camps and Detachments. In addition, agencies that used Jewish labor, such as CFR, came up with new guidelines for their own labor detachments, a further indication of cooperation between the military and civilian authorities in their attempts to improve the productivity of forced labor.

However, tensions between the military and civilian bureaucracy soon emerged. A central point of the reforms was the need to "review" the status of workers who had been exempted from forced labor and determine which workers were truly necessary to their employers and which could be sent to forced labor without harming the economy. The General Staff expected to have the final say in this process, but Antonescu instead permitted his commissar for Jewish affairs, Radu Lecca, to organize the commissions that would conduct the review. The infamously corrupt Lecca soon turned the review process into a moneymaking opportunity, enriching himself and his cronies by extorting exemption "fees" from Jews who wished to continue working in their jobs and avoid forced labor. The corrupt commissions undermined the review process, angering the military authorities, who felt that their control over the forced labor was being usurped.

In April 1942, Antonescu ordered the General Staff to come up with its own proposals for reorganizing the forced labor system, without input from the civilian authorities. While he gave them general guidelines to work from, they were largely able to compose policy as they saw fit. They concluded that the best course of action was to change the organizational structure of the labor system, moving away from smaller camps and detachments and toward larger detachments with greater numbers of supervisory personnel, believing that a smaller number of larger detachments would be easier to administer than a large number of smaller ones. In addition, they introduced harsher disciplinary measures, intended to intimidate the Jewish laborers and motivate them to work harder. However, for these measures to be successful, they would have to be implemented conscientiously by the lower-level actors who had demonstrated so much incompetence and corruption the year before, meaning that however ambitious the General Staff's changes to the forced labor system were, they still had the same failure point as in 1941.

The General Inspectorate of Labor Camps and Detachments was established as a new oversight body for forced labor on January 1, 1942, as the November 15, 1941, Decree-Law No. 1003 had ordered. Its creation was announced on New Year's Day by General Staff Order No. 70407, which delineated the responsibilities of the new General Inspectorate and those of the General Staff.[1] It was led by Theodor Mociulschi, a "notorious and corrupt antisemite"[2] who was a follower of Alexandru C. Cuza during his days as a law student in Iași, where he was president of the Association of Christian Students, a far-right antisemitic organization.[3]

The General Inspectorate was tasked with the establishment, organization, staffing, leadership, and inspection of labor camps and detachments; the deployment of Jewish laborers; and the creation of "programs of labor" for the camps and detachments in cooperation with the departments that employed them. The General Staff retained overall control of the forced labor system, the right to give directives and appoint personnel to the General Inspectorate, and responsibility for collecting statistical data on forced labor. The order also declared that the start date for the 1942 forced labor campaign would be pushed back to April 1, while Jews requisitioned by government and private businesses would return to work on January 8. All exemptions from forced labor for economic reasons were extended through January 20, pending further review.[4]

The General Inspectorate was given substantial power over the day-to-day administration of the labor camps and detachments and would hold significant power in determining how forced labor would be carried out. It also assumed other duties such as handling requests for more than fifty laborers, a task that had been assigned to the General Staff under the August 8, 1941, General Instructions; in this sense, the General Inspectorate partially took the place of the General Staff in the administrative hierarchy. The division of responsibilities between the two entities represented a compromise between the civilian and military authorities that would become increasingly rare as the "review" and reorganization of the forced labor system continued during the following six months.

The General Inspectorate immediately began preparing for the 1942 labor campaign. On January 5, Mociulschi issued Order No. 7, confirming the General Staff's earlier order that Jews working in industry, business, and government institutions were to return to the places where they had been working on December 20 by January 8. All Jews who had not worked in 1941 for whatever reason were required to report to their local recruitment center by January 20 to be reregistered and assigned to a labor detachment for 1942. The order also allocated additional administrative tasks to the recruitment centers, including the preparation of reports on the registration and deployment of laborers, which were to be sent to the General Inspectorate on the fifteenth and thirtieth of every month. These reports would enable the General Inspectorate to have precise knowledge of how many Jews were working, where they were assigned, and how many remained available to work.[5]

On January 20, the General Inspectorate announced that beginning the following day, every Jew eligible for forced labor would be required to report to clear snow from the streets and rail lines in the cities in which they were living. Each eligible worker would be required to complete at least five days of snow-clearing labor by February 15, working nine and a half hours a day, beginning at seven in the morning and ending at seven in the evening, with breaks for meals in between. Jews working in the snow-clearing detachments were allowed to eat and sleep at home like Jews in the regular local labor detachments. Jews between eighteen and twenty-four would be sent to work first, followed in turn by the other age cohorts (Jews under thirty-two on January 25, Jews under thirty-eight on January 26, Jews under forty-two on January 27, and all other Jews up to fifty years old on January 28).[6]

Each worker would be issued a pass indicating that he had performed his five days of snow removal work. Any Jew of military age found without a pass and without an exemption card after February 15 would be arrested and imprisoned. Although the minimum number of days of snow removal work to be performed was set at five, the General Inspectorate did not set an upper limit on the number of days an individual could be required to work; the minimum requirement was subsequently extended to ten days on February 23. The exemption tax for snow clearing was set at 1,000 lei per day. Thus, a complete exemption from snow clearing would cost 10,000 lei, beyond the means of most Romanian Jews at that time.[7]

Although snow removal was obviously useful work from the government's perspective, it was reminiscent of the National Legionary period, when the Iron Guard had forced Jews to sweep the streets solely to humiliate them. The General Inspectorate's order differed in that the obligation was restricted to Jewish men eligible for forced labor, precluding the use of elderly people, women, and children, who had not been spared by the Iron Guard. Nonetheless, the similarity was not lost on the Jews standing in the freezing cold and performing what felt like a fruitless task during an unusually snowy winter. Sometimes the snow fell more rapidly than they could remove it, and they were often reduced to shoveling snow back and forth from the roads to the tram tracks so that cars and trams could alternate passing through. Bica Bercovici said that it would have been impossible for their small group of men to clear all of the snow from the city's streets manually with shovels. He recalled that the men clearing snow were beaten by the guards if they did not work quickly enough or took breaks without permission.[8]

Figure 3.1. Romanian Jews are forced to clear snow during the winter of 1942 in Brașov, Romania. © United States Holocaust Memorial Museum, courtesy of George Joseph.

Bercovici and many of the other Jews required to clear snow during this time felt that the purpose of this work was primarily to humiliate them rather than to clear the streets, which they could not hope to do efficiently. Bercu Goldfain, a thirty-year-old survivor of the Iași pogrom and the death trains who had just returned from four months of internment in Călărași, remembered that the townspeople spit on and hit them and that the guards did not intervene.[9] Mihail Theodoru, who worked clearing snow in Craiova, believed that they were being forced to clear snow primarily for the purpose of "ostracism and ridicule." However, he also recalled that some of the city's non-Jewish residents showed compassion toward them and brought them bread and hot tea.[10] Mihail Sebastian, who was forced to clear snow in Bucharest, noted in his journal on March 4, 1942, that the worst part of the work was not the physical aspect (which he described as "a joke"), but the "standing around, the journey there, the waiting, [and] the formalities."[11] Though the survivors' testimony indicates that the work was often unproductive, it was nonetheless cost-effective for municipal governments, who no longer had to pay city employees to do the same tasks that the Jews were doing almost for free. As a result, the same requirement was imposed on Jewish men during the following two winters as well.

One of the most important recommendations of the General Staff's fall 1941 report was a "review" of the Jews who had been exempted from forced labor to continue working in private businesses and industry. The General Staff believed that too many Jews had been exempted and that many of them were not truly "economically necessary" and had been exempted only because they bribed local officials. This belief was not entirely unjustified, as some Jews had obtained exemptions, whether economic or medical, through bribery in 1941. As a result, the General Staff wished to appoint a commission to review these workers' exemptions on a case-by-case basis and determine which workers were truly "absolutely necessary" to their employers. Those who were not would be sent to bolster the ranks of the labor detachments.

However, as demonstrated by the extensive corruption involved in the exemption process in 1941, there was a significant financial incentive for the civilian authorities who had been entrusted with this responsibility to try to retain control over it. The General Staff, meanwhile, had envisioned that the review would be conducted by military personnel with input from the Ministry of Finance and Ministry of the National Economy. As a result, a power struggle broke out, from which the civilian bureaucracy, led by Radu Lecca, emerged victorious. Lecca, a veteran of the First World War, had been working as a Gestapo agent since 1933 (actually a double agent, as he was also working for the Romanian secret police, the Siguranța) and had ingratiated himself with Antonescu during the National Legionary period.[12] He was well-known as an antisemite and was extraordinarily corrupt, even by the standards of a country where government corruption was omnipresent. He had no qualms about using his position of power over the Jewish community to extort enormous sums of money from them for his own enrichment. By the end of the war, he had pocketed millions of lei extracted from the Jews of Romania and spread hundreds of millions more around to his associates in and outside the government. For Lecca, leading the review of Jewish workers and petitions from Jews and employers for extensions of exemptions was a highly desirable position, which he correctly determined to be a lucrative source of wealth. In the end, the process was entrusted to a commission of delegates from the interested sectors of the military, government, and economy, headed by Lecca.[13]

The review of exemptions from forced labor was officially announced on March 4 by a decree that declared the "review of the Jews in view of clarifying their situation in the national labor campaign." It stated that all Jews who had been given exemptions to continue working in their prewar jobs or professions would have their status reviewed by a special commission. The review would take place at two levels: the Central Commission for the Review of the Jews in Bucharest and local commissions established in each county, a model that resembled the commissions that had been established the previous September. The local commissions would review the cases in their respective counties and refer them to the Central Commission for final approval. The Central Commission was also responsible for the review of exemptions given to Jews living in Bucharest, including those granted by the General Staff.[14]

The Central Commission was composed of seven members: a president and six delegates. Radu Lecca served as the president of the commission. The delegates were Theodor Mociulschi, a man named Crant (representing the Ministry of Labor), Colonel Viorel Caragea (representing the General Staff), an engineer named Dulfu (representing the Ministry of Industry and Commerce), Nicolae Marinescu (representing the Ministry of Finance), and Ioan Roceric (representing the Chamber of Commerce).[15] The inspectors of the county branches of the Central Romanianization Office presided over the local commissions, with the heads of the county Chamber of Commerce and Chamber of Labor as delegates.[16]

The commissions were to create lists of Jews working in their respective counties, indicating which workers were exempted and which had been sent to forced labor. Jews who were exempted from forced labor (or their employers) were required to provide a statement declaring their professions, annual incomes, and any academic or professional qualifications, along with a copy of their contracts. This information had to be provided to the county commission or Central Commission (for Jews working in Bucharest) by March 31 for the applicant to be eligible for an exemption. The commission would then decide by a majority vote the merit of each person's claim that he was "absolutely necessary" to the economy and whether to grant an extension of the exemption. Those whose cases were deemed meritorious would receive an official document proving their status; anyone caught without one would be sent to a labor detachment and be "subject to the most severe regime." The commissions were expected to complete their work by May 31. The exemptions granted by the commission would be valid until the end of the year, with another review planned prior to the start of each subsequent year's labor campaign.[17]

According to Lecca in his self-exculpatory postwar memoirs—ludicrously titled *Eu i-am salvat pe evreilor din România* (I saved the Jews of Romania)—the new chief of the General Staff, Ilie Șteflea, reacted "with much hostility" to the establishment of the Central Commission. Șteflea wanted all Jews between eighteen and fifty years old to perform forced labor and felt that only the General Staff could competently make decisions about exemptions. Lecca said that Șteflea never forgot this slight and that he and the military authorities sought to oppose and obstruct him at every turn for the rest of the war (a true statement, although not for the reasons that Lecca alleged). Lecca claimed that this opposition was because the army had lost the ability to fleece the Jews by demanding payment for exemptions. However, Lecca openly admits in his memoirs that not only he but also the entire Central Commission and many of the county review commissions were corrupt, proving that Șteflea was correct in his assumptions about Lecca's motives and the inevitable result of his control of the review process.[18] Șteflea and the General Staff continued to pressure Antonescu to turn the process over to them throughout 1942.

The procedures of the Central Commission, as described by Lecca, were predicated on bribery and corruption. The files of Jews requesting exemptions were brought before the commission by a lawyer from the Jewish community (around one hundred per day) and the commission reviewed and voted on each. If an exemption was granted, the commission expected to receive an "honorarium" from the exempted person. The lawyer who presented their cases would also receive a small kickback for each exemption that was approved; according to Lecca, a lawyer named Pulca, who worked for the Ministry of Internal Affairs, became very rich through this process.[19]

Eventually, the state-appointed Jewish community leadership became the intermediary through which Lecca granted exemptions and received bribes. This role was filled by the Central Jewish Office, which had been established on December 16, 1941, at the urging of German officials in Bucharest, to act as the official organ of the state for the execution of its Jewish policy and as a replacement for the national Jewish community organizations led by Wilhelm Filderman. However, as Lecca was also the official head of the Central Jewish Office (superseding its nominal leader, Dr. Nandor Gingold), it was hardly acting in the interests of the Romanian Jews; it instead became Lecca's means of enriching himself and his patrons at their expense.[20] Lecca's use of the Central Jewish Office to drive personal profit is clear from the testimony of Haskal Brociner, who was granted an exemption from the external detachments through the Office so that he could work on Radu Lecca's farm near Bucharest. Brociner did note, however, that he was treated and fed well while working on Lecca's farm, and after about four weeks, he was allowed to return to Bucharest, where he used his exemption to avoid forced labor for the rest of the war, demonstrating the effectiveness of bribery as a means of resistance to the Antonescu regime's discriminatory policies.[21]

Lecca estimated that the Central Commission reviewed around 50,000 files in the spring of 1942 and granted around 30,000 exemptions, more than triple the number of exemptions that had been issued in 1941 (9,365). However, even this enormous figure was an understatement according to the General Staff's final assessment at the end of 1942, which counted more than 38,000 Jews exempted from forced labor.[22] Lecca also decided that women should be allowed to practice their professions without any special authorization from the government (although women were not being recruited for forced labor in substantial numbers at that time). Entrusting the process to Lecca had completely subverted the purpose of reviewing exemptions, just as the General Staff had feared it would. Furthermore, it redistributed the forced labor obligation largely onto poorer Jews who could not afford to pay the requisite bribes, even if they held jobs that were important to the economy. A lucrative black market for exemption cards emerged that allowed Jews eligible for conscription into forced labor to purchase them without going through the official review process.[23] Lecca viewed his role as a heroic one, writing in his memoirs, "When I realized that I was doing this review under an antisemitic dictator with the German Army at its apogee in the country and with a Himmlerist consul beside me, I asked myself who could have done more for the Jewish population being in my position at that that time?"[24] Lecca's claims to have been acting in the interest of the Jews are risible given the enormous amount of personal profit he obtained from brazenly exploiting them. However, despite the absurdity of his claims of humanitarian motives, his corrupt enterprise did in fact help thousands of Jews avoid forced labor.

While the Central Commission and county commissions were reviewing the status of exempted Jews, the remobilization of workers began. Jews working in private industry, businesses, and government had been remobilized in January, but the labor detachments were not re-formed until the beginning of April, as the General Inspectorate had ordered. By this time, the General Staff's plans for the organization of forced labor had moved away from stationary camps, and detachments of five hundred or more men became the preferred structure. The needs of the General Directorate of Roads and CFR were prioritized over those of other state institutions. CFR had worked with the General Staff during the preceding weeks on a very detailed organizational plan designed to maximize the productivity of the railway construction detachments in 1942. This effort reflected CFR's proactivity in regulating the use of Jewish forced labor, which its head, T. C. Orezeanu, had already demonstrated in 1941.

CFR's new plan took effect when its detachments were remobilized on April 7. It called for the creation of large detachments of several hundred men, subdivided into companies and then into platoons, each led by military personnel and supported by CFR technical staff. It clearly specified both the responsibilities and rights of the workers. They would be expected to work eight hours a day (increased to ten hours a day between May 1 and October 1). CFR would supply them with tools and clothing, and they were to be ensured decent housing conditions, with new barracks being constructed when possible. To solve the food supply issues that had been ubiquitous in 1941, the Ministry of National Defense would provide food, while utensils and cookware would be provided by CFR. CFR would also provide medications and requested a medic and two to three orderlies per one thousand workers. Each detachment was to have a separate infirmary with enough beds for 1 percent of its workers. The workers would be paid 40 lei per day, above the minimum pay established by the August 8, 1941, General Instructions. Family assistance of 300 lei (for those living outside the capital) or 1,000 lei (for those living in Bucharest) was to be provided to the laborers' dependents. However, strict standards were to be maintained for daily productivity with punitive measures taken against those who failed to meet them, including deductions in pay and loss of privileges. Detachment commanders were also responsible for keeping very detailed records of the presence of Jews at work and the amount of work performed each day.[25]

In theory, the CFR conventions represented a progressive step in the treatment of Jewish laborers and the organization of labor, one that would be influential in the General Staff's reforms to the forced labor system in 1942. Unfortunately, the changes in organization and the proactive efforts of CFR did not immediately benefit the Jews who returned to the labor detachments in the spring of 1942. Many of the same problems from 1941—substandard housing; inadequate supplies of food, medicine, and medical personnel; and dangerous working conditions—were still widespread.

These issues continued in detachments operated by other institutions as well. In the case of Haim Leizerovici, a nineteen-year-old Jew from Huși who was sent to a road detachment in Șuldanești, near Bălți (in present-day Moldova), the living conditions were just as bad as they had been in 1941, when he had worked in a stone quarry in Dobruja extracting rocks for track ballast. His detachment was assigned to help build a strategically important road toward the front, which would stretch from Bălți to the Dniester River. As work on the road progressed, the Jewish laborers faced an increasingly long walk to their work site each morning, which eventually stretched to more than ten kilometers. The poor quality of the food and cold weather, from which their poorly constructed barracks offered little protection, exacerbated their suffering. The men in Leizerovici's detachment were "encouraged" to work by whippings with a leather belt if productivity was not high enough.[26]

Natan Bron, who was eighteen years old at the time, reported a similar experience. He was part of a detachment of Jews from his hometown of Iași that was sent to work in a stone quarry in Ghidighici, near Chișinău. This quarry was one of the most important suppliers of ballast for road construction projects in eastern Romania and hundreds of Jewish laborers were employed there until the spring of 1944, when the approach of the Red Army forced their evacuation to the west. While Bron was working in the quarry, a wagon ran over his foot, seriously injuring him. However, the detachment did not have adequate medical supplies to treat his injury, and he had to trek to town along with the detachment's medic, Dr. Roșcovan, to acquire the necessary supplies. Beyond the carelessness that led to his injury, the working conditions were difficult and the detachment commander, an officer named Mihailovici, ordered that if one person failed to meet his daily work quota, no one in his group of fifty men would eat that night. Poor supplies and cruel treatment of workers at the Ghidighici quarry contributed to what Bron called an "atmosphere of depression."[27] Aurel Lupovici, who was working at Preda-Obor railway station in Bucharest loading wood onto trucks, reported another case of severe injury caused by negligence. A man in his detachment fell from a woodpile, suffering a permanent injury (although Lupovici did not specify what kind of injury it was).[28]

The corruption of the review process hampered the creation of labor detachments and impeded the General Staff's plans for the 1942 labor campaign. General Staff Order No. 89089, issued on May 2, indicated that Antonescu wanted ninety-five thousand Jews between twenty and forty years old to be mobilized for forced labor in road and railroad construction detachments; however, the General Staff noted that fewer than half that number were available due to the massive increase in exemptions granted by the Central Commission. It proposed that all Jews between twenty and forty years old be recalled from other work, whether they had been requisitioned by government or private employers or assigned to local labor detachments, and redistributed to the external construction detachments. They would be replaced at their previous workplaces by Jews between forty-one and fifty years old. The General Staff also proposed nullifying all existing exemptions on June 1; however, this proposal was not adopted due to protests from Lecca.[29]

On May 14, the General Staff noted that it could not fulfill its plan for 22,750 Jews to be sent to railroad detachments because too many had been exempted or simply had not reported for work. It stated that contrary to its intention to only create detachments of 500 or more men, it would instead form units of only 100 to 150 men due to the lack of available workers.[30] Plans announced on May 26 to create eight road detachments with 6,000 Jews total were also scrapped.[31] Similar complaints about the excessive numbers of exemptions were registered by the local recruitment centers, as they were unable to fulfill requests for workers. For example, on June 4, the recruitment center in Neamț County informed the Fifth Territorial Command that it was unable to create all the detachments the latter had requested due to the large numbers of Jews who had been exempted. The center stated that in many cases it was unsure why the Jews in question had been given exemptions—the answer, of course, being that they had successfully bribed either the local or Central Commission.[32]

It quickly became clear to both Antonescu and the military leadership that the reforms implemented during the winter of 1942 had failed to address the problems affecting the forced labor system and that additional changes would be necessary to improve its productivity. On April 21, Chief of the Military Cabinet Radu Davidescu informed the General Staff that Antonescu had demanded that they immediately prepare proposals for the utilization of Jewish laborers between the ages of twenty and forty. Antonescu offered some general "guidelines" for the General Staff's consideration:

1. Jews should be organized in large labor detachments (rather than small groups or camps), staffed with active and reserve officers and NCOs (noncommissioned officers).
2. Jewish workers should be paid and fed like soldiers.
3. All supplies for the Jewish workers should be "secured by the authorities of the state which use these detachments."
4. Sick Jews and "intellectuals" should pay taxes in place of working; a base rate should be established for Jews between twenty and thirty years old, which would be doubled for Jews thirty to fifty years old.
5. Jews who are unable to work and unable to pay these taxes would either have their taxes covered by the Jewish community or be deported to Transnistria.
6. Organization of detachments should be done by the recruitment centers.
7. Costs incurred for the upkeep of the workers in the detachments should be covered by the exemption taxes.[33]

These guidelines echoed the ideas Antonescu and the Council of Ministers had discussed during their November 19, 1941, meeting.

The chief of staff responded to this order on April 30 with a proposal for a set of new regulations. General Ștefleaʼs response openly acknowledged that the results of forced labor had been well below expectations. He noted that the output from workers between forty-one and fifty years old had been particularly poor, since health problems were more common among that group and they were past their physical prime. As a result, he proposed that the external labor detachments be composed primarily of men between eighteen and forty years old, while older men would be concentrated in the local detachments. Sick Jews and intellectuals would be charged a fixed tax for each day they did not work: 250 lei per day for Jews under thirty and 500 lei per day for Jews between thirty and fifty. Those who could not pay would be deported to Transnistria, as the Military Cabinet had suggested (although in reality this punishment was never enforced).[34]

To optimize their productivity, Jews with special skills or training would be sent to work in their areas of specialization; the concept of separate "teams" or "groups" of Jewish craftsmen in urban areas was introduced later. The number of officers and soldiers guarding detachments would be increased and detachments would be consolidated into groups of five hundred men. Their pay would be equal to 60 percent of the pay a non-Jewish Romanian worker would receive for the same work. Finally, Șteflea proposed the implementation of much harsher punishments for desertion and shirking, including deportation to Transnistria.

These proposals were deemed satisfactory by Antonescu and the Military Cabinet, and the General Staff was given permission to use them to create a new set of General Instructions.[35]

On May 12, General Staff Order No. 33911 expounded on the proposals sent to the Military Cabinet with a new set of plans for the organization of detachments. Each detachment would have a commanding officer, supported by two lower-ranking officers and three NCOs (all reservists) for every five hundred laborers, one enlisted man for every fifty laborers, one Jewish medic per five hundred laborers, and a Jewish reserve NCO responsible for coordinating supplies. The Territorial Commands would assign the officers, NCOs, and soldiers to the detachments, while the General Staff would coordinate the distribution of Jewish medics. The General Inspectorate was essentially sidelined only four months after its creation as the General Staff consolidated its control over the forced labor system. Housing would be secured by the authorities utilizing Jewish labor, as would food, medications, and transport for the workers. Their pay would come from the General Staff's general fund for forced labor, derived from the special military taxes paid by Jews. The detachments would be subject to the same disciplinary regulation as regular military units; however, deportation to Transnistria would be an option for punishing serious infractions such as escape attempts. Commanders and guards were urged to use "severe measures" to encourage "maximum productivity."[36]

On May 17, the General Staff reported that Jews were "search[ing] for all means by which to escape from work" and that the prevalence of reports of desertion and shirking (1,500 from Iași recruitment center alone) indicated a "severe lack of sanctions" for such acts. They again proposed court-martialing suspected deserters and deporting those who were convicted to Transnistria.[37] Antonescu agreed with this proposal, as indicated by a General Staff memo from May 31 that reported that he had ordered that all Jews who deserted (and any Romanians who aided them), as well as Jews who did not work "conscientiously" and any Jews who had relations with Romanian women, should be sent to hard labor in Transnistria. The memo also noted a further 103 Jews from Bucharest who had deserted, in addition to those reported in Iași.[38] Antonescu's approval gave the General Staff a free hand to introduce harsh punishments for desertion in the new forced labor regulations they were crafting.

The proposals outlined on April 30 and developed in the May 12 order formed the basis for the new General Instructions for the Use of Forced Labor, which were issued on June 27. These instructions were the most extensive set of reforms yet and led to a substantial reorganization of the forced labor system. Though there would be some amendments and later changes to these instructions, they would guide the use of Jewish labor for the remainder of the war. These instructions were a confirmation that control over the regulation and deployment of forced labor was once again solely entrusted to the General Staff, superseding the authority of the General Inspectorate and Ministry of Labor.[39]

The new General Instructions confirmed the "essence" of the General Staff's review of the forced labor system: that the labor camps and detachments as deployed in 1941 were both unproductive and harmful to the economy and that Jews should instead be deployed in large labor detachments, well staffed with military personnel, to ensure adequate supervision of workers, which the General Staff believed was the key to improved productivity.[40] The categories the General Staff had proposed in April were retained as the basis for the assignment of Jews to forced labor. However, the procedures and requirements for the exemption of Jewish workers were more detailed. Jews who held foreign citizenship, who were part of the leadership of the Central Jewish Office, who were unfit for physical labor, or who were disabled war veterans were exempted from any form of forced labor. Jews who held academic titles or leadership roles in the county Jewish offices were exempted from forced labor in external detachments but could be called to work if their services were needed by a government institution. Any Jews who obtained an exemption from forced labor would be required to pay the military taxes according to the scheme laid out in the initial proposals.[41]

Jews who had been exempted by the Central Commission would remain exempt through December 31, 1942. Skilled workers or graduates of technical schools would be made available to war-related industries (strictly defined as those that had contracts with the military) that requested their service; however, until such a request was made, they were eligible to be sent to external detachments that needed their skills.[42] Though this provision afforded protected status to workers exempted by the Central Commission, the General Staff later reviewed these exemptions and voided a number of them that were determined to have been granted through corrupt means. Lecca, to his frustration, was powerless to resist this decision because in this case, Antonescu chose to back the General Staff.[43]

As indicated in the April 30 proposals, external detachments would be assigned to major projects for the roads, railroads, or other concerns of strategic significance. These detachments would be composed of Jews between twenty-one and forty years old, and they could be created only with the approval of the General Staff. The local detachments would be made up of Jews forty-one to fifty years old, with younger Jews employed only if they were not needed for work in the external detachments. Local detachments were required to submit a work plan to the Territorial Command for approval. The Territorial Commands would also handle requests for the use of Jewish specialists in local detachments, state institutions, and private firms. However, requisitions of Jewish professionals (including doctors, veterinarians, and pharmacists) required direct approval from the General Staff, since they were also eligible for conscription into active military service. Any need for Jewish professionals for active duty would be prioritized above their use for forced labor.[44]

The instructions for the administration of the external detachments were similar to the General Staff's original proposals. For every five hundred workers in a detachment, there were to be three reserve officers (one of whom was to be the commander of the detachment), three reserve NCOs, a Jewish former officer or NCO (to be responsible for supply), one Jewish medic, ten additional soldiers of lower rank (one for every fifty Jews), and two additional soldiers to assist with supply. In local detachments, the number of administrative personnel was to be identical to that of the external detachments; however, aside from the commander, the other officers could be retired Jewish officers, if there was a shortage of non-Jewish officers.[45]

Jewish laborers were to be housed in barracks or isolated buildings, away from villages and towns. Under no circumstances were Jews to be housed in villages or allowed to enter the villages. Jews working in their own cities would be allowed to sleep at home, as had been the established practice for nearly a year. Food and medicine would be supplied by the authorities that employed workers in external detachments, while Jews in local detachments could eat at home and receive medical care from local doctors. The new instructions also specified that all workers were to have appropriate clothes for the time of year in which they were working. In practice, this meant that the laborers would either have to bring winter clothes from home or that the Jewish community would be required to collect clothing for the workers in the detachments, unlike the earlier CFR instructions in which the agency agreed to supply winter clothing to its Jewish laborers.[46]

Jewish workers in both local and external detachments would have the right to the same pay and food as regular soldiers of the equivalent rank. Each worker would receive fifteen lei a day in wages in addition to their food and other supplies, and their families would receive a support payment equal to half their monthly wages. They would also be granted fifteen days of leave every six months. The working day was decreased from between ten and twelve hours per day to nine hours per day; however, detachment commanders still had the authority to set daily quotas for the laborers and keep them at work beyond the nine-hour limit if those quotas were not met.[47]

At the work site, the commandant had the authority to determine the division of workers into groups within the labor detachment; generally, these groups would be composed of about fifty to a hundred men. Every group would have to be supervised by one of the officers or other soldiers in the detachment to ensure appropriate discipline and pace of work. The new instructions gave the detachment commanders the authority to mete out corporal punishment for violations of "minor importance," such as being late to the daily roll call, working too slowly, or having an "undisciplined attitude." Jews who repeatedly committed such violations, who failed to "work conscientiously," who had relations with Romanian women, or who attempted to desert from the labor detachments would be deported to Transnistria, along with their families (parents, spouses, and children).[48] On June 18, the governor of Transnistria, Gheorghe Alexianu, sent a note to the General Staff informing them of his plans to create special camps for deported forced laborers at Slivina and Oceacov.[49] Any non-Jews who assisted Jews in escaping from forced labor would also be deported to Transnistria.[50]

Finally, the new General Instructions prescribed procedures for the use of Jewish women as forced laborers. Prior to June 1942, there had been no provision for the employment of Jewish women in the labor system (although it was not explicitly prohibited). The Territorial Commands would have the authority to send Jewish women between eighteen and forty years old to perform both manual labor (as seamstresses, washwomen, etc.) and intellectual labor (as office workers) for businesses and military units in their cities. Jewish women would be organized into work groups like those for male specialists. They would have the same rights to supply and payment as Jewish men working in labor detachments and would be subject to the same penal code.[51]

While the program established by the new General Instructions was a logical step toward improving the productivity of the forced labor system, it was still dependent on consistent application of the new regulations by the personnel of the Territorial Commands and local recruitment centers, as well as the officers and soldiers in the detachments. Additionally, it did nothing to rein in corruption among Romanian officials at all levels of government, which continued to provide a means for Jews to escape forced labor. Finally, it did not adequately account for logistical shortcomings, such as the inability of the military authorities to distribute food supplies regularly.

Despite the provisions that would theoretically improve living and working conditions for the Jews, the new General Instructions also presented a more rigid approach to discipline in the labor detachments, with the expectation that harsher sanctions would lead to increased productivity. An article published in the newspaper *Curentul* on June 17 demonstrated the shift in the authorities' attitudes toward forced labor, announcing that the euphemism "work in the community interest" (*munca în folos obștesc*) was to be replaced with the more straightforward term "compulsory labor" (*munca obligatorie*).[52] While this change in terminology seemed like little more than a bureaucratic formality, it reflected a firmer attitude toward forced labor, which was in line with the accelerating trend of Antonescu's Jewish policy in mid-1942 as preparations for the "radical solution" of the Jewish question in Romania continued.

Notes

1. USHMMA, RG-25.003M, reel 138, file 2367, 69.
2. Ancel, *History of the Holocaust in Romania*, 531.
3. Clark, *Holy Legionary Youth*, 37 and 71.
4. USHMMA, RG-25.003M, reel 138, file 2367, 69.
5. Ibid., 68.
6. Ibid., 69–72.
7. Bărbulescu et al., *Munca obligatorie*, document 63, 212–213.
8. Bercovici, interview 50196.
9. Interview with Bercu Goldfain, USHMMA, RG-50.037*0026, Holocaust Resource Center of Buffalo Oral History Collection.
10. Theodoru, interview 49504, accessed on March 6, 2015.
11. Sebastian, *Journal*, 479.
12. Ancel, *History of the Holocaust in Romania*, 62.
13. Friling et al., *Final Report*, 118.
14. *Monitorul Oficial*, March 4, 1942.
15. Radu Lecca, *Eu i-am salvat pe evrei din România* (Bucharest: Editura Roza Vânturilor, 1994), 195–196.
16. *Monitorul Oficial* 54, March 4, 1942.
17. Ibid.
18. Lecca, *Eu i-am salvat pe evrei*, 197.
19. Ibid.
20. Deletant, *Hitler's Forgotten Ally*, 121–123.
21. Brociner, interview 21836.
22. USHMMA, RG-25.003M, reel 181, file 3001, 369–370.
23. Ancel, *Economic Destruction*, 334.
24. Lecca, *Eu i-am salvat pe evrei*, 198.
25. USHMMA, RG-25.003M, reel 174, file 2893, 2–26.
26. Leizerovici, interview 12250, accessed on February 5, 2015.
27. Natan Bron, interview 43924, Visual History Archive, USC Shoah Foundation, accessed online at the United States Holocaust Memorial Museum on February 5, 2015, http://vhaonline.usc.edu/viewingPage?testimonyID=46753&returnIndex=0.
28. Lupovici, interview 25432.
29. USHMMA, RG-25.003M, reel 138, file 2367, 20.
30. USHMMA, RG-25.003M, reel 174, file 2895, 31.
31. USHMMA, RG-25.003M, reel 157, file 2963, 109.
32. USHMMA, RG-25.003M, reel 153, file 2956, 128.
33. Bărbulescu et al., *Munca obligatorie*, document 66, 218–219.
34. Ibid., document 70, 231.
35. Ottmar Trașcă, ed., *"Chestiunea evreiască" în documentele militare române, 1941–1944* (Iași: Editura Institutul European, 2010), document 241, 510–512.
36. USHMMA, RG-25.003M, reel 174, file 2893, 58–61.
37. Trașcă, *"Chestiunea evreiască,"* document 255, 533.
38. Ibid., document 263, 546–547.

39. "Repartizarea evreilor la munca de folos obștesc, se face numai de Marele Stat Major," *Universul,* July 6, 1942, 3.
40. Friling et al., *Final Report,* 88.
41. USHMMA, RG-25.003M, reel 148, file 2825, 256.
42. Ibid., 256–257.
43. Lecca, *Eu i-am salvat pe evrei,* 230.
44. USHMMA, RG-25.003M, reel 148, file 2825, 258.
45. Ibid., 260.
46. Ibid., 262.
47. Ibid.
48. Ibid., 262–263.
49. Alexandru Climescu, "Sanctions and Interdictions Applicable to the Jews Subjected to the Mandatory Labor Regime in Romania," *Holocaust: Studii și cercetări* 4, no. 1 (2012): 69.
50. USHMMA, RG-25.003M, reel 148, file 2825, 262–263.
51. Ibid., 264.
52. "Repartizarea evreilor la munca obligatorie," *Curentul,* June 17, 1942, 1.

4 In the Shadow of Belzec

THE REORGANIZATION OF the labor detachments began shortly after the new General Instructions were issued. Many smaller detachments were consolidated into larger ones, following the General Staff's preference for greater numbers of workers per detachment with corresponding increases in supervisory personnel. However, this change did not produce immediate results in most cases. Reforms had been enacted at the top level, but their success still depended on proper implementation by lower-level actors. In the few cases where the detachment commanders and officers were competent and honest, some improvements in productivity and living conditions were reported both by official documents and in the testimony of Jewish survivors from those detachments. However, these detachments were the exception, not the rule. Many of the officers, soldiers, recruiters, and other officials did not apply the General Staff's instructions properly, and the reform process was further undercut by the shortages of personnel caused by the corrupt review commissions' exemptions.

The lack of substantial improvements in most detachments by the end of 1942 indicated that the problems caused by the forced labor system were structural rather than a matter of policy. No policy change could eliminate the skill mismatches, poor logistical capacity, or lack of motivation for laborers that undermined productivity and produced bad working and living conditions. Furthermore, the introduction of deportation for violators of forced labor regulations added a new level of cruelty to the system that exceeded that caused by negligent and incompetent authorities. From the perspective of most laborers, little about their living and working conditions had changed.

While the forced labor detachments were being reorganized, Antonescu and the members of his government were planning the "radical solution," which was to follow the "temporary solution" that forced labor provided. Their discussions included both autonomous Romanian plans to deport the Jews of the Old Kingdom and southern Transylvania to Transnistria, as well as negotiations with German representatives in Bucharest for Romania's participation in Nazi Germany's continent-wide Final Solution to the Jewish Question. Antonescu ultimately rebuffed the Germans and decided not to allow the deportation of the Jews living within the prewar borders of Romania. After this decision, his Jewish policy shifted away from deportation, favoring a more moderate approach in which the Jews would be allowed to emigrate from Romania. As a result of his rejection of the "radical solution," forced labor became a permanent fixture of his Jewish policy—one that would increase in importance as the war on the eastern front turned against the Axis.

On July 27, 1942, one month after the new General Instructions were issued, the General Staff reported to the Military Cabinet that the Jewish laborers working for CFR had been concentrated into twenty-two detachments, whose productivity was described as "good to very good." Eighteen detachments (out of thirty originally planned) with approximately nine thousand laborers working for the Ministry of Agriculture had harvested 14,200 wagons of wood.[1] Fourteen road construction detachments had been created (whether newly mobilized or through consolidation of smaller detachments) as of September 5.[2] Additionally, several detachments of "pioneers" (*pionieri*) were created, which built dams and dug canals and built and repaired defensive works near Romania's eastern and western borders. Work also continued on other military projects, such as the Cotroceni shooting range, where nearly eighteen hundred Jews were employed.[3] Finally, a number of general labor detachments were created to work on a wide variety of projects, such as cutting wood and improving military installations. Among them was Labor Battalion 120 (Batalionul 120 Lucru), one of the few military labor detachments that operated in the Transnistria Governorate.[4] The Jews in Battalion 120 were assigned to cut wood and dig antitank trenches near Balta, one of the major cities in Transnistria.[5]

On August 12, the General Staff added another component to the labor requirement. All Jews between eighteen and thirty who resided in Romanian cities were required to spend five to ten days cleaning the streets under the supervision of the local authorities before the end of the year. Jews who wished to avoid this requirement, including those classified unfit for physical labor and those with medical exemptions, were to pay 1,000 lei per day (up to 10,000 lei in total) by September 1. Those who did not pay and did not show up to clean the streets would be considered deserters and deported to Transnistria.[6]

The following month, the General Staff prepared a series of amendments and additions to the June 27 General Instructions, which were published on September 14 as Order No. 98.500, titled Explanations and Completions of the General Instructions. Among the changes it introduced was permission for local governments to force Jews of both sexes between fourteen and seventeen years old and between fifty-one and sixty-nine years old to work on projects of local significance (with the General Staff's approval). The main purpose of this measure was to allow the conscription of skilled workers and artisans who were above the upper age limit for forced labor, although the addition of healthy younger Jews to tasks requiring unskilled labor would have also been welcome to local governments struggling to find adequate numbers of workers for projects involving manual labor.[7]

Order No. 98.500 also provided additional clarification on the status of certain groups of laborers. Jews from the oil-producing regions of Romania, particularly those from Ploieşti who had been deported from the city and forbidden to return, had often escaped forced labor because they were not living in the territory of the recruitment centers that held their records. The author of the order, General Ion Arhip, made it clear that these Jews were still expected to perform forced labor and that reports on their status were to be transmitted to the appropriate Territorial Command. Exemptions granted by the Central Commission were to be respected, even though, as Arhip noted, many were given "without sufficient documentation." However, specialists and craftsmen could be requisitioned for military service even if they held exemption cards. Jews already working in labor detachments who were exempted by the Central Commission would not be allowed to leave until a replacement worker arrived, with severe sanctions (including deportation to Transnistria) prescribed for those who did otherwise.[8]

Order No. 98.500 also increased the responsibility of the detachment commanders for the inspection and control of workers and required more detailed record keeping. Arhip reminded the detachment commanders and military administrators that it was "the wish of [Antonescu] that [forced] labor not be trivialized, but instead carried out with total seriousness." He reiterated that corporal punishment was an option for the commanders of external detachments, though abuses committed by detachment personnel would be punished. Additionally, to ensure conformity with the General Staff's instructions, Arhip ordered detachment commanders to send semimonthly reports to their supervising Territorial Commands with information on the results of inspections, the presence and absence of workers, productivity, punishments, difficulties encountered during work, and proposals they wished to submit for consideration. These reports were also to include the names of Jews recommended for deportation to Transnistria because of flight attempts or repeated infractions.[9]

Some of the early reports from labor detachments after the issuance of the new General Instructions seemed to suggest—superficially at least—that the General Staff's reforms were having a positive effect on productivity and conditions in the labor detachments. At the end of August 1942, the Fourth Territorial Command reported that eleven new external detachments had been created in their territory. The author of the report, General Hugo Schwab, noted that each detachment had proper housing, food was abundant, and productivity was "approximately normal."[10] Shortages, where they existed, were covered by the local Jewish communities. Schwab also delivered positive news about the productivity of the local detachments, although he noted a shortage of skilled laborers. Traian Panaitescu, director of CFR detachments, also had some good news for the General Staff. His summary report for September 1942 stated that the food supplies, which were coordinated with the help of the Territorial Commands, were generally sufficient and most detachments had barracks to house their workers or had found suitable housing for them elsewhere.[11] However, as reports from detachment commanders and later inspections would indicate, these general conclusions were likely based on what the supervisory personnel wished were true or wanted the General Staff to believe rather than reality.

Some of the reports from inspection of individual detachments were also encouraging. Captain Teodor Diaconescu, who inspected the detachment at Ghidighici quarry in Bessarabia on September 13, reported that 288 of the 301 Jews in the detachment were at work, their housing and food adequate, and productivity good.[12] Diaconescu's report, based on an in-person examination is the most credible of these positive reports. However, Natan Bron, a survivor of the Ghidighici quarry detachment, recalled that the working conditions were still very hard and the improvement in productivity did not lead to better treatment for the workers.[13]

Despite the early cause for optimism, most of the reports the General Staff received during the fall of 1942, particularly in the later months, were mixed at best. The same September report from Panaitescu also noted that CFR Detachment 12 and CFR Detachment 18 were experiencing poor productivity, which he blamed on a "lack of vigilance" on the part of the detachment commanders. This negative report indicated that supervision of workers was still inadequate—a continuation of the problem that the General Instructions had targeted above all others. Furthermore, Detachment 12 reported a monthly average of 7.29 percent of its workers sick or absent, while CFR Detachment 17 was without 12.60 percent of its workforce on average.[14] By December 1942, Detachment 17 reported an average of 18.50 percent of its workers absent.[15] Concerns about the supervision of laborers were also expressed by commanders of road construction detachments. Colonel Radu Spânu, the commander of Roads Battalion 3 (Batalionul 3 Drumuri), which was deployed in eastern Romania, stated that substantial numbers of Jews were absent from the battalion's work sites, many of them without leave, although poor record keeping by the company commanders made it difficult to determine exactly how many. In his September 28 report for the preceding two weeks, Spânu noted that an average of 9.20 percent of the battalion's workers were absent, with more than a third of those absent "without reason."[16]

An earlier report from Spânu, filed on August 22, provided an example of the types of "lapses" by camp personnel that allowed Jews to escape. A Romanian soldier had taken a Jewish laborer with him to Focșani to buy cigarettes in direct contravention of the General Staff's order prohibiting Jewish laborers in external detachments from entering cities. When the soldier returned, the worker was gone, and the soldier said he could not find him. Spânu indicated that the soldier had not requested permission to take the laborer with him when he went into the city and that he had been reprimanded for his mistake.[17] Despite the official ban on Jews leaving their detachments to purchase supplies, detachment personnel continued to allow them to do so. Max Goldberger, who was working at the Cotroceni shooting range at the time, revealed that he and other workers bribed the guards to gain this privilege.[18] Marcel Floreanu, who was working in an excavation detachment near Urziceni, was also allowed to go into the city to purchase cornmeal so that the workers could make mămăligă to supplement their diet of soup they received in the detachment.[19] In other cases, absences had more mundane explanations, which nonetheless reflected poor supervision of workers. On October 1, a report to the General Staff revealed that a Jew named Herșcu Lupu, who had been working in a labor detachment near Bârlad, had been discovered missing during an inspection on August 25; only two weeks later did the detachment commander discover that he had been in a hospital in Bucharest since July 10.[20]

The General Staff received numerous complaints from Jewish workers and Romanian civilians alike about abusive soldiers meting out excessive corporal punishment, well beyond that permitted by the General Staff's regulations. Many Jewish survivors of the labor detachments recalled such incidents of abuse. For example, Pinchas Lipner, who worked cutting trees in the forests near Hațeg, in west-central Romania, was given twenty-five lashes across the back for missing work while ill.[21] Somewhat surprisingly, some officers and soldiers were reprimanded or even court-martialed for mistreating Jewish workers. On November 20, Sergeant Major Vasile Frațescu, who supervised a group of Jews working for the Council of Patronage—the "charitable" venture operated by Ion Antonescu's wife, Maria—was accused of repeatedly abusing his Jewish workers verbally and physically in full view of the children in the neighboring primary school. Because of these actions and his "vulgar attitude," he was sentenced to one hundred days of military arrest by a court martial on November 22.[22] However, such punishments were uncommon, and most officers and soldiers who abused Jews were never punished. Furthermore, most of those who were punished were from local detachments—particularly in Bucharest, as in Frațescu's case—indicating that the General Staff's actions in these cases were motivated primarily by concern for public opinion rather than any interest in the well-being of the workers.

Reports in the last weeks of the fall of 1942 revealed that many of the same problems encountered in the fall of 1941 were still present, despite the General Staff's attempts to eliminate them. For example, on August 18, the commander of Roads Battalion 1, Major Nicolae Ionescu, informed the General Staff of the issues he faced in his detachment. Although the General Instructions required that all Jews have two changes of clothes, warm clothing for winter, eating utensils, and bedding, many of these items were in short supply in the battalion; in one company, only about 20 Jews out of 450 were fully equipped according to the General Staff's requirements.[23] Roads Battalion 1 had a number of Jews who were either too old, too young, or too infirm to contribute to its work, and the productivity of the detachment was "below normal" in spite of the fact that "severe measures" were in place to encourage hard work. Eleven Jews from the Iași recruitment center who had been approved only for "light work" had been sent to the detachment. Ionescu contended that there was no "light work" in a road construction detachment, echoing Panaitescu's comment about railroad detachments in 1941. Ionescu's complaints indicated that workers were still being dispatched to detachments in a haphazard manner, without concern for adequate supplies or proper vetting of their health and capacity to work.[24]

Many detachments still did not have proper housing for their workers. On December 12, the Fourth Territorial Command informed the General Staff that the barracks of Roads Battalion 1 were overcrowded and that many workers lacked mattresses and blankets. The Jews in Roads Battalion 3 were housed in two abandoned synagogues, where some men had to sleep on the floor due to lack of beds. Most of them also lacked winter clothing.[25] Similarly, Jews in CFR Detachment 16 at Valea Homorodului slept in the train stations near their work sites or in abandoned schools. Few of the workers had warm clothes, and they were unable to work at all after November 12 due to heavy snow. CFR Detachment 12 had barracks for its workers, but they were of poor construction and leaked during rain and snow. Thirty-five percent of the workers in Detachment 12 were without winter clothes.[26] Panaitescu's general summary for December 1942 noted that hygienic conditions were "deplorable" in almost every detachment, as the workers had few opportunities to bathe and there were no procedures in place to control parasites (lice were particularly problematic).[27]

Even Colonel Diaconescu's generally positive report from the Ghidighici quarry acknowledged problems with supplies. During his visit, Diaconescu noted that about two-thirds of the detachment lacked winter clothing and that only some of these workers would be able to return to their homes to obtain warm clothes.[28] Although Diaconescu had stated that the workers' living quarters were in good condition, one of the Jews deployed in the detachment, Carol Segal, recalled that the men in the detachment slept in barracks that provided little insulation from the cold. Segal corroborated Diaconescu's statement that almost none of the workers at Ghidighici had winter clothing during the exceptionally cold months of late 1942.[29] Pinchas Lipner recalled that his brother, who also worked in the Ghidighici detachment, suffered from frostbite on his feet due to inadequate footwear.[30] The Council of Ministers, alarmed by a November 6 report that almost none of the Jews working on the Brașov-Ploiești highway had coats or blankets, ordered that detachment commanders and agencies using Jewish labor take "urgent" measures to ensure the availability of winter clothes for their workers.[31]

It is difficult to determine how common deaths of workers were during this time. The detachment commanders' reports were supposed to include statistics on fatalities. Taken at face value, these reports suggest that death rates were quite low, with most detachments experiencing no more than one or two deaths during the 1942 campaign. This assumption is obviously problematic, given both the poor quality of record keeping in many detachments and the incentive for detachment commanders not to report fatalities, since they would reflect badly on their leadership. Some Jewish survivors give corroborating evidence for these statistics. Leon Herscovici noted that he did not recall any deaths in his CFR detachment at the Preda-Obor rail station—though it is possible that Herscovici was simply unaware of fatalities that may have occurred.[32]

Conversely, survivor Martin Schottek, who worked in Jewish Labor Detachment 102 (Detașament 102 Evrei) digging a canal between the Criș and Mureș Rivers in western Romania, stated that there were several deaths in his detachment. At his detachment's work site, near the city of Arad, food was scarce. The work there was also very hard. According to Schottek, each worker was expected to remove four cubic meters of earth from the canal site each day, using only a shovel. As a result of the lack of food and the stringent work quotas, Schottek recalled, "a couple" of men died of heart problems and multiple other workers from different, unspecified ailments. He described the commanding officer of the detachment, Colonel Vitcu, as "harsh" and the other soldiers as "indoctrinated" with antisemitic propaganda. He received corporal punishment on multiple occasions. Unlike workers in many other detachments, who were sent home for the winter, Schottek's detachment remained deployed without any leave until February 1944.[33]

Based on survivor testimony, it is probable that deaths were not evenly distributed across detachments and that, unsurprisingly, detachments working on more dangerous tasks (such as quarrying and mining) experienced more fatalities than those with relatively safer responsibilities, such as unloading train wagons or harvesting crops. On average, the death rate for Jewish workers in the detachments was probably relatively low, and reports from survivors indicate that most of the deaths they witnessed were due to health problems—including both preexisting conditions exacerbated by hard labor and conditions that arose from working and living in the detachments—or due to accidents, most of which were caused by the failure of the Romanian officers to ensure safe working conditions and properly supervise workers, rather than excessive corporal punishment or executions.

Work in the reorganized local detachments was also problematic for the Romanian authorities. Absences were an issue for the local detachments just as they were in the external detachments. For example, in mid-August 1942, the Baia recruitment center reported that five Jews sent to work in a vegetable garden in Pașcani commune were absent without leave.[34] On October 26, the General Staff received a report on the inspection of local detachments in Bucharest that placed the rate of absence from work at 9.2 percent, noting more than one-third of these workers (3.5 percent of the total) were absent without leave. This problem was attributed primarily to the inattentiveness of the local authorities to the presence or absence of Jewish workers and the fact that they could travel freely in the city to perform various tasks without supervision. In other cases, Jews were being used as office workers without the required written approval from the General Staff, or in pharmacies and dental offices, which was strictly forbidden. Other Jews allegedly received "favorable treatment" from the authorities.[35]

Detachments in and around Bucharest were a frequent source of complaints. For example, the Jews in the railroad detachment at Valea Homorodului lacked adequate shelter even in mid-December. The workers slept at their work site (at Bucharest East station) or in old school buildings (at Dealul Spirei station) or had no fixed shelter at all (at Filaret station). The workers also did not have a canteen for meals as recommended by the June 27 instructions. Instead, they ate in their sleeping quarters or outside. Furthermore, nearly all Jews in this detachment were without winter clothing.[36]

The detachments in Bucharest presented further problems. On December 18, the General Staff produced a final report on the activity of a local detachment of 2,038 workers deemed fit only for "light work" who had been assigned to cultivate fruit and vegetable gardens in the city between June and October of that year. Many of these workers found ways to avoid work or were given preferential treatment by the authorities and only required to work during the morning hours. After the completion of the project in October, many of these Jews had not been given another work assignment, and of those who had been called up for further work, 695 had not presented at the Bucharest recruitment center. The General Staff ordered that this project not be repeated in 1943, as it was little more than a way for Jews to escape work and the undersecretary of state for provisions recommended that those who were discovered to have shirked from forced labor at the gardens be subjected to harsh punishments, including deportation.[37]

Louis Beno Nedeleanu, twenty-one years old at the time, was one of the workers in this detachment, and his recollections corroborate much of the General Staff's report. He had been assigned to the Olteniței Garden in Bucharest on July 17, after his father, a veteran of the First World War, had used his status to persuade a recruiter in Bucharest to give his son an easier job. During this time, he said, he worked from six in the morning to six in the evening harvesting tomatoes, with a one-hour break for lunch—a total work time two hours longer than that prescribed in the June 27 General Instructions. However, despite the long hours he worked, he did witness some of the "irregularities" documented in the December 18 report. He noted that, aside from the detachment commander, the gendarmes at the garden were not particularly interested in supervising the workers and frequently just "stood [around] and laughed and smoked." He said that he "got on well" with the commander at the garden.³⁸ However, the positive aspects of Nedeleanu's time in the local detachment—mainly due to lax enforcement of the rules and friendly relations between workers and supervisors rather than the result of any reforms—were not typical of the experiences of Jewish workers during the latter months of 1942.

In addition to the poor food and shortages of winter clothing he had previously experienced, Haim Leizerovici recalled difficulties with the authorities in Roads Battalion 8. By the end of 1942, Leizerovici was in poor health due to malnutrition and exposure, as well as exhaustion and stress. Because of his health problems, he was frequently unable to meet the daily production quotas imposed by the detachment's commander. As a result, he was frequently berated, usually by a Romanian soldier named Olaru, who referred to Leizerovici and the other Jewish workers as "insects." Leizerovici was also beaten by the soldiers at his work site. He recalled the beatings of other Jews, including one who attempted to escape and was given twenty-five lashes across the back with a whip. Leizerovici cites the Jewish workers' strong will in the face of difficult conditions and their psychological and moral drive to resist the Romanian authorities as the reason for his and others' survival.³⁹

The large number of people exempted by the review commissions continued to have a negative effect on productivity. The final total of workers exempted (both by the commissions and through the General Staff) was 38,123, 43.5 percent of the 87,591 Jews registered for forced labor in 1942; this figure was only slightly smaller than the 39,212 (44.8 percent) who were working.⁴⁰ The General Staff collected numerous reports of "irregularities" in the exemption process. For example, on October 13, it was discovered that a Jew named Szabo Lupu, who had obtained an exemption to remain at his job, working for an engineer named Zamfirescu in Călinești, was actually living in Râmnicu Vâlcea, sixty kilometers northwest of Călinești. His employment with his friend Zamfirescu was simply a ruse to allow him to receive an exemption.⁴¹ In another case, on November 16, a memo noted that a Jew named Ușer Haimovici had presented exemption card No. 6260 when called up for forced labor. However, the General Staff checked the exemption records and discovered that this card belonged to Rita David; this finding was confirmed by the Second Territorial Command.⁴² The numerous cases of fraud, in addition to the rampant bribery during the exemption process led to an inevitable confrontation between Radu Lecca and the military authorities, particularly his hated rival Ilie Șteflea, the chief of the General Staff.

On August 11, the judicial counselor of the General Directorate of Police, Mircea Busuioceanu, filed a report on his investigation into irregularities in exemptions granted by the review commissions and the General Inspectorate (prior to March 1942). Busuioceanu's investigative committee included Lieutenant Colonel Alex Mădârjac; Tunari Mucichescu, an architect; and Gheorghe

Popescu, a lawyer. However, the objectivity of this committee is questionable, as Lecca served as its nominal president. Nonetheless, Busuioceanu indicated that based on interviews members of the Central Commission, including Mociulschi and Dulfu, that numerous files were altered after the commission had voted against granting an exemption, and other cases were revisited in violation of regulations. None of the members of the commission interviewed said specifically who they believed had altered the files, but each heavily implied that they suspected Lecca was responsible.[43]

The report also exposed several cases in which lawyers had extorted money from Jews in exchange for arguing their case before the commission—as much as 175,000 lei in one case. The report conveniently omitted that a substantial portion of this money was then passed along to the commission in the form of bribes to Lecca and other members. Busuioceanu also reported cases in which a laborer obtained an exemption and then sold it to another person for profit, which was a common practice by mid-1942. Finally, eleven employees of the General Inspectorate were accused of accepting bribes for exemptions. The bribes paid to the Central Commission and local commissions were not mentioned in the report.[44]

Later that month, at Șteflea's insistence, Antonescu convened a meeting with Lecca and several members of the military leadership. Initially, Șteflea believed that he had convinced Antonescu to strip the power to grant exemptions from Lecca due to the enormous amount of corruption he had permitted in the process. Șteflea and the other army personnel present hurled accusations not only of corruption but of philosemitism as well, and the meeting devolved into a shouting match. Coming into the meeting, Antonescu was quite frustrated with Lecca's corruption and may have indeed intended to rein him in.

However, Lecca had an ace up his sleeve. Not only had Lecca enriched himself through bribery and extortion, but he had funneled money to hundreds of others as well, including many government officials. Among them were Mihai Antonescu and Maria Antonescu, the latter through substantial contributions to the Council of Patronage.[45] Records from the Central Jewish Office indicate that Lecca had spread at least 206,508,759 lei around to his various patrons in the government by December 1943.[46] The pressure exerted on Antonescu by these interests was greater than that applied by the military, and Lecca survived the second round of his power struggle with the army. Nonetheless, the military was given limited authority to cancel exemptions issued by the Central Commission in cooperation with the Central Romanianization Office (over Lecca's protests). In September 1942, the Territorial Commands annulled 824 exemptions on behalf of the General Staff, and another 342 were annulled in November 1942.[47] Further changes to the exemption process in 1943 would at least partially rein in Lecca's extortion enterprise; however, he found other methods for enriching himself and his associates.

After the dissolution of the Central Commission in May 1942, the Central Jewish Office became a central part of Lecca's system of corruption, replacing the middleman lawyers who had extorted the Jews on behalf of the commission. Requests for exemptions were submitted to the Central Jewish Office, which then passed them on to Lecca for approval. Lecca established the amount of the exemption tax to be paid and returned this information to the Central Jewish Office, which would then collect the tax from the petitioner (or pay it from the funds of the Jewish community if the petitioner could not pay). Hundreds of millions of lei passed through the Central Jewish Office into Lecca's hands during the final two years of Antonescu's rule. This role as the intermediary for extortion by corrupt officials earned its leadership the ire of both prominent Jewish leaders and ordinary Romanian Jews. According to the chief rabbi of Romania, Alexandru Șafran, he and many other Jews considered the head of the Central Jewish Office, Nandor Gingold—a Jewish convert to Catholicism, albeit a lapsed one—to have "assumed the role of public traitor." In his memoirs, Șafran opined that while Gingold was "an evil man, ruthless and severe," and "the leadership of the [Central Jewish Office] was composed of traitors and collaborators, the Central Jewish Office also included honest people, good Jews."[48]

In addition to supporting Lecca's extortion operation, the Central Jewish Office was also responsible for coordinating relief supplies of food and clothing to labor detachments (as well as to the camps and ghettos in Transnistria) and assistance to the families of men who were sent to forced labor. In this capacity, it assumed the role that the Jewish community organizations led by Filderman had filled prior to their dissolution at the end of 1941. On August 31, 1942, the head of the Jewish Office of the General Staff, Lieutenant Colonel Ilie Dumitrescu, sent a letter to the Central Jewish Office formally requesting that its county offices "send clothes and blankets to poor Jews [in the labor detachments] to replace deteriorated items."[49] On September 27, Dumitrescu's successor, Captain Apostolide, informed the Central Jewish Office that half of all Jews in the "pioneers" detachments lacked winter coats and blankets and that 80 percent had no change of clothes. He encouraged Gingold to "take urgent measures" to remedy the situation.[50] On October 29, Gingold announced to the commandant of CFR Detachment 12 in Valea Homorodului that the Central Jewish Office had sent one hundred pairs of wooden-soled canvas shoes, eighty-nine shirts, seventy-six pairs of underwear, sixty-seven pairs of wool stockings, forty-four pullovers, twenty-five vests, and eight pairs of pants for the workers.[51]

Although the Central Jewish Office and the local Jewish community leaders attempted to bridge gaps in the supply of winter clothing to the labor detachments, many Jews still went without coats, gloves, and boots in the later months of 1942. For example, of the 491 workers in Roads Battalion 8, located at Florești-Soroca, in northern Bessarabia, 212 lacked proper clothing. Roads Battalion 3, at

Cornești, in western Bessarabia, reported similar problems, with 199 of 272 workers without winter clothes.[52] Haim Leizerovici recalled that the weather was quite cold in late 1942 and that he and most of the other workers at that site lacked winter clothes, along with adequate food. He credited his and his comrades' survival to the fact that "[their] optimism was very strong."[53] On November 23, Antonescu issued a new order to the Central Jewish Office to compile stocks of clothing for Jewish workers who would be working throughout the winter.[54]

However, unlike its predecessor organizations and the local community bodies that remained intact, the primary function of the Central Jewish Office was not assistance to Jews and their families. Although it was the official representative of the Romanian Jews before the government, it was mostly concerned with carrying out Romania's Jewish policy as dictated by Antonescu and Lecca, in accordance with the will of the German legation.[55] As the exemption "taxes" demonstrated, the economic side of the regime's Jewish policy often amounted to outright extortion. In early September, the General Staff's Jewish Office held discussions with the Ministry of National Defense's undersecretary of accounting regarding the taxes paid by Jews for exemptions from forced labor. On September 2, the General Staff proposed two options for the collection of future exemption taxes. The first proposal included a daily rate of taxation—150 lei per day exempted for Jews under the age of thirty, and 300 lei per day exempted for Jews thirty and older—while the second consisted of a lump sum of 1.2 billion lei to be paid by the Central Jewish Office on behalf of all Jews who owed exemption taxes (a suggestion made by Radu Lecca).[56]

The General Staff and Ministry of National Defense agreed that Lecca's suggestion was the best option, and Antonescu approved the measure on October 9. The amount of the tax was later raised to 2.0 billion lei, of which 600 million was to be used to supply Jews at forced labor, while the remaining 1.4 billion would be given to the "needy [non-Jewish] population" of Romania.[57] The reality was quite different: half of the 1.4 billion lei was diverted into Maria Antonescu's Council of Patronage while the remainder was allegedly used to fund the operation of the labor detachments. In reality, most of it went directly into the pockets of Lecca and his associates.[58] Between August 1941 and August 1944, the Jews of Romania paid 3,178,172,516 lei in exemption taxes, hundreds of millions of which ended up in the accounts of Lecca and his associates within his network of patronage.[59]

Although many of the Jews who were exempted by Lecca had obtained their exemptions through illegal means, the large number of exemptions nonetheless accurately reflected the economic reality in Romania: the country still heavily depended on skilled Jewish laborers and professionals. Although Antonescu could not admit it publicly, he and his advisors were well aware of this fact, as demonstrated by his discussions with his cabinet in the summer of 1942. On July 23, Mihai Antonescu announced during a meeting of the Council of Ministers that the country was short some two thousand doctors and pharmacists since the Jews had been expelled from these positions. Minister of Culture Ion Petrovici informed him that the University of Iași wished to reestablish its Faculty of Pharmacy to train more ethnic Romanian pharmacists but did not have the necessary personnel. The university's administration requested permission from Petrovici to rehire their Jewish pharmacy professors. However, the council's decision on this question was not recorded.[60]

A week later, on August 1, the undersecretary of state for labor gave a report on the progress his department had made in the Romanianization of labor. He noted that while Antonescu had desired that "labor would become a new national religion," the removal of Jews from the workforce had not had the desired effect. While the number of Jews employed in the more than seven thousand Romanian businesses surveyed had decreased substantially, from 28,225 on November 16, 1940, to 17,134 on December 31, 1941 (the deadline for removal of all Jewish employees established by the November 16, 1940, Romanianization law), there had not been a corresponding increase in the number of non-Jewish ethnic Romanians employed in those firms. In fact, the number of ethnic Romanians employed in the surveyed businesses had decreased slightly as well, from 210,472 to 210,297. This disappointing result suggested that either the companies had downsized their workforces after their Jewish employees were dismissed or had simply replaced their Jewish employees with other people of non-Romanian ethnicity, such as Germans or Hungarians. In either case, these results were a major failure for Antonescu and his Jewish policy.[61]

The undersecretary's report also stated that one of the main problems facing Romanian firms wishing to replace their Jewish employees was the lack of qualified ethnic Romanian specialists, one of the problems that had sunk every preceding attempt at the Romanianization of labor through legislation. This situation had only been further exacerbated by the mobilization of Romanian men for military service when the war began. Several business leaders had suggested that the government should set up training programs to quickly prepare ethnic Romanians to replace skilled Jewish workers if the Romanianization of labor were to succeed.

While the undersecretary decried the corruption of Romanian officials in charge of Romanianization, he also pointed out that both employers and Jews "knew that [the government's] sanctions [for violating the Romanianization law] were almost inoperable, and could not be easily enforced because of the economic situation," leading many to openly flout the law without consequence.[62] However, the solutions he proposed (preventing Jews from obtaining professional qualifications and expelling them from unskilled labor) were impractical given the stress the economy was under due to the war. In reality, there was no mechanism through which the Romanianization of labor could be carried out, at least not to

Table 4.1. Daily wages established by the October 16, 1942, Law on Requisitions.

Personnel Type	Daily Wage
Apprentices	140 lei
Unskilled Workers	170–190 lei (men); 140–160 lei (women)
Skilled Workers	250–350 lei
Drivers	300 lei
Machine Operators	400 lei
Foremen	450–550 lei
Professionals	Less than fifteen years' experience: 650 lei
	Fifteen to thirty years' experience: 750 lei
	More than thirty years' experience: 850 lei

Antonescu's standards for completion and quickness, in a labor market that was constrained due to the war and already lacking skilled workers beforehand.

The October 16, 1942, Law on Requisitions, developed by the General Staff, established a new pay scale for Jewish workers requisitioned by private firms and government institutions through the military labor system. The law encouraged workers not to seek exemptions by providing a financial incentive for requisition, since the wages paid under the law were comparable to those paid by private employers.[63]

In practice, however, workers were probably disinclined to leave their jobs with their prewar employers to work for the military, where their activity would be subject to surveillance and military discipline. With such a weak incentive and no stick to follow up the General Staff's carrot, the October 16 law was ineffective in convincing workers to agree to its terms. The General Staff did not collect statistics on the number of Jews who decided to forgo exemption requests and come to work for the military. However, the mere existence of such a law indicated how badly the Romanianization of labor was failing. Economic necessity forced Antonescu to further delay the implementation of a central part of his antisemitic program.

The procedures for the deportation of deserters to Transnistria were amended in the fall of 1942. On August 29, the General Staff issued a directive that Jews who were to be deported would be allowed to take only hand baggage and cash (which would be exchanged for German marks, minus a conversion "tax").[64] On September 17, the General Staff ordered that if a worker deserted and was not found by the police or military authorities, then his family would still be deported without him.[65] The family members subject to deportation along with the violator included his spouse, parents, and children. The General Staff drew up a list of 14,247 Jews (later reduced to 12,588) who were to be deported for either deserting from forced labor or for not showing up for work. Two transports of alleged deserters departed from Bucharest for Transnistria in late September.[66] However, despite the large number of forced labor violators calculated by the General Staff, only 2,216 Jews were deported to Transnistria in September 1942, most of them for reasons unrelated to forced labor.[67] The small number of deportees was attributable to both the failure of the Romanian authorities to pursue forced labor violators thoroughly and changes in Jewish policy on a larger scale in the fall of 1942.

On October 12, the General Staff reported that 555 Jews (306 men and 249 relatives) had been deported to Transnistria for violating the forced labor regulations. Another 124 who were on the deportation list could not be found by the police and gendarmes. Some of the men who were arrested and deported with their families were not even on the General Staff's list; they had simply been in the wrong place at the wrong time or were arrested for being absent with leave. In other cases, the people who were arrested had legitimate excuses for their absence but were deported anyway. Froica Wainstein, a twenty-four-year-old laborer from Secureni who had been assigned to dig antitank ditches near Târgu Neamț, was deported with his family after he missed work because he was in the detachment infirmary.[68]

After the two transports departed in September, the General Staff noted that there were still 12,086 people who were in violation of the regulations who had not been deported. However, all deportations to Transnistria were suspended indefinitely in mid-October 1942. The General Staff expected that the deportations would resume at some point and the remaining violators and relatives were next in line, but the suspension remained in place and no more forced laborers were deported to Transnistria.[69] In his *Black Book* (*Cartea neagră*), Matatias Carp reported that 200 additional Jews were deported to Bogdanovca on February 5, 1943, of whom 7 died; however, these Jews are not included in the official lists of deported compiled by the General Staff in late 1943 and early 1944, and their fates are therefore difficult to corroborate.[70]

The experiences of those who were deported in the September transports were harrowing. Among the deportees were fourteen-year-old Sonia Palty and her family. Like the other deported Jews, they were arrested by the police on the night of September 15. Her father's arrest, however, was a mistake—he had been present at work for the required periods, both during the winter and summer labor campaigns (and had proven this to the police during two previous visits with his stamped identification card). Nonetheless, the family was taken to an abandoned school in Bucharest where the other arrested Jews were gathered. They waited there a week before being loaded onto freight cars and deported to the Alexandrovca camp in the Golta district of Transnistria via Tiraspol and Odessa, a journey that took another week.[71]

The deportees in Sonia Palty's transport were housed in a makeshift camp on the site of a former collective farm (*kolkhoz*), where they worked harvesting the sunflower crop. Palty described life in the camp in her memoirs: "Cold. Rain. Wind. The cold blew through the boards and window railings into the rooms. Into the bones. Outside, in the field, we were soaked with rain, beaten by the wind. In the rooms, we shivered from the cold. . . . At night, we lay on the floor, one against the other, trying to warm ourselves. We didn't have anything with which to make fire. We also suffered from hunger. But worse, from cold."[72] On December 26, 1942, Palty and 195 other deportees were taken by train to Bogdanovca, the site where the largest single massacre of Jews by Romanian forces had taken place exactly one year earlier.[73] Others were sent to different ghettos in Transnistria, such as Domanovca. The journey from Alexandrovca to Bogdanovca took nineteen days, during which the deportees received little food, water, or protection from the extreme conditions.[74] Palty's family was repatriated to Romania in October 1943 along with most of the surviving Jews deported from Bucharest; others would have to wait until early 1944 to return.[75]

Forced labor ended in most external detachments on December 1, 1942. As in 1941, the laborers were not allowed to return to their homes but instead were sent back to the capitals of their counties of origin. Jews working in certain detachments, such as the road construction battalions, were granted fifteen days of leave and then required to return to work, despite the winter conditions. Antonescu also requested the creation of detachments for unloading wagons and clearing snow throughout the winter months.[76] Jews who were requisitioned by private or government employers were not given leave and remained at work during the winter. However, they, like all other Jews residing in Romanian cities, were required to clear snow from the streets, as they had been in the winter of 1942. The formal order for this work was given on January 10, 1943.[77]

Despite the regulations established by the General Staff in the spring and early summer, forced labor in the fall of 1942 still returned mostly disappointing results. Though they insisted in meetings in early 1943 that the results in the large external labor detachments had been desirable where the supervision of workers had been good, they could not escape the fact that in most cases, forced labor had still failed to yield the desired results.[78] They would introduce further policy changes that, combined with the mobilization of more Jewish laborers than at any other point during the war, would lead to the most intensive of the four labor campaigns and the numerical peak of the forced labor system. However, this peak was reached only after a dramatic shift in Antonescu's Jewish policy.

Shortly after the Wannsee Conference in January 1942, Gustav Richter, the Reich Main Security Office representative in Bucharest, informed Antonescu that the Final Solution to the Jewish Question was set to begin and requested the end of the deportations to Transnistria, in view of the impending "continental" solution. It was at this point that the Antonescu regime's antisemitic policy began to deviate from that of the Third Reich. Despite the pervasive Nazi influence over Romania's Jewish policy, Antonescu continued to pursue an independent line in the persecution of Romania's Jews. Romania took more initiative in violence against its Jewish population than any of the other satellite states of Nazi Germany. During the spring and summer of 1942, the Antonescu government developed multiple, sometimes conflicting, plans for the extermination of the Romanian Jews, all of which were based on the continuation of deportations to Transnistria. On the other hand, the German authorities were focused on the deportation of the Jews of the Romanian Old Kingdom and southern Transylvania to the Belzec extermination camp in the General Government (in the southeastern part of present-day Poland, near the border with Ukraine). Antonescu's audacity and the single-mindedness of the Nazi authorities inevitably led to conflict.

One of the primary goals of the German delegation in their efforts to ensure the full cooperation of the Romanian authorities with the Final Solution was to sabotage the deportations to Transnistria. The responsibility for convincing the Antonescu regime to comply with the Nazi plans for the deportation of the Romanian Jews to Belzec belonged to Richter. In his capacity as the representative of Adolf Eichmann in Romania, he dealt with the Romanian foreign minister Mihai Antonescu, while Ambassador Manfred Freiherr von Killinger was responsible for direct communications with Ion Antonescu. The negotiations with the Romanian government began in earnest at the end of May 1942, when Richter met with Mihai Antonescu and Radu Lecca to discuss the "solution to the Jewish question" in a broad sense. Richter interpreted Mihai Antonescu's comments at this meeting as an indication that Romania wished to cooperate with the Nazis in the Final Solution, though he did not secure a verbal or written confirmation from Ion Antonescu.[79]

Two months later, on July 22, Richter finally received this confirmation in the form of a letter dictated by Mihai Antonescu, which communicated to Richter that it was "the wish of Marshal Antonescu" that the deportation of the Jews from Arad, Timiș-Torontal, and Turda Counties (in western Romania, near the Hungarian border) commence according to the German plan. Richter was so excited by this letter that when he returned to Berlin for a meeting with his superiors on July 24, he proudly presented it to Eichmann personally. Two days later, Eichmann gave Richter permission to return to Romania to begin "technical preparations" for the deportation of the Romanian Jews.[80] Eichmann also informed Richter that he had invited Radu Lecca to Berlin for a meeting the following month to make further arrangements regarding the Final Solution. In this meeting, Lecca requested permission from Eichmann to retain a total of seventeen thousand Jewish men between fifteen and forty-five years old deemed to be useful for work. Eichmann granted him no guarantee that such exemptions would be allowed, indicating that the Nazis had no interest in the continuation of the use of Jewish labor in Romania, irrespective of economic needs.[81]

Two weeks after receiving Mihai Antonescu's assurance of Romania's cooperation, Richter made his first major blunder in his mission to secure Romania's participation in the Final Solution. In a measure that demonstrated his overconfidence, on August 8, he published an article in the official German-language Nazi newspaper in Romania, the *Bukarester Tageblatt*, that announced, "Romania will be Jew-Free" (*Rumänien wird Judenrein*).[82] This article was not only a direct violation of Eichmann's orders that the Jews of Romania be kept unaware of their fate as long as possible but also a major embarrassment for Ion Antonescu, who had promised the former leader of the Jewish community in Romania, Wilhelm Filderman, that the Jews of the Romanian Old Kingdom would be protected from deportation.

Additionally, it led to vigorous protests from Jewish leaders, as well as other religious and political figures, which would also influence Antonescu's decision regarding Romania's role in the Final Solution. The first person to protest to Antonescu against the deportations in person was Nandor Gingold, the head of the Central Jewish Office. He met with Antonescu on August 22, 1942, after Antonescu had given orders to the Jewish Offices in Arad, Timișoara, and Turda to draw up lists of the Jews living in those counties in preparation for the "resettlement" of the Jews. Gingold also involved other Jewish community leaders in the process, including Mișu Benvenisti, Efraim Froimescu, and Arnold Schwefelberg.[83] Armed with information about the deportation plans obtained from discussions with Radu Lecca, Gingold also recruited Filderman and Chief Rabbi Alexandru Șafran, two of his most vocal detractors, to protest to Antonescu.[84] Other important people in Romania, including Antonescu's political opponents, such as Iuliu Maniu, leader of the National Peasant Party, and religious figures, like Metropolitan Nicolae Bălan of the Romanian Orthodox Church, also made their disapproval known to Antonescu.[85]

Ion Antonescu was rarely directly involved in the negotiations with the German authorities during the late summer and fall of 1942 due to an undisclosed illness. Most of the negotiating was handled by Mihai Antonescu on his behalf. The deportations were originally slated to commence on September 10, 1942. Eichmann had told Richter that the Jews of Romania would be deported to Lublin in the General Government and either be sent to forced labor or subjected to "special treatment" (*Sonderbehandlung*), a Nazi euphemism for gassing.[86] However, when the date came, preparations had not been completed, and the deportations did not begin as scheduled. The Romanian administration did not reply to German requests for information regarding an actual start date for the deportations.[87]

On September 22 and 23, Mihai Antonescu met with Nazi foreign minister Joachim von Ribbentrop at Hitler's eastern front military headquarters in Vinnytsia, in occupied Ukraine. At this meeting, Ribbentrop urged him to begin the deportations as soon as possible, to no avail.[88] As a result, Eichmann and the German Ostbahn railway agency planned a conference for September 26 to 28 in Berlin, at which they requested the presence of the Romanian state railway agency, CFR. However, due to a bureaucratic mix-up, T. C. Orezeanu, the director of CFR, was incorrectly informed by Radu Lecca that CFR's attendance of the conference was *not* needed. As a result, the logistics of the deportations were planned without any input from the Romanians.[89]

According to the plan developed during the conference, one transport of 2,000 Jews in fifty freight cars was to depart Romania every forty-eight hours. These transports would embark from the Adjud rail station in eastern Romania and follow the Orășeni-Sniatyn rail line to Belzec. Nearly 280,000 Jews from the Old Kingdom were to be deported in this manner.[90] The extermination facilities at Belzec had been expanded in July 1942 as the Nazis prepared for the "liquidation" of the Lwów (L'viv) Ghetto and the arrival of the Romanian Jews. The camp's six new gas chambers could murder between 1,000 and 1,200 people in twenty to thirty minutes.[91] Despite Radu Lecca's proposal to Eichmann to allow "useful" Jews to remain, Richter's plan excluded only a small number of Jews from the deportations. Almost the entire Jewish population of Romania, including the vast majority of the forced laborers, was to be deported.[92]

Richter was outraged that the Romanians continued sending Jews to Transnistria (including forced labor violators) while ignoring German requests to begin the deportations to Belzec. On October 7, he met with Mihai Antonescu and demanded the immediate end of the deportations to Transnistria, accusing the Romanian authorities of collaborating with the Jews to sabotage the Nazi Final Solution. After receiving no response from Mihai Antonescu, Richter became further enraged. On October 11, he published an article in the *Bukarester Tageblatt* decrying the presence of "Jewish lackeys" (*Judenknechte*) within the Antonescu government and implying that Romania's place within the "new Europe" that was to follow the Nazi victory would be determined by its handling of the "Jewish question."[93]

Nonetheless, two days later, in a meeting of the Council of Ministers, Mihai Antonescu announced that deportations to Transnistria and cooperation with the German deportation plans were "postponed" indefinitely. Richter was informed of this decision on October 22.[94] On November 11, he met with Mihai Antonescu and Lecca to convince the Romanians to change their position, but he was rebuffed by the deputy prime minister, who informed him that the Romanian government would no longer be participating in the "barbaric mass actions and acts of terror" against the Jews and indicated that the primary focus of Romania's antisemitic policy after that time would be against Jewish economic activity.[95]

The decision not to deport the Jews of the Old Kingdom was a watershed moment for Antonescu's Jewish policy. Having lost faith in an eventual Axis victory in the war, Antonescu adopted a more conciliatory stance toward the Jewish community. This change was reflected in Mihai Antonescu's remarks in the Council of Ministers' meeting on October 13, 1942, that if Romania was to fight against the Soviets in the name of "civilization," then it could not simultaneously use "barbaric" means against the Jews. Hildrun Glass noted that this statement does not indicate that Mihai Antonescu had become a philosemite but rather that he, too, realized that the Axis would likely lose the war and that Romania would be held accountable for its treatment of the Jews.[96] After the "postponement" of the deportations, Ion Antonescu's new preferred "solution" was to allow the Jews to immigrate to Palestine. Ambassador von Killinger referred to this plan as a "partial solution" (*Teillösung*) that "must be stopped by all means."[97] However, Antonescu was unmoved by his complaints, and emigration remained the focus of Romania's Jewish policy for the rest of the war.

The shift in the Antonescu regime's plans for the Romanian Jews also had important implications for forced labor. Prior to the "postponement" of the deportations, forced labor had been viewed as a temporary solution to the Jewish question, which would end when the permanent solution of deportation and extermination could be realized, as noted in the Popescu memo in November 1941. However, after the rejection of the German deportation plans and the end of large-scale deportations to Transnistria, there was no longer an imminent permanent solution via extermination, and forced labor became a permanent part of Antonescu's Jewish policy by default. Though the regime's plans still involved the eventual removal of as many Jews as possible from Romanian territory, the process of allowing all the Jews in the country to immigrate to Palestine would inevitably be very long due to immigration restrictions imposed by the British and the costs incurred by the transport of Jewish emigrants by sea. Thus, Jewish forced labor continued in Romania from October 1942 until the collapse of the Antonescu government twenty-two months later.

After the cancellation of the deportations, the importance of Jewish forced labor to the war effort increased, particularly as the tide turned against the Axis on the eastern front. On November 19, 1942, the Soviet Twenty-First and Sixty-Fifth Armies and Fifth Tank Army launched an assault on the Romanian Third Army, which was protecting the left flank of the German Sixth Army at Stalingrad. The following day, the Soviet Fifty-First Army attacked the southern flank of the Sixth Army, defended by the German Fourth Panzer Army and the Romanian Fourth Army. Both Romanian armies, with equipment and training that was inferior to those of their German counterparts, collapsed shortly after the operation began, allowing a breakthrough by both Soviet pincers that resulted in the encirclement of almost the entire combined German-Romanian force at Stalingrad.[98] Though they attempted to hold out against the Red Army and the Russian winter, on February 2, 1943, the commander of the Axis forces in Stalingrad, Field Marshal Friedrich Paulus, surrendered the German Sixth Army, along with the allied Romanian forces remaining in the city, completing a decisive Soviet victory in the largest battle of the war. Romania suffered almost 160,000 casualties during the Battle of Stalingrad, as well as the loss of a large amount of materiel—a disaster from which its armed forces would not recover.[99]

After the crushing Axis defeat at Stalingrad, the initiative in the war shifted into Soviet hands. Germany's allies had been crippled by Soviet counteroffensives in the winter of 1943. The Hungarian Second Army, its largest force on the eastern front, was almost completely destroyed at Ostrogozhsk, while the Romanian Third and Fourth Armies had to be rebuilt almost from scratch after their destruction at Stalingrad. Following another decisive Soviet victory in the Battle of Kursk in July 1943, the Axis forces were no longer capable of mounting meaningful offensive actions in the east. Antonescu's government put out peace feelers to the Western Allies in 1943, but to no avail. As the Red Army rolled back the German gains in Russia and Ukraine, it became clear to the Antonescu and the military leadership that Romania would soon have to defend its eastern border. As a result, the need for labor on military projects increased, meaning that the labor of the Romanian Jews became much more valuable.

The increasing needs of the Romanian military led to a reorientation of Jewish forced labor toward projects of immediate military significance, such as the improvement of fortifications and pillboxes and the construction of antitank ditches in eastern Romania and along the Hungarian border. As the Red Army drew closer and Romanian cities came within range of Soviet bombers, Jewish workers in local detachments also became involved in the war effort as part of both civil defense measures and as manual laborers removing debris from areas devastated by aerial assaults. Thus, by late 1943, Jewish forced labor was much more important to the Romanian military than it had been when the labor campaign began two years earlier.

One additional consequence of the end of the deportations of Jews from the Old Kingdom and the simultaneous postponement of mass deportations to Transnistria was that the option of deportation as a punishment for deserters was no longer available. However, detachment commanders and the Territorial Commands continued to recommend accused deserters for deportation, and individual people occasionally were still deported. The removal of deportation as a viable option for punishing the large number of known and suspected deserters caused some consternation in the Jewish Office of the General Staff, which had to find a new means by which to deter Jews from evading forced labor. The issue was raised at an October 10 meeting (three days before Mihai Antonescu formally announced the end of the deportations), during which it was decided that the punishment for desertion should be "similar to [that for] soldiers who ... desert during a time of war."[100] The Romanian army's punishment for desertion was execution.

However, Antonescu intervened with a proposal that those deserters who were caught would be sent to external labor detachments to do the most difficult work possible. This proposal was officially adopted on December 31, 1942.[101] In practice, the shift in the Romanian authorities' objectives for forced labor resulted in an intensification of the labor campaign and a dramatic increase in the number of Jews mobilized for work, nearly doubling the number deployed in 1942. This increase in the number of workers employed in 1943 can be attributed both to the military authorities' decreased tolerance of corruption by military and civilian officials and a more vigorous effort to pursue Jews who had not presented for forced labor as required.

The about-face in Antonescu's Jewish policy, the increased need to improve Romania's defenses after the reversal of the Axis's fortunes on the eastern front, and the full application of the regulations established by the June 27, 1942, General Instructions meant that the labor campaign of 1943 had a different character than that of the fall of 1942. This new atmosphere was reflected not only in the number of Jews deployed and the types of labor performed but also in the attitudes of the Romanian military personnel involved in the forced labor system, who no longer saw forced labor as merely an economic opportunity but as a vital part of Romania's national defense.

Notes

1. USHMMA, RG-25.013M, reel 22, file 48, folder 32, 303–304.
2. USHMMA, RG-25.003M, reel 180, file 2999, 63.
3. USHMMA, RG-25.003M, reel 180, file 2997, 46.
4. Only a small number of Jews were sent to work in Transnistria by the Romanian military. Forced labor in the camps and ghettos in Transnistria was administered directly by the government of Transnistria and was separate from the military system; therefore it is not treated in detail here. For information about forced labor in Transnistria outside the military system, see Viorel Achim, *Munca forțată în Transnistria: "Organizarea muncii" evreilor și romilor, decembrie 1942–martie 1944* (Târgoviște: Editura Cetatea de Scaun, 2015).
5. Ovidiu Creangă, "Balta/120 Labor Battalion," in Megargee, White, and Hecker, *United States Holocaust Memorial Museum Encyclopedia*, 3:599–600.
6. Trașcă, *"Chestiunea evreiască,"* document 300, 632–633.
7. Bărbulescu et al., *Munca obligatorie*, document 94, 286.
8. Ibid., document 94, 288.

9. Ibid., document 94, 293–294.
10. Bărbulescu et al., *Munca obligatorie*, document 90, 273–274.
11. USHMMA, RG-25.003M, reel 180, file 2999, 78.
12. USHMMA, RG-25.003M, reel 154, file 2958, 114.
13. Bron, interview 43924.
14. USHMMA, RG-25.003M, reel 180, file 2999, 79.
15. Ibid., 143.
16. USHMMA, RG-25.011, Romanian Forced Labor Camps, box 1, folder 2, 3–5.
17. USHMMA, RG-25.011, box 3, folder 13, file 132.
18. Goldberger, interview 25547.
19. Marcel Floreanu, interview 50019, Visual History Archive, USC Shoah Foundation, accessed online at the United States Holocaust Memorial Museum on March 5, 2015, http://vhaonline.usc.edu/viewingPage?testimonyID=52836&returnIndex=0.
20. USHMMA, RG-25.003M, reel 154, file 2960, 106.
21. Pinchas Lipner, interview 9713, Visual History Archive, USC Shoah Foundation, accessed online at the United States Holocaust Memorial Museum on March 7, 2015, http://vhaonline.usc.edu/viewingPage?testimonyID=8650&returnIndex=0.
22. Bărbulescu et al., *Munca obligatorie*, document 108, 312–313.
23. Ibid., document 90, 276–277.
24. Ibid., document 90, 271.
25. USHMMA, RG-25.003M, reel 157, file 2963, 196–197.
26. Ibid., 251, 256.
27. USHMMA, RG-25.003M, reel 180, file 2999, 143–144.
28. USHMMA, RG-25.003M, reel 154, file 2957, 114.
29. Carol Segal, interview 50164, Visual History Archive, USC Shoah Foundation, accessed online at the United States Holocaust Memorial Museum on February 5, 2015, http://vhaonline.usc.edu/viewingPage?testimonyID=53017&returnIndex=0.
30. Lipner, interview 9713.
31. USHMMA, RG-25.003M, reel 181, file 3001, 298–299.
32. Leizerovici, interview 12250.
33. Schottek, interview 49548.
34. USHMMA, RG-25.003M, reel 84, file 87, 291.
35. USHMMA, RG-25.003M, reel 154, file 2958, 135.
36. USHMMA, RG-25.003M, reel 157, file 2963, 107.
37. USHMMA, RG-25.003M, reel 154, file 2958, 149–168.
38. Louis Beno N., interview from Projekt Zwangsarbeit 1939–1945, za279, video interview.
39. Leizerovici, interview 12250.
40. USHMMA, RG-25.003M, reel 181, file 3001, 369–370.
41. USHMMA, RG-25.003M, reel 157, file 2963, 50–59.
42. Ibid., 26–27.
43. USHMMA, RG-25.002M, reel 16, file 43–42, 7–8.
44. Ibid., 26–32.
45. Ancel, *Economic Destruction*, 338–339.
46. USHMMA, RG-25.021M, selected records relating to the Holocaust in Romania, reel 7, file 134, 2.
47. USHMMA, RG-25.003M, reel 181, file 3001, 314.

48. Alexandru Şafran, *Resisting the Storm: Romania, 1940–1947, Memoirs* (Jerusalem: Yad Vashem, 1987), 87–89.
49. USHMMA, RG-25.016M, Centrala Evreilor, reel 4, file 32, 4.
50. USHMMA, RG-25.016M, Centrala Evreilor, reel 4, file 32, 6.
51. USHMMA, RG-25.016M, reel 8, file 70, 133.
52. USHMMA, RG-25.003M, reel 157, file 2963, 197.
53. Leizerovici, interview 12250.
54. USHMMA, RG-25.003M, reel 187, file 3014, 2.
55. Deletant, *Hitler's Forgotten Ally*, 122.
56. Traşcă, "*Chestiunea evreiască,*" document 300, 645.
57. Bărbulescu et al., *Munca obligatorie*, document 99, 301–302.
58. Deletant, *Hitler's Forgotten Ally*, 123.
59. Friling et al., *Final Report*, 203.
60. Benjamin, *Problema evreiască*, document 140, 422.
61. Ibid., document 140, 423–424.
62. Ibid., document 141, 425–426.
63. USHMMA, RG-25.003M, reel 185, file 3009, 3.
64. USHMMA, RG-25.003M, reel 181, file 3001, 186–187.
65. USHMMA, RG-25.003M, reel 181, file 3002, 102.
66. Ancel, *History of the Holocaust in Romania*, 476.
67. Glass, *Deutschland und die Verfolgung der Juden*, 218.
68. Froica Wainstein, interview 49829, Visual History Archive, USC Shoah Foundation, accessed online at the United States Holocaust Memorial Museum on March 6, 2015, http://vhaonline.usc.edu/viewingPage?testimonyID=52659&returnIndex=0.
69. USHMMA, RG-25.003M, reel 148, file 2946, 331.
70. Matatias Carp, *Cartea neagră: suferintele evreilor din România in timpul dictaturei fasciste, 1940–1944* (Bucharest: Ateliere grafice Socec, 1948), 3:304.
71. Sonia Palty, *Evrei, treceți Nistrul!* (Cluj-Napoca: Editura Dacia, 2006), 13–14.
72. Ibid., 61.
73. Ioanid, *Holocaust in Romania*, xxii.
74. Ovidiu Creangă, "Bogdanovca," in Megargee, White, and Hecker, *United States Holocaust Memorial Museum Encyclopedia*, 3:612.
75. Palty, *Evrei, treceți Nistrul!*, 173–175.
76. USHMMA, RG-25.003M, reel 174, file 2988, 11.
77. Bărbulescu et al., *Munca obligatorie*, document 113, 320–321.
78. Ibid., document 127, 350–352.
79. Palty, *Evrei, treceți Nistrul!*, 152.
80. Balta, *Rumänien und die Großmächte*, 291.
81. Friling et al., *Final Report*, 171.
82. Ancel, *History of the Holocaust in Romania*, 479.
83. Balta, *Rumänien und die Großmächte*, 293.
84. Glass, *Deutschland und die Verfolgung der Juden*, 171–173.
85. Ancel, *History of the Holocaust in Romania*, 498.
86. Jean Ancel, "The German-Romanian Relationship and the Final Solution," *Holocaust and Genocide Studies* 19, no. 2 (Fall 2005): 262.
87. Friling et al., *Final Report*, 170.

88. Ancel, *History of the Holocaust in Romania*, 482.
89. Vladimir Solonari, *Purifying the Nation: Population Exchange and Ethnic Cleansing in Nazi-Allied Romania, 1940–1944* (Baltimore: Johns Hopkins University Press, 2009), 292.
90. USHMMA, RG-25.003M, reel 185, file 3009, 36–38.
91. Ancel, *History of the Holocaust in Romania*, 501–502.
92. Ibid., 481.
93. Ibid., 477.
94. Friling et al., *Final Report*, 172.
95. Ioanid, *Holocaust in Romania*, 247.
96. Glass, *Deutschland und die Verfolgung der Juden*, 193–195.
97. Balta, *Rumänien und die Großmächte*, 339.
98. Anthony Beevor, *Stalingrad: The Fateful Siege: 1942–1943* (New York: Penguin Books, 1998), 239–265.
99. Axworthy, Crăciunoiu, and Scafeș, *Third Axis, Fourth Ally*, 113.
100. USHMMA, RG-25.003M, reel 181, file 3001, 272.
101. USHMMA, RG-25.003M, reel 181, file 3002, 109.

5 The Apogee

THE CANCELLATION OF the plans to deport and murder the Romanian Jews transformed forced labor from a temporary, intermediate phase of Antonescu's approach to the Jewish question into a permanent feature. The rapid deterioration of the situation at the front after Stalingrad forced Antonescu and his military advisers to recognize that Romania would soon have to mount a defense of its eastern border against the Red Army. To prepare for this defense would require an enormous amount of labor for the construction and enhancement of fortifications, antitank ditches, and other impediments to an advancing army, as well as improvement of the road and railway networks connecting these positions. This need for labor motivated the military to increase the recruitment of Jewish laborers and to craft more stringent policies for the supervision of Jewish workers in order to achieve maximum productivity.

The need to intensify the exploitation of Jewish labor coincided with a general de-escalation of Romania's Jewish policy. With deportation and extermination off the table, Antonescu and his allies in government increasingly viewed Romania's Jews as a bargaining chip in a potential separate peace with the Western Allies, seemingly their last hope for saving Romania from being overrun by the Red Army. While Antonescu continued to make antisemitic statements—and even had Wilhelm Filderman briefly deported to Transnistria for perceived insolence—his government decreased its antisemitic propaganda, and by the end of 1943, some of the Jews deported to Transnistria had been repatriated. The end of large-scale deportations to Transnistria removed the General Staff's strongest form of punishment under the 1942 General Instructions, forcing the government to find other measures that would promote discipline and productivity in the labor detachments. Antonescu supported these measures but also intervened at crucial times, including expressing opposition to the use of Jewish laborers at the front—a decision that may have prevented the deaths of hundreds or even thousands of people.

Although the military attempted to both increase the number of Jews working and induce them to work harder, the same problems that had arisen in 1941 and 1942 were present. Conditions and productivity in different detachments were still variable, but the overall results achieved by the forced labor system were not substantially improved. Furthermore, the need for increased production for the war effort forced Antonescu's government to admit defeat in the

Romanianization of labor. It acknowledged that the country could not immediately end its dependence on the skills of Jewish workers and professionals, proving that the fundamental premise of the economic side of Antonescu's Jewish policy—that Jews were harmful to the country's economy and Romania would benefit if they were removed—was fatally flawed. However, by that point in the war, there was no chance that Romania's economy could produce enough materiel to compensate for its losses at the front regardless of Antonescu's policy choices.

After the changes in Romania's political and military situation and Antonescu's Jewish policy in the fall of 1942, the General Staff and civilian authorities spent the first months of 1943 reworking certain aspects of forced labor policy so that it would be better suited to its new role. The end of deportations to Transnistria required new methods for punishing deserters and shirkers, while the increased labor needs of the military and state required a better system for recruiting and deploying skilled laborers and craftsmen. Furthermore, the need to increase the number of people mobilized for forced labor necessitated changes to the exemption of workers both for medical and economic reasons, even though such changes would inevitably lead to conflict with Radu Lecca. Although they were in some sense the continuation of the reform process initiated in 1942, the new policies enacted in 1943 were crafted in a distinctly different context.

One of the first policy choices Antonescu and the General Staff made in 1943 was the most important one for preventing the mass murder of Romanian Jewish laborers. On January 22, 1943, the General Staff met to discuss the potential value of sending Jewish laborers to build defensive fortifications for Romanian infantry formations at the front, noting that the Hungarians had done so the year before. For the General Staff, having Jewish laborers instead of regular soldiers perform such dangerous tasks was an appealing option. They agreed that the question should be studied and that a decision would be made based on that study.[1] However, at the exact time they were debating the proposal to emulate the Hungarians, the Hungarian Second Army was being overwhelmed by the Red Army at Ostrogozhsk; at least 18,550 Jewish laborers were killed or went missing during the battle.[2]

The study resulted in two plans for the organization of frontal detachments, which were based on the number of Jews registered for forced labor in external detachments as of February 1943. The first of these proposals (Hypothesis A) included all 27,500 registered Jews aged twenty to forty. This proposal noted that 12,200 of them were already assigned to external detachments and another 9,500 were working in local detachments, leaving 5,800 still available. Using these figures, the authors of the study calculated that six battalions of 900 men could be created from the available Jews twenty to forty years old. If the men in the local detachments were also included, seventeen detachments of 900 men could be formed, while if those already in external detachments were included, it would be possible to create thirty such detachments. The second proposal (Hypothesis B) included only the 17,750 registered Jews between twenty and thirty years old. Of these men, 6,000 were in external detachments, 9,000 were in local detachments, and 2,750 remained available. It would be possible to form three battalions of 900 men from those still available, thirteen including those in local detachments, and nineteen including all men aged twenty to thirty.[3]

However, the study also noted that either of these plans would be difficult to execute in practice, primarily due to lack of supplies. Antonescu had declared that all workers must be fully equipped with adequate clothing and provided with tools, neither of which could be guaranteed for the detachments sent to the front because to do so would divert valuable supplies from the troops. While the option of sending Jews to the front in civilian clothes was available, the General Staff opposed such an action, as it might draw "unfavorable comments from abroad" and any Jews who fled would be able to easily blend in with the local population.[4] In the end, the whole idea was abandoned, likely sparing thousands of Romanian laborers a fate similar to that of the approximately thirty-three thousand Hungarian Jewish laborers who died on the eastern front.[5] Even without the use of laborers at the front, however, conditions were generally worse in detachments that were farther from the Bucharest and were particularly bad in those deployed outside the Old Kingdom. For example, conditions Labor Battalion 120, under the control of the military Command of the Eastern Areas were among the worst in any Romanian labor detachment, although they were certainly far less dangerous than they would have been in the immediate vicinity of the front.[6]

With deportation to Transnistria and deployment to the front both off the table, the government and General Staff had to find a new way to punish deserters from forced labor detachments. On December 31, 1942, Antonescu had given his assent to a proposal to enforce the military punishment for desertion— court-martial with a maximum penalty of execution—for forced laborers as well. This proposal was enacted by Law No. 59 on February 3, 1943. Under this law, Jews called up for forced labor would have four days to report to their local recruitment centers after receiving their conscription notice (for Jews living abroad still under Romanian jurisdiction, the deadline was thirty days), after which they would be considered "insubordinate" (*nesupuși*). In peacetime, the penalty for insubordination was imprisonment of two months to one year; in wartime, it was death. Law No. 59 defined desertion as being absent without leave for more than two days, or failure to report to the assigned detachment within four days. The penalty for desertion in peacetime was imprisonment of six months to two years; in wartime, as for insubordination, it was death. Law No. 59 was the strictest measure yet to prevent desertion, though, as with previous policies, it was dependent on vigilant enforcement by detachment personnel.[7]

On February 24, the General Staff issued Order No. 21456, which contained additional instructions on the application of Law No. 59. Detachment commanders and government and private employers of Jewish workers were told to keep detailed records of each Jew working under them and his presence or absence from work. If these records indicated that someone was in violation of Law No. 59, the commander was to report the violation to their Territorial Command. The Territorial Commands were responsible for giving orders to find deserters, coordinating the searches with police and military authorities, and preparing the formal legal complaints against deserters. These instructions also stated that Jews were required to carry their military identification cards with proof of registration for forced labor at all times, to notify their recruitment centers in writing of any change of address, and to inform their employers immediately of any illness or injury that would prevent them from working, or if they were arrested or detained by the police.[8]

Although the General Staff's estimate of more than twelve thousand Jews violating the forced labor regulations (either as "insubordinates" or deserters) in 1942 was inflated by errors and poor record keeping, they were not mistaken in their belief that desertion was widespread. For Jews who could not pay the exemption taxes or obtain exemption cards on the black market, desertion was the most viable option for resistance against forced labor. Desertion as a means of resistance took many forms. Some Jews were simply absent without leave, such as a group of three Jews working for the natural gas company Gaz Metan who were reported missing in January 1943.[9] However, such tactics could backfire, as they did for a Jew named Constantin Ardeleanu, who was working for a private employer in Bacău when he decided to desert. After he disappeared for five days, the labor inspector of Bacău declared him to be "a recalcitrant element" and reported that his employer no longer wanted his services, meaning that even if he escaped court-martial, he would likely be sent to an external labor detachment.[10]

Other Jews found more subtle methods to avoid being sent to the labor detachments. William Farkas admitted that after he returned from a railway labor detachment in Valea Homorodului, he and a friend lied to the recruitment authorities, claiming that they were trained electricians, even though neither of them had had any professional training and Farkas was afraid of the idea of working with electricity. However, the ruse worked, and they were given an assignment in a mechanic's garage rather than being sent back to the railroad detachment.[11] Other Jews evaded forced labor through requisitions by confederate non-Jewish business owners. One such case was reported in Bacău in March 1943, where three Jews—Solomon Sächter, Iosif Rotenberg, and Bernard Galantar—had been granted exemptions to work in the business of Iulius Cerbu, an army reserve captain. However, when the local labor inspector arrived at Cerbu's business on December 15, 1942, he found only Cerbu and his receptionist present. The three requisitioned Jews had not been to work there in months, and records of their presence had been falsified dating back to at least the previous August. The inspector ordered that they be sent to Galați to face court-martial. His report did not specify what punishment Cerbu would face.[12]

One of the most extreme cases of fraud occurred at Întreprinderile Metalurgice (Metallurgical Enterprises) in Iași, to which forty-four Jews, mostly skilled laborers, had been assigned. After an investigation by the Fourth Territorial Command in July 1943, it was determined that the entire company was a sham, set up to facilitate the exemption of these workers and defraud the government of money by obtaining military contracts. All the Jews allegedly working for Întreprinderile Metalurgice were returned to the Territorial Command to be sent elsewhere. The report did not specify the punishment for the operators of the fake company.[13]

Cases like that of Întreprinderile Metalurgice, as well as other incidents of fraud—such as twenty-eight Jews who were granted false exemptions by the Chamber of Labor in Cernăuți—aggravated the already acute shortage of craftsmen and skilled laborers the military was facing.[14] Because Jews still made up a substantial proportion of the country's craftsmen, there was high demand for their services from both government and private employers, far outpacing the number available. Although the shortage of skilled laborers was not a new problem—it had been a thorn in the General Staff's side since the earliest days of the forced labor system—it was particularly acute by 1943, when the war had placed the Romanian economy under tremendous stress and the need for skilled labor on projects of immediate importance for national defense increased. Jews with specialized skills had been used in local detachments or in "teams" since at least May 1942, when the General Staff ordered the recruitment centers to create "homogeneous groups" of certain types of skilled laborers (such as barbers, tailors, and cobblers), which consisted of no more than ten people and performed tasks of local significance in cooperation with the county prefect.[15]

On May 14, 1943, the General Staff introduced new regulations on the use of these valuable workers to maximize their productivity. Jews classified as skilled laborers or craftsmen (and registered as such with the recruitment centers) were divided into two categories. Category A consisted of skilled laborers between the ages of twenty and thirty-five. Their deployment would be regulated by the General Staff and the Territorial Commands, who would send them to areas where their services were needed. Category B comprised skilled Jews from eighteen to nineteen and thirty-six to fifty years old who would be at the disposal of their local governments and military units. Jews in category A who were deemed fit only for "light work" would be moved into category B. Plans for Jews in category B would be drawn up by local commissions made up of the commander of the Territorial Command (or his delegate), the county prefect, the mayor, the commander of the local recruitment center, the president of the local chamber of labor, and representatives from other relevant local authorities. Workers in category A would be made available to local governments only if they were not needed elsewhere.[16]

This new system was designed to increase the mobility of skilled laborers and hasten their deployment to places where they were needed. It also allowed the General Staff to ensure that they were used on projects of the most immediate military significance. It followed a previous decision from February 28 that restricted the requisition of craftsmen and professionals by the military to ten per unit, with exceptions for larger needs granted on a case-by-case basis.[17] This new regulation further demonstrated how desperate the need for skilled Jewish labor was on the home front.

Despite the importance of Jewish craftsmen, professionals, and skilled laborers to the economy, Antonescu nonetheless remained opposed to their presence in certain situations, such as military hospitals, where he feared they would spread "communist propaganda" and demoralize wounded soldiers returning from the front. Antonescu's paranoia extended to Jewish laborers requisitioned for private use as well, and his attitudes were shared by lower-level officials. For example, a Jew working for a mechanic's shop in Timișoara that repaired military vehicles was accused of collecting information on the Romanian army's motorized formations for the Soviets. It was also alleged that he was only there because of his friendship with the owner, Nicolae Criștian.[18] No evidence was presented for either of these allegations, but they nonetheless demonstrate the conflict between Antonescu's suspicions toward Jewish workers and the military's understanding that the war economy relied heavily on their skilled labor. While a conscious effort was made to minimize the number of Jewish craftsmen being used in sensitive war-related industries—as revealed by a memo circulated by the Second Territorial Command, proposing "to reduce the number of craftsmen in all military enterprises and units"—such measures proved impossible, particularly as the situation at the front worsened and ideological preferences had to be sacrificed in the interests of national defense.[19]

The need to set ideology aside and gain as much benefit as possible from Jewish labor motivated Antonescu and the General Staff to reexamine the results of the labor campaign in the fall of 1942 in search of other ways to streamline the recruitment of laborers and increase productivity in the labor detachments. On March 11, Antonescu held a conference with the leadership of the General Staff and several government ministers to evaluate the previous year's results and develop new policy based on them. Despite the mixed reports from the detachments in the last months of 1942 and the continuation of major problems with housing and supplies, the General Staff told Antonescu that the results in the external detachments had been very good due to the vigilance of supervision but that the local detachments had performed poorly due to lax supervision by civilian authorities, which were "easily corrupted." Their report lamented the abuse of workers by local commanders, which they believed had damaged public opinion of forced labor.[20] Furthermore, the number of Jews whose status was listed as "unknown," which had climbed to 19,742, was deemed far too high relative to the number of Jews registered and eligible for labor in 1943. Nonetheless, there were already significantly more Jews registered than in the previous two years—98,466 by March 11.[21] By May 1943, 102,139 Jews had been registered, of whom 42,025 had been sent to work in local and external labor detachments, and by June 30, 50,246 Jews were working in the detachments.[22]

The General Staff made several proposals to maximize the number of Jews available for work. First, it requested that as many twenty- to forty-year-old Jews as possible be sent to labor detachments, unless they were truly indispensable. Second, it called for the annulment of exemptions for Jews working in public institutions and the right to requisition Jews with academic degrees (even those holding exemptions) for ninety days a year. Third, it asked that work be found for Jewish women of military age. Finally, it requested that the police and gendarmes be more vigilant in pursuing Jews who violated Law No. 59 and bringing them to justice.[23] The second request was implemented almost immediately, with a decree-law appearing in the official gazette of the Romanian government, *Monitorul Oficial*, just five days after the conference. The other requests, which were more open-ended, were only partially enacted; information on work performed by Jewish women in particular is very limited, and it is difficult to determine the extent of their involvement in the labor campaign precisely.

Intensified recruitment of Jewish laborers and pursuit of forced labor violators, however, ran concurrently with the de-escalation of Antonescu's post-1942 Jewish policy. Noting the General Staff's complaints about the abuse of workers by military and civilian supervisors, and concerned, as the General Staff was, about public opinion, on March 17 he ordered that Romanian personnel were not to physically abuse Jews or use "vulgar" language toward them, as Romania would not "treat our minorities like the Hungarians treat our Romanians in Northern Transylvania"—referencing the massacres of ethnic Romanians and Jews committed during the Hungarian reoccupation of the region following the Second Vienna Award. The decree also explicitly referred to "Romanian citizens of any ethnic origin," a departure from the terminology and rhetoric that Antonescu had used toward the Jews during the preceding two and a half years.[24]

Antonescu's displeasure with the mistreatment of workers and its negative impact on productivity was best demonstrated by an incident that took place in June 1943. During his observation of Roads Battalion 1, in the Carpathian foothills, Antonescu encountered a Jew named David Margulius, who was physically disabled and not capable of performing manual labor. Antonescu was angered that someone in such a condition had been sent to a labor detachment. General Radu Davidescu relayed Antonescu's report to the General Staff: "At Roads Battalion 1 at Predeal, the marshal saw the Jew David Margulius, sent from the Iași recruitment center. The Jew was in such a physical state that he could not be used for labor. He traveled [to the detachment] for no reason and was costing the detachment expenses while not being of use. Because of what the Iași recruitment center has done in this case, they shall take action against those responsible. . . . [Antonescu] has ordered [the General Staff] to investigate this case and report [back to him]."[25] In the subsequent investigation, it was determined that when Roads Battalion 1 sent its laborers on leave for the winter, only 73 of the 177 Jews assigned to the detachment from Iași had returned; 55 had been sent to work elsewhere by the recruitment center, while 49 had deserted (or their whereabouts were unknown). In response, the recruitment center officials sent replacements back to the detachment to avoid a reprimand from their superiors for losing track of so many workers. Some, like Margulius, who had previously been classified as unfit for labor were reclassified as fit (without medical clearance from a doctor) and sent to the detachment. Colonel Gheorghe Zamfirescu, who prepared the investigation report, informed the General Staff that those responsible at the recruitment center would be court-martialed for their actions. The commanders at the detachment were sentenced to punishment at the discretion of the Ministry of National Defense, while the Jewish medic in the detachment was sent to a camp in Transnistria.[26]

In the wake of this incident and continued controversy over medical exemptions, the General Staff issued new instructions on medical examinations and exemptions on October 7. Jews in local detachments who became ill were to be sent to the detachment infirmary, while those requisitioned by private or government employers were to visit the recruitment center infirmary (or a local doctor). All employers of Jewish laborers were required to keep records of medical visits in the detachment infirmary. Jews granted sick leave from work were required to sign a form indicating that they were on sick leave, which was to be reported to the recruitment center or Territorial Command. Detachment medics could grant a maximum of five days of sick leave; further leave would require the approval of the Territorial Command (after examination by their doctors), which could grant leave of up to eight additional days. Jews who repeatedly received sick leave were subject to investigation by the Territorial Command's medical staff. Jews who were injured and required hospitalization would first need approval from a medic at the recruitment center or Territorial Command. Medications for Jews treated in detachment infirmaries or private clinics would be paid for by their employers.[27]

Each external detachment was required to have a medic (in spite of an acute shortage of Jewish medics who could be deployed to the detachments) and an infirmary with enough beds to hold 1 percent of the detachment's workers. Leave could be granted only by a detachment medic with the approval of the military commander of the detachment, the recruitment center, or Territorial Command medic. The detachment commander would keep a record of all medical leave granted to his workers, and the medical staff of the recruitment center or Territorial Command would make periodic visits to inspect sanitary conditions in the detachment. Jews needing hospitalization would be sent to the nearest civilian hospital at the expense of their employer. Jews bitten by suspected rabid dogs would be sent to the nearest rabies treatment facility at the cost of the local Jewish community (an attempt to discourage feigned dog bites). Jews requiring extended hospital stays or unable to return to work after their hospitalization were to be inspected and approved by the Territorial Command. If a Jew died in the detachment or in a hospital from injuries received in the detachment, the cost of the burial would be paid by the local Jewish community.[28]

Medical exemptions could be granted only by the Territorial Command (or the General Staff), and the head of the Territorial Command was responsible for determining what work a person could be sent to after his exemption expired. Jews eligible for labor would be divided into five categories:

- A. fit for hard labor
- B. fit for light labor
- C. fit only for intellectual work
- D. unfit for any work
- E. conditionally unfit (for a period of 180 days)

Jews could be classified unfit for any work only if they had a well-documented chronic illness or handicap. Workers were classified by the medical staff of the Territorial Command or the army's medical review commission. Those in categories B, C, and D would be subject to review and reclassification every three years until they reached the age of fifty; those in category E would be reevaluated every 180 days, and if they were classified as conditionally unfit for two consecutive 180-day periods, they would be reviewed by the army medical commission.[29]

The Territorial Command and detachment commanders were expected to supervise their medical personnel, and any deliberate falsification on their part or simulation of illness by workers would be punished severely by the Territorial Command. Anyone who committed deliberate self-harm would face court-martial, just like regular soldiers.[30] These harsh penalties were designed to keep fraudulent medical exemptions, which the General Staff believed to be a serious problem, to a minimum. However, it also created bureaucratic impediments to emergency care needed by workers. From the General Staff's perspective, the new measures were a success: nearly half the 7,710 medical exemptions granted in 1942 were canceled in 1943.[31]

The General Staff also sought to increase the number of available Jewish laborers by eliminating corruption in the exemption of "economically necessary" Jews. Lecca still had the authority to grant exemptions based on requests made via the Central Jewish Office—including the power to exempt Jewish religious leaders and employees of the Central Jewish Office, as well as Jews with academic and professional degrees—but since the Central Commission had been dissolved at the end of May 1942, most of the exemption requests were handled by the county commissions, supervised by the Ministry of Justice. According to statistics presented to the Council of Ministers on April 13, 1943, a total of 25,895 exemptions were granted (4,495 by Lecca and the rest by the county commissions), of which 21,124 were to Jews between eighteen and fifty years old and 4,771 to Jews over fifty. While the number of exemptions had increased by 5,859 over the number granted in 1942, on further review by the Central Romanianization Office, undersecretary of state for labor, and General Staff, 4,495 of the exemptions for Jews between eighteen and fifty were canceled, leaving a total of 16,629 Jews of military age exempt from forced labor for economic reasons, a net decrease from 1942.[32]

The exemptions granted by the county commissions expired on June 30, 1943, when a commission including representatives from the General Staff, Ministry of the National Economy, Ministry of National Defense, and Ministry of Labor convened to determine which exemptions would be extended and which would be canceled. The Central Romanianization Office provided input to the commission, which was responsible for the removal of Jews from Romanian businesses. Lecca's power to exempt Jews with academic and professional degrees frustrated the General Staff because it only worsened the shortage of skilled Jewish laborers. For example, of 211 construction engineers in the country, 132 had been exempted by Lecca. The General Staff proposed that Jews with academic degrees who held exemptions still be required to perform ninety days of forced labor per year, as Jewish academics without exemptions were. Lecca rejected this proposal, suggesting instead the extension of the time that Jewish professionals without exemption could be required to work. On August 14, the General Staff ordered that Jews with academic degrees who did not have exemptions would be required to work six months a year (double the requirement established in 1942). It also demanded that the number of exemptions given to Jewish specialists be reduced by half.[33]

The General Staff's efforts to increase recruitment of Jewish workers were successful. As of June 30, 107,601 Jews had been registered for forced labor, of whom 50,246 were working in labor detachments (17,967 in external detachments), 52,909 were requisitioned or exempted, and 4,446 were available to be called up. In addition, 4,668 Jewish women had been registered for work.[34] The number of Jews registered for forced labor had increased by more than 20,000

Table 5.1. Jewish labor detachments as of November 3, 1943.

Detachment Type	Number of Detachments	Total Jewish Laborers
CFR (Railroads)	4	1,040
D. G. Drumuri (Roads)	8	6,000
Engineering	5	6,623
Civilian Authorities	32	8,414
Total	49	22,077

over 1942, while the number of Jews deployed in the detachments increased by more than 10,000, and bested 1941's total by more than 8,000. At least 75,000 people performed forced labor in some form in 1943, by far the highest number of the four labor campaigns. By November 3, the number of Jews in external detachments had increased to 22,077 working in a total of forty-seven detachments.[35] With a roughly comparable number of Jews working in the local detachments, which were generally smaller than the external detachments, it is likely that well over one hundred detachments had been created by the end of 1943.[36]

The effects (or lack thereof) of the General Staff's policy changes in 1943 on both the productivity of the labor detachments and the experiences of the laborers are best illustrated through case studies of several labor detachments. It is easier to examine the conditions in the detachments during this period than earlier in the war because detachment commanders were (in theory) keeping more detailed records. Some commanders were more diligent than others in preparing and filing their reports, and those who did a better job are obviously more thoroughly represented in the archival records, potentially biasing the sample in favor of those detachments that were under more competent supervision. However, these records still indicate variable conditions between detachments, demonstrating the diversity of experiences in the Romanian forced labor system. The case studies presented in this and the following chapter will be broken down by the types of work each group of detachment was engaged in, including railroad, road construction, and engineering (i.e., fortifications and waterways) detachments.

During the first two years of the forced labor system, the Romanian railway system had been one of the primary beneficiaries of Jewish labor. Several thousand Jews had worked in the detachments of the Romanian state railway agency throughout the country, laying new track and repairing existing lines, as well as performing other tasks like quarrying and moving stone and clearing snow from the tracks in winter. These jobs were important to the war effort as they maintained or improved transportation of goods within Romania and toward the front. However, beginning in 1943, the number of Jews working on the Romanian railways began to decline as workers were reoriented to tasks of direct military importance, such as the improvement of existing fortifications and construction of new ones. Most of the laborers in CFR detachments in 1943, which totaled more than fifty-seven thousand workers, were non-Jewish Romanians (many of them ethnic minorities) working as civilian labor servicemen. Most of the remainder were Soviet prisoners of war, who were in many cases treated worse than Jewish laborers.[37]

The largest Jewish railroad detachment was CFR Detachment 49. Formed in Timișoara in April 1943, Detachment 49 had 778 Jewish workers at its peak, approximately 400 of whom were deportees from Bessarabia.[38] Most Jewish railroad detachments—such as CFR Detachment 106/107, to which memoirist Andrei Voinea was assigned—numbered no more than a few hundred workers. CFR Detachment 49 was dispatched from the Timiș-Torontal recruitment center on April 1, 1943, with 494 Jewish workers divided between four platoons, six officers, three noncommissioned officers, and a Jewish medic, under the command of Reserve Captain Constantin Budu. The detachment had been assigned to work extending the forty-kilometer rail line between the cities of Caransebeș and Reșița in Severin County, in southwestern Romania. In the first two weeks of April, no work was performed, as the workers were building their barracks and the infrastructure of the detachment's base camp. Nonetheless, ninety-three men made trips to the infirmary and three men were sent to the hospital, including Mateiu Kunț, who broke his tibia after falling out of his bunk on the morning of April 10. During this period, one man, described in the official report as a "gypsy," deserted from the detachment.[39] By mid-May, the size of the detachment had increased to 580 men and work on the rail line had commenced, with generally good productivity. However, on May 26 the assistant commander of the detachment was sent to the hospital and replaced with a Sergeant Olteanu. Additionally, one Jewish worker was hospitalized with a suspected case of typhus.[40]

In addition to the loss of the assistant commander for medical reasons and the threat of typhus, the detachment was faced with other problems. On June 15, Captain Budu reported that approximately 75 percent of the four hundred Jews from the city of Orhei (in present-day Moldova) who were working in the detachment had no change of clothing, and two months of hard work had left their clothes badly tattered.[41] Despite their lack of adequate clothing, Captain Budu noted that these men were the hardest workers in the detachment. However, he neglected to mention that the Jews from Orhei, unlike those from the Old Kingdom, had seen the massacres committed by the Romanians in their city in July 1941 and were, therefore, likely motivated by a fear of the Romanian soldiers that was not present in the workers from the Old Kingdom.[42] CFR officials noted that the productivity of the Jewish workers was lower than that of the ethnic Romanian workers in the civilian labor detachments.[43]

Andrei Voinea's experience in Detachment 106/107 illuminates some of the reasons the lower productivity of the Jewish labor detachments. In his detachment—which was sent to a stone quarry in Abrud, in west-central Romania, in February 1943—every two men were required to fill a ten-ton wagon with stone every day, work that Voinea described as "very hard." Sometimes the men were forced to work well into the nighttime hours to finish their task.[44] Voinea's experience suggests that the General Staff and Territorial Commands had assigned some of the most difficult tasks to the Jewish workers. Jewish workers were increasingly shifted away from work on the rail lines and toward work in quarries, road construction, digging canals, and reinforcing fortifications, all among the most difficult tasks performed by military laborers during the war.

Because of the strenuous nature of the work, many men in the CFR labor detachments missed work due to injury and illness. For example, from July 16 to 31, the 587 men in Detachment 49 made 219 visits to the detachment infirmary. Of these men, 7 were excused from work in the detachment due to injury, while 9 others were kept in the infirmary and 4 were sent to the hospital (of whom one was believed to be a case of deliberate self-injury).[45] The number of infirmary visits continued to be high throughout the 1943 labor campaign, including 386 in the month of September. Some of these accidents resulted in serious injuries (for example, one of the four men hospitalized in the first two weeks of July had suffered a skull fracture). However, Detachment 49 reported only one fatal injury in 1943, which occurred in early October. The reason for the man's death was not given, as the detachment commander was still awaiting the results of his autopsy, and it was not revealed in subsequent reports.[46] As with records from earlier years, it is not possible to determine whether additional deaths were concealed in the detachment commander's reports or whether Captain Budu's reports are accurate; the lack of available worker testimony from this detachment prevents corroboration of his statements.

The level of discipline enforced on the workers varied from detachment to detachment and commander to commander. Aside from the incident of desertion in early April, Captain Budu did not report any major violations of the labor regulations in his detachment that resulted in corporal punishment or court-martial; however, he did note that the men's morale "left much to be desired."[47] Meanwhile, the leadership personnel of Detachment 106/107 apparently enforced rules and order more rigidly. Voinea reported that, while the officers did not speak or behave in an antisemitic manner, the workers were expected to work in an orderly, disciplined fashion, keep their mouths shut unless they were spoken to, and maintain their hygiene rigorously to avoid disease. Luckily for Voinea, his detachment was quartered near the Ariestal River, which allowed them to bathe and wash their clothes and bedding regularly, as well as providing a consistent source of clean drinking water, luxuries not available to most Jews working in the labor detachments.[48] However, these luxuries were not the result of good planning on the part of the detachment leadership, but simply a consequence of a fortuitous location. Neither Voinea nor Captain Budu reported any cases in which the punishments prescribed by Law No. 59 were carried out. In fact, no official documentation exists from any detachments of executions under Law No. 59.

Food supplies in the railroad detachments were generally adequate in early 1943, a marked improvement over the prior two years. At the beginning of the 1943 campaign, the quality of food provided to the workers in Detachment 49 was very good: the men received coffee and bread with marmalade in the morning and mămăligă at their two evening meals, with meat provided six times per week.[49] However, by the fall, the men were receiving only five meals with meat per week (approximately one hundred grams per meal) and were given mămăligă only on Saturdays.[50] High supply costs earlier in the year, in addition to the strain of wartime rationing and the diversion of additional resources toward the front in late 1943 contributed to the decline in quality of food provided in the detachments. Andrei Voinea recalled that the men in Detachment 106/107 were more fortunate than those in many other detachments because the Jewish community in Turda had arranged for the men to have kosher meat for their meals. However, their housing conditions were less than comfortable, as they were quartered in old, abandoned houses near the river.[51]

By the fall of 1943, the hard work and declining conditions began to take a toll on the workers in Detachment 49. Captain Budu reported that productivity had dropped off dramatically in October and November and that by that point, the men were looking forward to their expected release at the end of the year rather than focusing on work.[52] Apparently, the workers in that detachment were unaware of the situation at the front. The men in Detachment 49 were allowed to return home on December 13, 1943.[53] By contrast, in Detachment 106/107, the men had learned from the soldiers supervising the detachment that the war was going badly for the Axis and about the defeat at Stalingrad. Voinea stated that by the fall of that year, the soldiers and even civilian bystanders had begun to treat the workers better, and the workers' morale improved with the expectation that the war would soon end. Voinea's detachment was disbanded in November 1943, and the workers received new assignments for the next year.[54]

As the cases of Detachment 49 and Detachment 106/107 demonstrate, the experiences of workers could vary greatly from detachment to detachment, depending on the attitudes of their leaders, the availability of supply, and the strictness with which disciplinary measures were enforced. While workers in Detachment 106/107 were somewhat more fortunate than those in Detachment 49, both cases indicate that the reforms of 1942 had had little practical effect and events external to the General Staff's policymaking, particularly the actions of the employers, were more important in determining the availability of supplies and quality of life in the detachments.

In 1941 and 1942, the second-largest employer of Jewish forced laborers was the General Directorate of Roads. The Jews in these detachments worked building new roads, as well as repairing and maintaining existing roads and gathering and transporting construction materials. Several of the larger detachments worked on highways connecting major cities or providing quicker access to the front, although the productivity of these detachments—and thus their benefit to the war effort—had been uneven. Jews continued to work in these detachments in 1943 in approximately the same numbers as the previous two years. Most Jews employed in road construction were returned to their same detachments rather than being reassigned to other tasks as many of the Jews working in railroad detachments had been. In some cases, Jewish workers had remained in their detachments throughout the winter and work continued uninterrupted into the next spring.

One of the latter detachments was Roads Battalion 3 under the command of Lieutenant Colonel Radu Spânu. Roads Battalion 3 was responsible for building a highway between Corneşti and Chişnău, near the current course of European Route E58. The battalion was an integral part of one of the Romanian military's most important construction projects: a series of strategic highways connecting the city of Roman, in eastern Romania, to Bălţi and Chişinău via Iaşi and Corneşti, which would allow quicker movement of men and materiel toward the front, in addition to connecting several major cities. Perhaps owing to the strategic significance of this highway, additional workers were added to the detachment in 1943, increasing its strength from fewer than 300 workers to almost 500 by late spring. Around 450 of these men were Jews, while the remaining 50 were Soviet prisoners of war, who were placed in a separate company.[55] Government policy required complete separation of prisoners of war from other laborers because of their presumed communist affiliations. In fact, in June 1942, Antonescu had ordered that a group of Soviet prisoners of war who had been assigned to work at the Cotroceni shooting range should be replaced with Jews, since they were more trustworthy; despite Antonescu's antisemitic attitudes, he still had more faith in native-born Jews than non-Jewish Soviet prisoners.[56]

The battalion was divided into five companies, four of which were composed of Jews, with the Soviet prisoners of war placed in the fifth. The first company, which began the 1943 campaign with 141 men, worked near the village of Pârliţa-Ungheni unloading and breaking up stones from a nearby quarry for ballast. The second, which consisted of the Bessarabian penal laborers, worked

Figure 5.1. Jewish forced laborers shovel gravel at a construction site. United States Holocaust Memorial Museum, courtesy of Federation of Jewish Communities.

at Călărași-Lăpușna, resurfacing the highway toward Sipoteni. The third company, with 218 workers at the beginning of April, worked unloading stones and sand and repairing a stretch of highway near Fălești. The fourth company worked between Grinăuți and Bălți, with 80 men digging stones in a quarry and breaking up bedrock. Finally, the fifth company (known as Company 5/2) continued the previous year's work at the Ghidighici quarry, from which much of the stone used in the construction of the highway was harvested. Most of the Jewish laborers in the detachment had been sent from the Putna recruitment center, supplemented by additional workers from Iași.[57]

The men of the Pârlița and Fălești companies were housed in former synagogues in their respective villages. The Bessarabian workers in the Călărași-Lăpușna company had slightly better accommodations, in the form of a purpose-built wooden barrack near their work sites. The laborers at Ghidighici were also housed in wooden barracks. Finally, the Jewish workers in the Grinăuți company were quartered in property that had formerly belonged to local ethnic Germans who had since moved out of the area. The Jews in Roads Battalion 3 had been required to provide their own tools when they were deployed in 1942, and the same requirement was imposed on those who were sent there in 1943, despite Antonescu's orders to the contrary.[58]

The program of work established for May to July 1943 prescribed the following daily schedule for the Jews in Battalion 3:

4:30 a.m.: Wake up
4:30 a.m.–4:50 a.m.: Bathe and dress
4:50 a.m.–5:15 a.m.: Clean quarters and prepare tea
5:15 a.m.–5:30 a.m.: Tea
5:30 a.m.–6:00 a.m.: March to work site
6:00 a.m.–12:00 p.m.: Work
12:00 p.m.–12:30 p.m.: Lunch
12:30 p.m.–2:00 p.m.: Break
2:00 p.m.–7:00 p.m.: Work
7:00 p.m.–7:30 p.m.: March back to quarters
7:30 p.m.–8:30 p.m.: Dinner and evening roll call
8:30 p.m.–9:00 p.m.: Clean clothes, inspection of quarters
9:00 p.m.: Lights out[59]

In theory, the men of Battalion 3 worked eleven hours per day, even though the June 27, 1942, General Instructions limited the working day for Jewish laborers to nine hours. The extra two hours were built into the work schedule to allow for flexibility according to the amount of available daylight and other factors, including the distance the men had to walk to and from the work site. Unlike the workers in most of the CFR detachments, the workers of Battalion 3 received only two meals per day, plus tea in the morning. These meals were supposed to consist of vegetable soup, with a *friptură* (a piece of fried meat) provided six to eight times a week—"preferably lamb," though pork was to be substituted if lamb was unavailable. On Easter weekend, the workers would also receive two eggs and half a bottle of wine each.[60]

During the spring and early summer of 1943, productivity in Battalion 3 was in line with the projected norms, with no major delays in work. At the Pârlița site, the workers had progressed enough in their primary task of unloading and breaking up rocks that some of the men were put to work digging and smoothing over the foundation for the section of the highway that was to run through that area.[61] Similarly, work at Fălești had shifted from unloading stones and spreading sand to laying down foundation stones for that section of the highway and building intersections for lateral roads.[62] At Grinăuți and Ghidighici, the men continued working in the quarries. Work continued at a normal level of productivity throughout the summer and early fall of 1943. By September 1943, the Fălești company and the two quarry companies had completed their work, and all 432 workers in the battalion were consolidated into the company at Pârlița, where they continued laying down the roadbed and spreading bedrock and sand. The addition of the workers from the other companies in the battalion accelerated the pace of work at Pârlița to the extent that by November 1943, only 177 workers remained, as the other 255 had been redistributed to other companies.[63]

However, in December 1943, in preparation for the projects to be completed in the 1944 work campaign—which included a connecting highway from Roman to the main highway at Pârlița—three additional companies were integrated into Battalion 3. These companies, located at Dragalina-Tutova, Roman, and Berezeni-Falciu, brought the total number of workers in Battalion 3 back up to 528. Additionally, the headquarters of Battalion 3 were relocated to Roman, closer to both the starting point of the project and closer to the Romanian interior as the Red Army continued to advance. The battalion would be centered at Roman until its dissolution in April 1944, though the locations and strengths of its subordinate companies changed several times in early 1944.[64]

As with the CFR detachments, the conditions endured by the road construction workers varied from detachment to detachment. This variation was evident even between the companies of Roads Battalion 3. The greatest discrepancies in conditions between the companies of Battalion 3 were in housing and the laborers' health. The problems encountered in Battalion 3 were representative of those affecting most labor detachments in Romania at the time, particularly the lack of proper clothing for workers and large numbers of men missing work due to illness. One chronic issue for every company of Battalion 3 was the lack of adequate clothing for winter, as well as the deterioration of the workers' clothes, which were not replaced during the 1943 labor campaign. The lack of winter clothing had been a problem for the battalion at the end of 1942 as well; it had substantially slowed the pace of work during the last two months of the year.[65] Many of the men sent to the Ghidighici company from the Bacău recruitment center were not equipped with appropriate clothes or tools, which Lieutenant Colonel Spânu attributed to the fact that they had been organized and dispatched in the span of two hours, the same kind of hasty organization that had caused problems in the fall of 1941.[66]

In the initial reports from the battalion in April 1943, Spânu reported that the status of the workers' clothing and equipment in all the Jewish companies was "poor" and even the non-Jewish workers' clothes were "somewhat worn."[67] The condition of the workers' clothing did not improve during the spring and summer, as the Jewish community of Putna was not able to collect enough clothing to help them. As late as September 1943, the clothing of the workers at Pârlița was reported to be in a poor state.[68] Despite Antonescu's order that all Jewish workers be supplied with the necessary clothing, these needs were never adequately met in Battalion 3 or in many other Jewish labor detachments. Health and sanitation issues were not distributed as widely across the detachments as the problem of clothing. While Spânu's reports indicated that the sanitary conditions in the detachment were good, many workers were absent from work for medical reasons, suggesting that either Spânu was overly optimistic about the conditions in the detachments or that the workers experienced many work-related injuries; the latter would be consistent with the cases of CFR Detachments 49 and 106/107.

For example, in the April 1943 report on the Fălești company, 13 of the 218 workers were hospitalized, with another on medical leave, representing 6 percent of the total effective, slightly above the permissible level established by the General Staff. In the same month, 13 of the 80 workers in the Grinăuți company, 16 percent of the total, were in the hospital. The same report, however, describes the sanitary conditions at that location as "excellent" and "the best in the entire battalion."[69] Therefore, it is possible that most of the absences of workers in these detachments were attributable to work-related injuries. However, such a high rate of injury among the workers would suggest a major problem with workplace safety. In August 1943, the Pârlița company had 16 men hospitalized and 1 on medical leave, more than 8 percent of its workers. Similarly, in the Fălești company, 16 workers were in the hospital, 8 percent of the 200 workers there.[70] Nonetheless, sanitary conditions were reported to be good until November 1943, after all of the workers in Battalion 3 had been consolidated at the Pârlița site; in his report for that month, Spânu acknowledged that cleanliness and sanitation in the workers' quarters were only "mediocre."[71]

In spite of the generally positive picture of the battalion's health indicated in Spânu's reports for the first ten months of 1943, there were several notable cases of serious illness among the workers in the detachment, suggesting that the health of the workers was at least somewhat worse than the commander claimed. Some of these events were beyond the control of Spânu and the officers in charge of the battalion. For example, in February, a number of Jews were sent to the Anti-rabies Institute in Focșani after being bitten by dogs that were suspected to be rabid. In an early March report, Spânu accused these men of having devised an "ingenious" system for escaping forced labor by faking the bites and using the lengthy treatment process to prolong their periods of leave.[72] However, Spânu's allegations are questionable. Rabies treatment in 1943 consisted of a series of injections into the abdomen, which required the use of a large needle and were very painful, making it an unappealing choice for men who were seeking to get out of work.

Other cases of serious illness in the battalion suggest that Spânu's statements about the sanitary conditions were inaccurate. On February 11, 1943, Spânu reported that a Jewish laborer named Isaac Ghelerter was sent to the hospital to be treated for meningococcal meningitis, a life-threatening bacterial disease that is spread through contact with respiratory secretions of infected persons.[73] While Ghelerter survived, the presence of such an illness suggests that men in the detachment who became ill were not properly quarantined and that the workers' living quarters and eating utensils were not properly cleaned. Many other men were hospitalized due to less serious conditions. For example, a man named Şmil Barat was sent to the Jewish hospital in Galați in late October 1943 for treatment of bronchitis.[74] Despite the strict new desertion law and Spânu's paranoia about workers feigning illness, desertion remained one of the main methods by which Romanian Jews could resist the forced labor system and Battalion 3 experienced a significant number of them. However, these desertions were not uniformly distributed across the individual companies. The Fălești company seems to have had a high rate of desertion compared to the companies at Pârlița and Grinăuți, which had relatively few. For example, in April 1943, the Fălești company experienced 13 desertions out of 218 workers present, while at Pârlița and Grinăuți, no desertions were reported.[75]

Through the end of August 1943, just prior to the consolidation of the companies of Battalion 3 at Pârlița, the Fălești company reported twenty-nine desertions, while Pârlița had only eleven and Grinăuți had none. Though the Fălești company was the largest of the five in Battalion 3, the number of desertions that occurred at that site was still disproportionately high. Spânu's reports do not account for this discrepancy, outside of vague statements about the quality of supervision, the default explanation for desertions from labor detachments.[76] It is apparent that the same problems with lax supervision of workers that persisted throughout 1941 and 1942 continued into 1943 and provided the Jews in the labor detachments with the opportunity for resistance, not only through desertion but also through deliberately working slowly and, on rare occasions, sabotaging labor projects. While the experiences of the workers of Battalion 3 varied between the five companies under its control, the living and working conditions in this battalion were generally representative of those in other detachments, and the extensive documentation provided by Lieutenant Colonel Spânu's meticulous record keeping makes it a valuable case study.

Both the CFR and road construction detachments were primarily carried over from the 1941 and 1942 labor campaigns, with some reduction in the number of Jews assigned to each between 1942 and 1943. In 1943, many Jewish workers were assigned to new projects which had begun in mid-1942, after the new General Instructions. While some new road and railroad detachments were created (or existing detachments reorganized) after that date, several of the new detachments were engineering and general labor detachments, reflecting the shift in the General Staff's priorities for Jewish labor toward projects of more direct military significance.

Because of the situation at the front, one of the General Staff's highest priorities for the 1943 labor campaign was the construction and improvement of fortifications (including casemates, pillboxes, and antitank ditches) in eastern

Romania and along the Hungarian border, as well as supplemental projects requested by the Ministry of National Defense's Fortifications Service. One such project was the creation of a series of canals to divert several of Romania's rivers and the strengthening of existing riverbanks, both for flood control and to protect fortifications and pillboxes from inundation in the event of heavy rain or snow melt. These tasks would require thousands of workers. On March 2, 1943, the General Staff issued Order No. 105.461, which authorized the creation of five detachments with a total of sixty-five hundred Jewish laborers who were to work on the Fortifications Service's river management projects.[77] These numbers would remain relatively constant through the end of the year, as reflected in the statistical report from November 3, 1943.[78]

The first of these detachments, Jewish Labor Detachment 100 (Detașamentul 100 Evrei), was to consist of two thousand Jews, who were deployed to the Siret River Valley project near the city of Focșani in eastern Romania. However, soon after this order was issued, Detachment 100 was reassigned to a new project regulating the flow of the Siret River in the area near the villages of Cotu Lung and Voinești in Brăila County. The second detachment, Labor Detachment 101, was also deployed to the Siret Valley, near the city of Galați, with two thousand men. Both of these detachments were supervised by the Fifth Pioneers Regiment (Regimentul 5 Pionieri). The third detachment, Labor Detachment 102, with one thousand men, was sent to the Mureș River Valley in western Romania, near the city of Siria, Arad County, under the Seventh Pioneers Regiment. Though Siria was on the opposite side of the country, near the Hungarian border, Antonescu's constant fear of Hungarian expansionism and aggression led to several projects during the course of the war that were designed to prepare defensive works along Romania's western border. The fourth fortification detachment, Labor Detachment 103, with one thousand men, was sent to the Sihna River Valley, near the city of Botoșani, in northeastern Romania. The fifth fortification detachment, Labor Detachment 104, was sent to the community of Pașcani, near Târgu Neamț, also in northeastern Romania. Detachments 103 and 104 were under the command of the Fourth Pioneers Regiment.[79]

The initial survey of the areas in which these detachments were working was conducted by the chief of the Fortifications Service's Technical Service, T. V. Angelescu.[80] The estimated cost of the project as of March 1943 was approximately 70 million lei; however, the General Staff (correctly) anticipated that the actual cost of the projects may exceed this initial estimate, and therefore budgeted 100 million lei for the year.[81] The General Staff gave its approval on March 30, and the five new detachments were dispatched the following day by Order No. 965.555. All of them were working by late April. However, in most locations, the exact specifications of the work to be done had not yet been confirmed with the Ministry of Public Works and Communications and the local Water Service office. Thus, many of the excavation and construction projects began without complete certainty of the planned final dimensions of the canals or embankments on which they were working. At most of the work sites, it would take several weeks for these details to be finalized with the Ministry of Public Works and Communications.[82]

According to Order No. 965.555, the fortifications detachments, like other large Jewish forced labor detachments, would consist of men between twenty to forty years old, including unskilled workers, students, and—with the General Staff's approval—skilled workers. Each detachment would have Jewish medical personnel proportionate to the number of workers in the detachment (one medic for every five hundred workers), as well as a tailor, a carpenter, a blacksmith, and two barbers. The Romanian soldiers supervising the workers would be, ideally, forty-one to forty-three years old, though men as young as thirty-six could be recruited for this purpose if necessary. These soldiers would be granted leave every three months.[83]

Each detachment was divided into companies of approximately 500 men, though the actual composition and size of the companies was at the discretion of the detachment commander. Detachment 100, with 1,990 workers, was divided into four companies. The first of these was deployed near the village of Corbu, where 640 men worked consolidating the right bank of the Siret River. The second was located near Voinești, northwest of Galați, where 350 men were constructing a canal to redirect the river and prevent flooding of the pillbox near the village. The third was at Cotu Lung, where 650 workers were digging a canal to regulate the confluence of the Buzău River with the Siret. Finally, the fourth company, with 200 men, was responsible for extracting rock from the Tifești quarry for use by the other companies.[84]

Detachment 101, consisting of 1,509 men, was also divided into four companies, which were split between two major projects. The first project was the creation of a canal along the Șușița River, near the village of Doaga, north of Bacău—the site of the by-then-infamous labor camp—where the river frequently flooded otherwise fertile farmland. The engineer in charge of the project estimated that the completion of the canal would preserve some 217 hectares of arable land. The remaining workers were sent to the village of Balta-Rădulești, in Ciușlea commune, where they were tasked with reinforcing the right bank of the Siret River with wooden cylinders in order to prevent its collapse, which would undermine the pillbox located on that bank.[85]

Detachment 102, with a strength of 985 workers, was divided into just two companies. However, these two companies were asked to cover a total of four work sites over the course of the project, which was to control the flooding of the Mureș River and its tributaries near the city of Arad. The first of these tasks was the reinforcement of the thirteen-kilometer Arad-Pecica canal, which would flood during heavy rain near its confluence with the Crișul Alb River. The canal was to be expanded to allow 6.6 cubic meters per second above its existing maximum flow rate so that it could more easily drain runoff from heavy rainfall and prevent flooding of the surrounding area. The canal at Sânpaul needed an expansion of the right bank to increase the maximum flow rate to 13.0 cubic meters per second at a depth of 2.8 meters. Similar improvements were to be made to the Gai-Ier canal, an extension of the Păuliș-Utviniș canal.[86] Finally, the detachment would be responsible for digging an 87,000-cubic-meter canal bed near the village of Matca, 50,000 cubic meters of which was to be done by hand, with the remaining 37,000 cubic meters completed with a dragline excavator.[87]

Records of the division of workers in the one-thousand-man Detachment 103 are not available, though, presumably, this detachment was also divided into two companies of approximately five hundred men. Finally, Detachment 104, with just under five hundred men, was assigned to conduct various excavation projects near Târgu Neamț, some of which had been initiated, but not completed, during the previous year. These projects included the reinforcement of a dig site near the city with concrete slabs and the consolidation of the riverbanks at Strunga-Găureana, Timișești-Păstrăveni, Heleștieni-Valea Humăriei, and Moțca-Soci to protect pillboxes, or, in the latter case, a national highway between Roman and Fălticeni.[88]

The tasks assigned to the laborers in the engineering detachments were important for the defense of Romania's eastern border. In many cases, the consolidation of riverbanks or redirection of water were the only ways the existing fortifications could be sustained and avoid subsidence, flooding, or total collapse. However, despite the sensitive nature and urgency of the fortifications projects, many of the same issues that affected other Jewish forced labor detachments occurred at the Fortifications Service detachments as well. The financing of the detachments was problematic from the outset. The commander of Detachment 101, for example, projected a monthly cost for the detachment of 4 million lei, including food and pay for the workers (60 lei per day), fuel and maintenance costs for equipment and vehicles, and food and shelter for the horses.[89]

Such high costs inevitably encouraged the detachment commanders to economize in terms of supplies of food and other goods for the workers, causing their welfare to suffer. In order to offset some of these costs prior to the beginning of the Ministry of National Defense's and Ministry of Public Works and Communications' funding of the projects, the General Staff issued advances of several million lei to each detachment. For example, Detachment 104 received a 3 million lei advance on May 30.[90] However, even prior to these advances, on May 22, the commander of Detachment 101 informed the General Staff that his unit needed 13 million lei simply to acquire the materials to complete their assigned tasks.⁹¹ Budget shortfalls and excess costs beyond those initially projected were a problem for the fortifications detachments throughout the 1943 and 1944 labor campaigns.

A related issue for the fortifications detachments was shortages of building materials and transportation, which first manifested during the construction of housing for Jewish workers in the detachments. On April 24, Detachment 101 reported that it could not build housing for its workers because of a lack of materials and the lack of money to purchase materials. In addition, the detachment commander, Lieutenant Chiriac, reported that there was nowhere for the workers to prepare their food, as there were no materials to construct a kitchen for the workers.⁹² To house all the workers in the detachment, the men would need to construct eighty wooden huts, at a cost of 11.2 million lei; by late July, this problem had been solved.⁹³ However, that same month, the detachment commander reported that the companies at Doaga and Nămaloasa did not have enough money to pay for materials or their transport, and that as a result of the lack of materials, work had come to a halt there.⁹⁴ As the issues with funding and the procurement of materials suggest, the productivity of the fortifications detachments was inconsistent; while some projects were completed in a timely manner, others were never completed for various reasons. Some of these delays were beyond the control of the workers or their commanders, but others were directly attributable to the inefficiency of the labor detachments' administration and its negative effects on the welfare of the workers.

Despite these problems, most of the fortifications detachments had periods in which work was relatively productive. In his mid-June 1943 report to the General Staff, the commander of Detachment 102, Lieutenant Ioan Nicolaescu, stated that productivity in his detachment was satisfactory. Nicolaescu's workers had put in about half an hour per day of work above the nine-hour limit set by the General Staff over the prior two weeks. Of his 985 men, 20 were hospitalized and 4 had deserted, but discipline and health in the detachment were generally good. The workers' housing and food was also reported to be adequate.⁹⁵ In Detachment 104, as of August 20, 1943, all the work at the Strunga-Găureana site had been completed, while the excavation work at Heleștieni had been completed as well, allowing the workers there to move on to the creation of concrete barriers along the riverbank. Additionally, at Valea Ozanei, only a small complement of workers remained consolidating the banks of the recently constructed canal.⁹⁶

Nonetheless, most reports regarding the progress of the fortifications detachments' progress were marked by shortcomings, caused by a variety of natural and human factors. One such problem was the incompetence and negligence of the officers tasked with supervising the workers. In his inspection of Detachments 103 and 104, the commander of the Second Pioneers Brigade, Colonel Ion Grigorovici, reported that the soldiers in both detachments fell short of the expectations for their behavior and work. In Detachment 103, he stated, the number of supervising personnel was "far too low"—one per thirty workers rather than the prescribed one per ten. He described the men as poorly trained, and remarked that he found the older soldiers in the detachment to be "uneducated." His report was hardly kinder to the commanders of Detachment 104, as he stated that the men in that detachment were clearly lacking in professional military preparation and that many of them were too old for their assigned task.[97] Another report from Colonel Grigorovici indicates that this problem was not isolated or temporary. On June 29, he informed the General Staff of the unsatisfactory performance of the officers in Detachment 104. He singled out one of the company commanders, Captain Dumitru Cincu of the Valea Ozanei company, who sat in his barrack half-dressed and uninvolved as the workers carried stone without his instruction. Colonel Grigorovici also alleged that Captain Cincu was frequently drunk.[98]

While the possibility exists that Colonel Grigorovici had some dislike of Captain Cincu or someone else in Detachment 103 or 104, other officials' observations regarding the soldiers in the fortifications detachments were similarly scathing, such as a September 19 report by a different inspector that declared that the infantry reservists in Detachment 100 were mostly "alcoholics" who were "no longer useful."[99] One of the few positive reports regarding detachment commanders' efforts came from a June 15 inspection of the Matca company of Detachment 102, where the laborers appeared to be working very hard, which was credited to their supervisors.[100] However, despite the increased disciplinary measures taken against soldiers and officers supervising labor detachments after June 27, 1942, problems stemming from poor supervision of workers remained; although they were often made the scapegoats for larger systemic failures, incompetence among the supervisory personnel seems to have been a legitimate problem in the fortifications detachments.

The labor detachments were also plagued by mechanical issues that were beyond the control of the commanding officers or the laborers. For example, the dragline used by Detachment 102 to excavate a canal bed broke down at least four times between July and November 1943. The July 31 report from the Matca company indicated that the dragline had been in a repair shop in Arad for the previous two weeks, during which time the workers did all the necessary digging with shovels in temperatures that were above thirty-five degrees Celsius.[101] On April 16, it was reported that the quoted price for the repair of the dragline was 16,348 lei, an additional expense that the already cash-strapped project could ill afford.[102]

Despite this expensive repair of the dragline, it broke down again in early September. Because all of the excavation work had to be done by hand once again, the productivity of the Matca company suffered—the men in that company had dug only 2.57 cubic meters of earth per man-day, well below the stated goal of 3.43 cubic meters per man-day. Prior to the failure of the dragline, the output of Detachment 102 as a whole and the Matca company in particular had previously been so high that the Seventh Pioneers Regiment command considered doubling the daily goal for earth excavated per man-day.[103] Production was hampered again in mid-October after the dragline broke down for a third time. The commander of the detachment gave great credit to the workers, as they nearly achieved the expected level of productivity even after the loss of the dragline.[104] The dragline was returned to service again on October 26, only to fail once more in late November 1943. However, in this final instance, the problem was only a broken cable, which was repaired quickly, and the machine was returned to service within four days. Again, the detachment commander praised the "perseverance" of his men, who met their work quotas despite the fact that only about 13 percent of that work had been accomplished by the use of the dragline, compared to the projected 43 percent.[105]

Work on the fortifications projects was also hindered by inclement weather. In addition to extreme heat slowing work, heavy rain and, eventually, cold weather interfered with the detachments. For example, in the first two weeks of October, Detachment 100 lost two days to rain. In a more extreme example, Detachment 104 lost seven of fifteen possible work days in the period between September 4 and 18 to torrential rain.[106] Meanwhile, on October 31, Detachment 102's commander reported that the cold morning temperatures in the area around Arad had slowed work during the early part of the day for the last two weeks.[107]

However, perhaps the greatest contributors to low productivity in the fortification detachments were poor living and working conditions, which led to decreased worker welfare and low morale. The relationship between the conditions and the laborers' efforts was identified as early as the first of June, when the commander of Detachment 100 reported that the productivity of his workers had been "insufficient" to that date. He blamed low worker morale, stemming from the bad conditions in the detachment.[108] The specific problems he cited included the high workload (including heavy physical labor, such as carrying stones long distances) and the workers' exposure to the elements. Additionally, while supplies of food were generally good in the detachments, housing was often substandard due to the lack of construction materials and the fact that the workers were usually required to construct their own living quarters on their arrival at their places of work.

Furthermore, the supply of medical equipment and number of medical personnel were generally inadequate as well, meaning that men frequently missed work due to illness, and many were hospitalized for serious illnesses. For example, in Detachment 100 during the first two weeks of August, there were 333 cases of illness, 114 of which required visits to the detachment infirmary.[109] Malaria was most common illness reported among the workers—they often worked in low-lying areas with standing water, which allowed mosquitoes to proliferate. This period was not an isolated example: in the latter half of that month, the same detachment reported 520 total cases of illness, 228 of which were attributable to malaria. Meanwhile, in Detachment 102, four men were sent to receive rabies prophylaxis after contact with suspected rabid animals.[110]

The large number of sick workers obviously had a negative effect on the detachments' productivity. Colonel Grigorovici reported that in September, as many as 20 percent of the men in Detachments 103 and 104 were ill and not at work.[111] The situation was even worse in Detachment 101, where it was reported that as of September 25, 35 percent of the workers were sick and little medical assistance had been received from the Central Jewish Office in Bucharest.[112] Grigorovici concluded that many of these men should never have been sent to forced labor in the first place, as they were not physically fit for work in such harsh conditions, and that it was unsurprising that so many of them had fallen ill.[113] However, none of the available reports from the detachment commanders included fatalities. It is impossible to determine whether these reports were accurate or whether fatalities were deliberately obscured; these casualty reports are difficult to verify independently because of the lack of systematic, centralized personnel records for Jewish laborers.

While the General Staff had succeeded in curtailing Radu Lecca's corrupt exemption enterprise to some extent, he continued to wield great power over Romania's Jews and to profit abundantly from this power. In addition to granting exemptions for forced laborers and collecting the exemption taxes, he also sought to extort the Jews through a second large levy on the Jewish community. In April 1943, he proposed to Antonescu that the Jews should make an additional "extraordinary contribution" of four billion lei in exchange for the "comfort" they lived in since they did not have to serve in combat. The measure was approved by Antonescu, and Lecca sent formal notice of the levy to the Central Jewish Office on May 11.[114]

After Wilhelm Filderman protested the additional tax, Antonescu had him deported to Transnistria at the end of May. He was allowed to return three months later after widespread complaints from both Jewish community leaders, including Mișu Benvenisti and Alexandru Șafran, and Romanian politicians, most notably Iuliu Maniu.[115] Lecca also attempted to profit off the regime's new emigration policy by reaching agreements with smugglers through which he would receive a sum of money for each Jew allowed to leave for Palestine. However, he did allow fifteen percent of revenues from the exemption taxes and other taxes levied against the Jews to be distributed for aid to forced laborers and Jews deported to Transnistria via the Central Jewish Office at the end of 1943.[116]

Even before these funds were freed up, the Central Jewish Office was spending tens of thousands of lei per month on aid to Jewish laborers. In 1943 and 1944, the amount of aid provided to the labor detachment each month varied between 120,000 and 150,000 lei.[117] The Central Jewish Office also provided aid in kind to individuals who needed it. For example, in December 1943, it purchased a train ticket for a Jewish dentist named Arcadie Andrei Bergher, who needed to return home to Timișoara from Bucharest, where he had been working (although in this case, Bergher later repaid the Central Jewish Office).[118] Large-scale aid-in-kind programs, such as the collection of winter clothes for laborers, also continued in 1943. These programs were one of the most important humanitarian functions of the Central Jewish Office.

The presence of over fifty-two thousand Jews working in Romanian business, industry, and government institutions eighteen months after they should have been removed and replaced with ethnic Romanians (under the November 16, 1940, Law for the Romanianization of Labor) forced Antonescu to acknowledge that his efforts to remove Jews from the Romanian economy had failed. No amount of legislation or rhetoric could counter the inescapable fact that the Romanian economy was still highly dependent on Jewish labor. This fact was readily apparent even before the deadline for removing Romanian personnel (December 31, 1941) had passed. After Jews were deported from Bukovina, commerce ground to a halt in many villages and towns (as well as some major cities, including Suceava) and others went without the vital services of doctors and pharmacists because these roles had been previously filled by Jews.[119] Furthermore, many of the Jews who had been forced out of their jobs had not been replaced with ethnic Romanians but instead by other "foreigners," including Hungarians and Germans. While the number of Jews working in some areas of the economy had declined, there had not been corresponding increases in ethnic Romanians employed in those fields.[120]

The General Staff presented a particularly unfavorable report on the status of the Romanianization of labor to Antonescu on November 16, 1943. It noted that of 369 Jews working in forty-nine militarized industrial concerns in Bucharest, nearly 60 percent (211 workers) were in leadership or administrative roles despite the official ban on Jews holding administrative positions in Romanian businesses. Nearly one in four (86 of them) had no Romanian "double," while 94 had been "doubled" on a "permanent" basis since 1941, revealing the inability of Romanian "doubles" to learn the jobs of the Jews they were supposed to replace and the lack of qualified ethnic Romanians who were available to "double" Jews.[121] This report made it clear to Antonescu that the Romanianization of labor had failed, though the Romanianization laws remained on the books until his ouster nine months later. Despite what the law said, Jews continued to have an important role in the Romanian economy as administrators, professionals, and skilled laborers—whether exempted to work freely or requisitioned by Romanian firms—throughout the rest of Antonescu's rule.

As Antonescu's Jewish policy moderated in the face of Romania's impending military defeat, he decided to allow some of the Jews deported for forced labor violations to return from Transnistria in October 1943. A November 22, 1943, census of those who had been deported for violating the forced labor regulations and their family members counted a total of 594 deportees. By December 8, 1943, 348 people had returned: 215 to Bucharest, 32 to Cernăuți, 31 to Roman, 20 to Iași, 12 to Botoșani, 10 to Arad, and 28 to other locations in Romania.[122] It was determined that, as of December 1943, 88 of the deportees, including 7 children under the age of five, had died in Transnistria. The locations of 49 of these deaths were known: 21 deportees had died in Golta, 8 in Bogdanovca, 5 in Ananiev, 4 in Acmecetca, 4 in Covaliovca, 3 in Slivina, and 1 each in Chirinaco, Cocrasca, Domanovca, and Moghilev. The locations of the remaining 39 deaths were not listed.[123] It is possible that these deaths occurred during transit either during the original deportations or one of the transfers of prisoners between camps that took place in late 1942 and early 1943. Another 43 Jews were stated to have "fled" from the camps in Transnistria, and their whereabouts were unknown.[124] These figures leave a remainder of 115 Jews still alive in Transnistria after the first wave of repatriations. These last remaining deportees were allowed to return in February 1944; the General Staff's records do not specify whether there were any additional deaths among those who remained in Transnistria during this time. Many of the returnees were subsequently sent back to labor detachments, including 11 men from Iași and 7 from Roman who were redeployed in the spring of 1944.[125]

Sonia Palty and her family were among those repatriated in October 1943. She described the journey home in her memoirs, recalling that "the train raced along. We watched out the window of the wagon. None of us spoke. Every station reminded us of the journey we had made in the cattle wagons [in 1942]. Memories. . . . Wounds still fresh, unforgettable. I wanted to cry. I wanted to put my head on my mother's shoulder and cry. . . . Home! Fourteen months ago I had been a little girl of fourteen years and two months. . . . I had returned a mature, weary woman . . . at only fifteen and a half years old."[126] Unlike many of the victims of the deportations, Palty remained in Romania after the war, living there until 1975, when she immigrated to Israel.[127]

As the reports from the railroad, road construction, and engineering detachments indicate, the results of Jewish forced labor in 1943 were mixed. Despite the June 27, 1942, General Instructions and the additional regulations in early 1943, productivity improved in only some instances, due to a variety of both human and environmental factors. However, it is clear that the new regulations did little to improve the welfare of the Jewish workers in most of the labor detachments. For example, in October 1943, the commander of Labor Battalion 120 in

Transnistria informed the General Staff that the Jews in his detachment lived in a "detestable situation" due to the lack of warm clothes and a constant state of poor hygiene.[128] While Battalion 120 was an exceptional case since it was located in Transnistria rather than within Romania proper, reports from detachments in the Old Kingdom and Bessarabia demonstrate that the workers' experiences were in many cases just as bad as they had been in 1941 and 1942, leading to both low productivity and continued suffering due to poor healthcare, inadequate supplies of food and clothing, primitive living quarters, and grueling working conditions.

Thus, while the forced labor system reached its peak in terms of the number of Jews employed and the intensity at which Jewish labor was exploited in 1943, the efforts of the General Staff to increase productivity were still ineffective in many cases. Although results improved in some detachments, others continued to report the same problems that had been present in the previous two years, suggesting that the failings of the labor service were systemic and not merely a matter of flawed policy or implementation of that policy. From the workers' perspective, the cruelty of forced labor did not abate in 1943 and, because of the General Staff's efforts to increase the number of workers mobilized for work, more people than in the previous two years were subjected to the same terrible experiences. Many forced laborers remained at work throughout the winter and were still in the same detachments in the spring of 1944. Meanwhile, the Red Army pushed across the Dniester River and was preparing to deliver its final blow to Antonescu's Romania the following summer.

Notes

1. Benjamin, *Problema evreiască*, document 151, 479.
2. Rozett, *Conscripted Slaves*, 62.
3. USHMMA, RG-25.003M, reel 185, file 3274, 10.
4. Ibid., 11.
5. Rozett, *Conscripted Slaves*, 60–62.
6. Bărbulescu et al., *Munca obligatorie*, document 172, 426.
7. Ibid., document 118, 328.
8. USHMMA, RG-25.002M, reel 10, file 21b, 10–11.
9. USHMMA, RG-25.003M, reel 154, file 2957, 181.
10. Ibid., 101.
11. Interview with William Farkas, USHMMA, RG-50.030*0026, USHMM Oral History Collection.
12. USHMMA, RG-25.003M, reel 211, file 3726, 5–8.
13. USHMMA, RG-25.003M, reel 49, file 7263, 90–97.
14. USHMMA, RG-31.006M, Czernowitz Oblast Archive Records, reel 2, 848–858.
15. Trașcă, *"Chestiunea evreiască,"* document 252, 528.
16. Bărbulescu et al., *Munca obligatorie*, document 139, 376–377.

17. Ibid., document 124, 341.
18. USHMMA, RG-25.003M, reel 211, file 3727, 416.
19. USHMMA, RG-25.003M, reel 196, file 3708, 3.
20. Bărbulescu et al., *Munca obligatorie*, document 237, 350–351.
21. Ibid., document 237, 352.
22. USHMMA, RG-25.003M, reel 192, file 3698, 12–13.
23. Bărbulescu et al., *Munca obligatorie*, document 237, 353–355.
24. Benjamin, *Problema evreiască*, document 163, 506.
25. USHMMA, RG-25.002M, reel 16, file 59–43, 157.
26. Ibid., 159–160.
27. Bărbulescu et al., *Munca obligatorie*, document 169, 415–416.
28. Ibid., document 169, 416–417.
29. Ibid., document 169, 419.
30. Ibid., document 169, 422.
31. Ibid., document 127, 351.
32. Trașcă, *"Chestiunea evreiască,"* document 381, 769–770.
33. Ibid., document 397, 796–797.
34. USHMMA, RG-25.003M, reel 192, file 3698, 24–30.
35. Arhivele Naționale Istorice Centrale (ANIC), Fond Președintele Consiliului de Miniștrii, Cabinetul Militar (PCM CM), dosar 35–1944, f. 7.
36. ANIC Fond PCM CM, dosar 35–1944, f. 7.
37. USHMMA, RG-25.013M, reel 31, file 59, 140.
38. USHMMA, RG-25.011, file 25, folder 3, 137.
39. Ibid., 19.
40. Ibid., 47.
41. Ibid., 58.
42. Friling et al., *Final Report*, 132.
43. USHMMA, RG-25.003M, reel 188, file 3278, 42.
44. Andrei Voinea, *Sanduhr aus Steinen: Jüdische Zwangsarbeiter in Rumänien, 1940–1944* (Konstanz: Hartung-Gorre, 2000), 58.
45. USHMMA, RG-25.011, file 25, folder 3, 119.
46. Ibid., 137–153.
47. Ibid., 166.
48. Voinea, *Sanduhr aus Steinen*, 57–60.
49. USHMMA, RG-25.011, file 25, folder 3, 19.
50. Ibid., 166.
51. Voinea, *Sanduhr aus Steinen*, 57.
52. USHMMA, RG-25.011, file 25, folder 3, 190.
53. Ibid., 277.
54. Voinea, *Sanduhr aus Steinen*, 61.
55. USHMMA, RG-25.011, folder 13, Fond Batalionul 3 Drumuri, file 236, 39–40.
56. USHMMA, RG-25.003M, reel 161, file 2790, 247.
57. USHMMA, RG-25.011, folder 13, Fond Batalionul 3 Drumuri, file 214, 2–5.
58. Ibid., 2–5.
59. Ibid., 188.
60. Ibid., 135.

61. USHMMA, RG-25.011, folder 13, Fond Batalionul 3 Drumuri, file 236, 28.
62. Ibid., 37.
63. Ibid., 136.
64. Ibid., 161–164.
65. Ibid., 160.
66. Ibid., 380–385.
67. Ibid., 2–5.
68. Ibid., 134.
69. Ibid., 5.
70. Ibid., 95.
71. Ibid., 136.
72. USHMMA, RG-25.011, folder 8, Fond Batalionul 3 Drumuri, 303–304.
73. USHMMA, RG-25.011, folder 7, Fond Batalionul 3 Drumuri, 253.
74. USHMMA, RG-25.011, folder 13, Fond Batalionul 3 Drumuri, file 275, 77.
75. USHMMA, RG-25.011, folder 13, Fond Batalionul 3 Drumuri, file 236, 2–5.
76. Ibid., 95–97.
77. USHMMA, RG-25.003M, reel 101, file 4185, 62.
78. ANIC Fond PCM CM, dosar 35–1944, f. 7.
79. USHMMA, RG-25.003M, reel 101, file 4185, 62.
80. Ibid., 141.
81. Ibid., 63.
82. Ibid., 157.
83. USHMMA, RG-25.003M, reel 111, file 4252, 9–10.
84. USHMMA, RG-25.003M, reel 101, file 4185, 3–16.
85. USHMMA, RG-25.003M, reel 103, file 4190, 47–61.
86. USHMMA, RG-25.003M, reel 105, file 4193, 19–21.
87. Ibid., 38.
88. USHMMA, RG-25.003M, reel 108, file 4201, 15.
89. USHMMA, RG-25.003M, reel 111, file 4252, 49.
90. Ibid., 107.
91. Ibid., 192.
92. USHMMA, RG-25.003M, reel 103, file 4190, 289.
93. Ibid., 269.
94. Ibid., 388.
95. USHMMA, RG-25.003M, reel 105, file 4193, 118–119.
96. USHMMA, RG-25.003M, reel 108, file 4201, 60–61.
97. USHMMA, RG-25.003M, reel 105, file 4193, 434–436.
98. USHMMA, RG-25.003M, reel 108, file 4201, 247.
99. USHMMA, RG-25.003M, reel 102, file 4186, 432.
100. USHMMA, RG-25.003M, reel 105, file 4193, 124.
101. USHMMA, RG-25.003M, reel 106, file 4194, 99–100.
102. USHMMA, RG-25.003M, reel 106, file 4195, 48–50.
103. USHMMA, RG-25.003M, reel 106, file 4194, 23–26.
104. USHMMA, RG-25.003M, reel 106, file 4195, 87–89.
105. Ibid., 125–127.
106. USHMMA, RG-25.003M, reel 108, file 4201, 232.

107. USHMMA, RG-25.003M, reel 106, file 4195, 99.
108. USHMMA, RG-25.003M, reel 101, file 4185, 373.
109. Ibid., 294.
110. Ibid., 99.
111. USHMMA, RG-25.003M, reel 102, file 4186, 437.
112. Ibid., 459.
113. Ibid., 437.
114. Ancel, *History of the Holocaust in Romania*, 527.
115. Friling et al., *Final Report*, 215–216.
116. Deletant, *Hitler's Forgotten Ally*, 124.
117. USHMMA, RG-25.021M, reel 8, file 152, 1–9, 14–20, and 54–60.
118. Ibid., 11–12.
119. USHMMA, RG-31.006M, reel 37, fond 307, opis 3, files 3 and 6.
120. Ancel, *Economic Destruction*, 165–167.
121. USHMMA, RG-25.002M, reel 16, file 199-43, 154–161.
122. USHMMA, RG-25.003M, reel 291, file 4597, 15.
123. Ibid., 82–83.
124. Ibid., 71.
125. Ibid., 8.
126. Palty, *Evrei treceți Nistrul!*, 175 (ellipses in the original).
127. Ibid., 205.
128. Bărbulescu et al., *Munca obligatorie*, document 172, 426.

6 Travails Ended, Justice Averted

By the spring of 1944, it was obvious that Romania would be on the losing side of the war. The Red Army had reached the country's eastern border, and its final breakthrough seemed only a matter of time. Because of this dire situation, the General Staff redoubled its efforts to recruit Jewish laborers for projects directly related to national defense, such as constructing and reinforcing defensive installations and digging antitank ditches. However, by this time, it was also clear that there was little they could do to meaningfully increase the productivity of forced labor, as the sweeping reforms of 1942 and the additional regulations created in 1943 had been largely ineffective.

Furthermore, the proximity of the most important labor detachments to the front and the awareness of the Romanian officers supervising the detachments that the war was soon to be over on unfavorable terms led to a decline in organization and productivity. Several detachments were disbanded by their commanders without orders from the General Staff even before the final Soviet breakthrough in mid-August, and in many others, productivity dropped to negligible levels. After the collapse of the Antonescu government in late August, General Constantin Sănătescu's new government dissolved the labor detachments and repealed the previous regime's antisemitic laws. However, for many Jews, their suffering did not end, as they found themselves far from home and with little to return to after as much as three years of forced labor.

The end of the Jewish forced labor system did not begin in Bucharest with Ion Antonescu or the General Staff but hundreds of kilometers away at the front. On March 5, 1944, Marshal Ivan Konev's Second Ukrainian Front attacked the German Eighth Army and the scattered Romanian forces in southwestern Ukraine, driving the Axis troops back across the Dniester River. Bălți fell on March 17, and within a few days, the Soviets had crossed the Prut River into the Romanian Old Kingdom. Botoșani was captured on April 7, but after Axis victories at Târgu Frumos and Podu Iloaiei, their defensive positions stabilized along a line that passed just north of the major cities of Iași and Chișinău.[1] The Soviets attempted to press their advantage and break through the Axis defensive lines with attacks toward Iași and Chișinău by the Second and Third Ukrainian Fronts in mid-April. This time, however, the Axis forces held their ground, repulsing Konev's forces in a second battle at Târgu Frumos, forty-five kilometers northwest of Iași. The Soviets suffered substantial losses, more than three times those experienced by the German and Romanian defenders, and the offensive was eventually halted in early June. The battered German and Romanian troops had managed to check the Soviet advance temporarily, buying Antonescu a few more weeks in power.²

Although the Red Army could not break the Axis lines in northeastern Romania in the spring of 1944, Allied aerial operations over Romania continued. Combined German and Romanian fighter defenses and antiaircraft gunners had repulsed the American bombers that had attacked the oil refineries at Ploiești and Câmpina in 1942 and 1943, but heavy losses in aircraft and airmen meant that by early 1944, Romania was largely at the mercy of Allied bombers. Unlike the 1942 and 1943 American campaigns, which had to be launched from Libya, Allied bombers could now attack Romania from newly captured air bases in southern Italy, greatly increasing the frequency and intensity of their attacks. Between April 4 and August 23, American and British air forces conducted at least seven major bombing operations against rail and oil industry targets in Bucharest, Ploiești, and Târgoviște, with devastating effects on both infrastructure and civilian morale.³

Because of the Red Army's advance into Romanian territory and the intensification of aerial assaults on Romanian cities, the General Staff pulled as many Jewish laborers as possible onto military tasks. Jews who had been working in local detachments in late 1943 and early 1944 were pressed into service in civil defense (*apărăre pasivă*) battalions or sent to clean up bombing debris and participate in search-and-rescue operations in their cities. Some Jews were exempted from snow removal work to participate in civil defense efforts, while others were sent to clear snow under the command of the civil defense battalions.⁴ In the spring, substantial numbers of Jews were exempted from regular labor in local detachments in Bucharest on the request of the city's military commanders in order to clean up debris left behind by Allied bombings.⁵

Other workers deemed vital to the war effort were also exempted from snow removal. On January 15, the General Staff issued Order No. 436.219, exempting all Jews working for the military clothing manufacturer APACA (Atelierul Publice Autonome de Confecții de Armatei) in Bucharest from being conscripted for this purpose. This order was based on experience in November 1943, when APACA workers in Iași were sent to snow-clearing labor, leading to a dramatic reduction in productivity. By the winter of 1944, the demand for supplies of clothing and other goods for the Romanian military had greatly increased, and another loss of production could not be tolerated, in the General Staff's view.⁶ In another case, on January 18, the General Staff ordered the exemption of all workers at the Queen Elizabeth Central Military Hospital from snow removal in the streets of Bucharest, as they were needed to clear snow on the hospital grounds instead. Some businesses complained that siphoning off laborers to snow removal and civil defense was hurting productivity, but the General Staff mostly ignored these complaints—including one from Solex, an important supplier of various metal products for CFR.[7] However, all workers in war-related industries were eventually excused from clearing snow and the exemption tax for this work.[8]

Some snow removal labor was directed toward military purposes. In certain cases, the General Staff made provisions for the use of Jews at snow removal at certain firms or military installations by specifically requisitioning Jews for that location. For example, the military airfield at Pipera, in the northern section of Bucharest, which was under the command of Aerial Regiment III, requested the use of five hundred Jewish workers for three days to clear snow from the runways and other facilities at the airport. On January 11, the General Staff reallocated five hundred workers from the shooting range at Cotroceni to Pipera.[9] To compensate for the loss of manpower for snow removal due to military necessity, the obligation to work on snow removal was expanded to include all Jews between fifteen and sixty years old, as announced in the Bucharest newspaper *Viața* on January 8.[10] All Jewish students were required to report to their local recruitment centers on January 13, with all other Jews to report on the following day. As in previous years, exemptions from snow removal could be obtained by paying a tax of 3,500 lei per week. While the mayor of Bucharest had proposed that Jews be required to clear snow for three weeks, in most cities, the requirement was only two weeks, and thus the total exemption tax was set at 7,000 lei.[11]

Aside from the reorientation of Jewish labor toward civil defense, the other major forced labor-related development in the winter of 1944 was the decision to allow the remaining 115 deportees to return from Transnistria. Most of them were finally allowed to return home by the authorities in February 1944, once it became clear that the Soviet Union would soon recapture Transnistria. In early February, each Territorial Command reported to the General Staff on the Jews who had been returned to their areas of control to that point. For example, the Fourth Army Command relayed the Baia Territorial Command's February 6 report that 4 Jews, Iosub Smilovici and 3 relatives of other deportees, had returned from Transnistria, but the 11 remaining deportees from that city—including Solomon Grisaru, Butun Herșcu, Strul Reven, and David Sloim, as well as 7 of their relatives—were still unaccounted for. On February 10, the General Staff reported that 4 former deportees—Matilda Bercu, Diamant Burah, Iosip Iosipovici, and Iosef Volansk—who had been detained in Tiraspol for undisclosed reasons, were allowed to return to their homes in Bucharest.[12] Repatriations continued over the coming weeks, though the exact number of persons repatriated during this period was not recorded by the General Staff, and it is unclear whether all 115 remaining deportees returned to Romania or what happened to those who were unaccounted for as of early February.

On December 29, 1943, General Staff ordered that Jews returning from Transnistria in the late fall of 1943 could not be sent to forced labor (aside from snow removal) until March 15, 1944.[13] However, there were no specific instructions provided for the Jews who returned in February 1944. As a result, the Territorial Commands made different decisions. For example, the Territorial Command in Cernăuți ordered that the Jews repatriated in February should not be returned to work (Cernăuți was captured by the Red Army only a few weeks later). However, the Territorial Command in Iași ordered five skilled laborers who had returned from Transnistria to work in local detachments, and six other unskilled laborers were assigned to external detachments. In Roman, five workers were sent to Roads Battalion 8 and two were sent to Roads Battalion 3, while one other person was granted medical leave.[14]

As in 1943, some Jews had remained in their assigned detachments and continued working throughout the winter months of 1944, although most had been allowed to return home for the winter and were returned to the same detachment in the spring of 1944. Registration and remobilization of Jewish laborers began in most of Romania in February 1944, earlier than in previous years. During this time, some new detachments were created, and some existing detachments were reorganized or consolidated. The creation of new detachments was prompted in part by the return of large numbers of Jews who had been deported to Transnistria in 1941 and 1942 (for reasons unrelated to forced labor) in early 1944. They were required to register on their return, and many of them were sent to work almost immediately. For example, in Dorohoi, a new detachment was formed with 288 Jews recently repatriated from Transnistria. However, these detachments were fraught with problems, as most of the returned Jews were destitute; the Jews of the Dorohoi detachment were "naked," without clothes or winter coats. An intervention from the Jewish community in Dorohoi convinced the recruitment center officials to replace them with other Jews who had spent a total of less than one year in external detachments.[15]

Another problem facing the military authorities was the immediate threat of the Red Army's advance, which necessitated several evacuations of Jewish labor detachments during the first months of 1944. The first evacuations took place in March and April during the Uman-Botoșani Offensive, as Jews were brought southward from northern Bessarabia and Bukovina, which were subsequently captured by the Soviets, into northeastern Romania. On June 7, 1944, near the end of the First Iași-Chișinău Offensive, a second wave of evacuations was declared by the Ministry of Internal Affairs' Directorate of Public Order, in which all Jews (including forced laborers) in the Romanian-held areas of northern Moldavia and Bessarabia were to be moved south and west, safely behind the Axis front lines. However, the officials of the Fourth Army Command, who were responsible for the evacuations, were forbidden to take the Jews to Iași, which was deemed to have too many Jews already; instead, the Jews were to be taken to other cities farther south in Moldavia, such as Vaslui, Huși, Bârlad, and Tecuci.[16] A final evacuation was ordered on August 17—immediately before the Soviets launched the Second Iași-Chișinău Offensive—in which Jews were to be taken from the eastern "zone of operations" and placed in ghettos in major cities in eastern Romania; however, the Soviet advance in August 1944 was so rapid that this plan was never enacted.[17]

While the situation at the front deteriorated, the army sought once again to maximize the number of Jews who were available for labor. The strength of the Jewish labor force had been badly depleted by the loss of territory during the winter and spring Soviet offensives. As many laborers as possible were evacuated south and west, but these evacuations were carried out in such a disorganized fashion that there was substantial uncertainty about where many of the evacuees were. The military authorities resorted to drastic measures to try to increase the number of Jews eligible for conscription, including the first attempt at a large-scale mobilization of Jewish women. Between October 1, 1942, and December 1, 1943, only 2,565 women had been sent to work in Bucharest, most of them as office workers or as nurses, seamstresses, and washwomen in government institutions—less than 12 percent of the 21,906 Jewish women in the city who were eligible for forced labor.[18] On May 7, 1944, the Fourth Army Command ordered the conscription of all men and women between the ages of fifteen and fifty-five (beyond the normal age range for forced labor) without respect to sex or aptitude for work on military projects, including highways, trenches, antitank ditches, and bridges. The only exceptions were for those who held exemption cards for economic necessity and women with small or ill children.[19] On May 19, Antonescu approved a decree that specified the tasks for which women could be mobilized. They were permitted to work as seamstresses, washwomen, and in "other work of a similar nature where their use [could] be of greater value than at hard labor on the land." This measure also annulled exemptions granted to both men and women by the review commissions, as their work was no longer forced labor "but the defense of the life of the country."[20]

In the same order, Antonescu also approved the execution of anyone caught fleeing a labor detachment.[21] This command reversed those given earlier in 1944 by certain recruitment centers that the pursuit of deserters was secondary to maintaining supervision of the remaining workers. For example, on February 15, the Bucharest recruitment center had instructed Detachment 1016 in Baldovinești that the commanders were not to "occupy [themselves] with the pursuit of deserters, but . . . with work at the work site." Deserters who were caught were to be sent to the most distant labor detachment from their homes.[22] However, on April 27, the Bucharest recruitment center ordered Detachment 1016 to take "severe measures" to curtail desertion, and by late May, mild punishments were gone, replaced once again by the threat of execution and the intent to motivate Jewish laborers by making them fear for their lives.[23]

Disorganization and a desire to increase the number of Jews working at all costs led the General Staff to forgo its established procedures for the distribution and exemption of individual workers as well. For example, on May 28, it was reported to the General Staff that Artur Goldstein, a thirty-nine-year-old Jew from Deva, was sent to an engineering detachment (Detachment 102) on May 18, despite the fact that he had been designated as fit only for light work on November 26, 1943, after he was diagnosed with chronic myocarditis, an inflammatory condition of the heart that can cause chest pain and irregular heartbeat. Goldstein also had a family with three young children. On June 6, the Hunedoara Territorial Command informed the General Staff that Goldstein would not be sent to Detachment 102 but instead to the Jewish hospital in Arad for treatment.[24]

With Romania in a desperate position militarily and economically, the General Staff was forced to reject the ideologically motivated exclusion of Jews from certain professions and types of work. On May 9, its Jewish Office approved a request from the prefect of Putna County to allow a Jewish dentist, Nathan Kaner, to return to the city of Falciu "to satisfy the needs of the population."[25] The lower-level military authorities were often pressed into similar decisions. On February 14, the Fourth Army Command allowed the transfer of six Jewish workers to Military Hospital No. 179 in Iași, contradicting Antonescu's previous order that Jews not be used in military hospitals.[26] These measures were combined with an attempt to press as many Jews as possible into forced labor through the rejection of all but the most necessary exemptions, including medical exemptions. For example, when presented with a report that 440 men had been found unfit for hard labor according to the October 7, 1943, regulations on medical exemptions by the Fourth Army Command, it ordered the Command to review this "enormously large number" of exemptions and reclassify as many Jews as possible for labor in the detachments.[27]

The orders issued by the Fourth Army Command and by Antonescu, as well as the decisions made by the General Staff, reveal that the regime had largely abandoned the principles established by the June 27, 1942, General Instructions by May 1944 because of how fraught the situation in Romania was. The idea of a highly regulated, disciplined, and productive labor service was replaced with simply throwing as many laborers as possible at the problems that existed and hoping that they could help the armed forces achieve an improbable victory. While Antonescu and the military leadership surely knew their situation was hopeless, their desperation and the resulting disorganization in the administration of the forced labor system filtered down to the individual detachments; the vast majority of them experienced a marked decrease in productivity and discipline during the final months of their existence. The chaos in the upper levels of command and in the detachments' leadership resulted in even worse logistics and more frequent shortages of supplies for the workers. As a result, they suffered some of the worst conditions of the entire war during the final weeks before their liberation.

The Fourth Army Command retained control over eight road construction battalions into the spring of 1944. These battalions—Roads Battalions 1, 2, 3, 4, 5, and 8; Labor Battalion 1017; and Maciu quarry company 5/7—were made up of Jews from the eastern territories of Romania, including the Iași, Baia, and Botoșani Territorial Commands. As of May 1, these battalions composed of a total of 1,541 Jewish laborers, some of whom had been removed from businesses in the cities to be sent to external labor detachments.[28] Information from the individual battalions is inconsistent; however, the surviving reports demonstrate the state of disarray in the forced labor detachments in eastern Romania.

The only road labor unit in this region from which reports are available prior to the commencement of the Soviet offensives is Battalion 3, which remained under the command of Lieutenant Colonel Radu Spânu. It was headquartered at Roman, in northeastern Romania, prior to the first Soviet offensive actions late in the winter of 1944. As of January 1944, three companies were under Spânu's command: Dragalina-Tutova, with 148 men employed clearing snow and excavating earth; Berezeni-Falciu, with 136 men extracting ballast from a quarry; and Straja-Neamț, with 44 men breaking ballast stones. However, the nominal strengths of these detachments did not reflect the actual number of workers present. For example, 60 of the workers from Dragalina-Tutova were on leave, as were 84 of the workers from Berezeni-Falciu, while 9 workers from Dragalina-Tutova, 5 from Berezeni-Falciu, and 1 from Straja-Neamț were ill and in infirmaries or hospitals. Two further workers from Dragalina-Tutova and 1 from Berezeni-Falciu had deserted, while equal numbers from each detachment were facing court-martial for desertion. Therefore, the actual strengths of these detachments were 75 workers (51 percent of the total) at Dragalina-Tutova, 45 (33 percent) at Berezeni-Falciu, and 43 (98 percent) at Straja-Neamț. The health of the workers in these detachments was reported to be good, although many workers' clothing was inadequate for the weather.[29]

In February 1944, Battalion 3 underwent a major reorganization. In response to Soviet advances in Ukraine and the imminent invasion of northern and eastern Romania, the battalion's headquarters were moved from Roman to the city of Tecuci, 125 kilometers to the south. Additionally, the battalion's three existing companies were split into five new companies. Companies 1, 2, and 3, under the leadership of Lieutenant Nicolae Dumitrescu, Lieutenant Lazăr D. Lazăr, and Captain Nicolae Petcu, respectively, were responsible for road construction projects between Tecuci and Bârlad, Bârlad and Falciu, Bârlad and Adjud, Bârlad and Bacău, Piatra Neamț and Bicaz, and Iași and Târgu Frumos. Company 4, under the command of Lieutenant Constantin Toma, worked on the construction of the Brătianu Bridge (Pod Brătianu) in Roman. Company 5, led by Lieutenant Mircea Gagiu remained at the Maciu quarry. As in 1943, the roads the battalion was working on were of strategic importance because they connected major cities to areas near the front.[30]

Spânu's February report indicated that the men in his detachments were employed in excavation, spreading stone and antifreeze, removing snow, and unloading wagons. The health of the workers in the battalion was reported to be good, with only minor illnesses and injuries present; each of the five companies had a Jewish medic to attend to the needs of the workers on its work sites. Most of the individual companies' reports corroborate Spânu's statements, though the company at Serbaneşti-Bacău reported only "mediocre" sanitary conditions, and several other companies noted that the condition of the workers' clothes was poor, especially among those who had been sent from the Iaşi Territorial Command.[31]

Despite the reorganization of the battalion, problems with desertion and administration continued. For example, on March 7, Lieutenant Toma reported that eleven workers from the Company 4 were absent without leave, while five had deserted.[32] Additionally, a General Staff report sent to Lieutenant Colonel Spânu on March 8 criticized the transportation of Jews between the various work sites of Battalion 3. The report cited a lack of supervision of the workers on the trains, combined with the failure of commanding officers to keep a roll of those on the train, which allowed Jews to freely hop off the trains and enter cities. The General Staff ordered Spânu to increase the number of officers on these transport trains to better supervise the workers during their movements.[33]

There were also problems with the conscription and distribution of workers. For example, as early as December 1943, the Health Service reported that as many as 12 percent of the workers in the Pod Brătianu company were too old or too sick to be sent to forced labor and should be recalled to the Roman Territorial Command.[34] Despite the unfitness of many of its workers, discipline in Company 4 was perhaps the harshest in the battalion. In multiple cases, workers in Company 4 were subjected to corporal punishment for violations of rules or failure to meet work quotas. For example, on January 19, a Jew named Iancu Leiba received twenty-five lashes for falling short of his daily quota, while on February 3, three Jews from Company 4 received the same punishment for unspecified rules violations.[35]

Organization and working and living conditions varied widely between the other detachments in the Fourth Army Command's territory, and perhaps surprisingly, negative reports did not necessarily correlate with proximity to the front. For example, the relocated Botoşani Territorial Command reported that in Roads Battalion 6, while 31 workers had deserted, food supplies, as well as productivity and discipline, were in good shape. Other partially positive reports came from Roads Battalion 1, farther from the front, which reported few desertions and good supplies of food and a nearly clean bill of worker health. However, this report did note the lack of adequate clothing for many workers and the overcrowding of the workers' barracks (200 men living in barracks with a capacity of 120).[36]

By contrast, Roads Battalion 4, located at Simileasca-Buzău, 250 kilometers from the front, reported that only 228 of its 445 workers (just over 51 percent) were currently with the detachment, and that, of those, only 90 percent were present at work. Battalion 4 did report, however, that food supplies were adequate and the workers' health was generally good. Much closer to the front, in Iași County, Roads Battalion 8 also reported large numbers of workers absent, with only 556 of 812 workers (68 percent) present, though, again, the detachment's commander reported that food, housing, and worker health were all in good order.[37]

The testimony of Jewish laborer Natan Bron provides some insight into the experiences of the Jewish workers in the road detachments during the final days and weeks of the war. The then-twenty-year-old Bron was assigned to Roads Battalion 2 in 1942, and had worked at the Ghidighici quarry through the winter of 1944, during which time he suffered a serious foot injury in a wagon accident. In March 1944, he and his company from Ghidighici were sent on a forced march to the city of Huși, more than seventy kilometers away, to escape the advancing Red Army. From there, they were taken by train to Brăila and then to Constanța, where they were assigned to work at another stone quarry near Hârșova. Bron described harsher conditions than those presented in most of the official reports.[38]

While that month's report from the Hârșova detachment's commander (whom Bron described as "severe") indicated that food and other supplies were "good,"[39] Bron indicated that the workers were merely "fed enough not to be hungry."[40] Furthermore, Bron noted, if any worker failed to meet his work quota for the day, everyone in the detachment (a total of 111 men) would be denied their evening meal. The men at Hârșova worked from sunrise to sunset with a short break for lunch, contrary to regulations that established a nine-hour workday for Jews in labor detachments. The men slept in peasant cottages in Hârșova, which was, in theory, strictly forbidden by the General Staff. He described his relationship with the other Jewish laborers there as being very close, stating that they were "like brothers." Bron remained at Hârșova until August 23; he was released after Romania switched sides in the war.[41] The hardships Bron and his comrades in the Hârșova detachment endured demonstrate the variability of conditions in individual labor detachments as well as the decline in worker welfare precipitated by the worsening of the Romanian army's situation in the last weeks of the war.

In 1943, the General Staff prioritized the construction of fortifications and other defensive works projects in Romania above even road and railroad construction projects. In 1944, this preference was even more evident, as these projects became even more critical. By the spring of 1944, some of the fortifications detachments created under Order No. 965.555 had either completed or very nearly completed their tasks. Detachment 103 was dissolved at the end of 1943, while Detachment 100 had been greatly reduced in numbers by that time, as its assignments were nearly finished. Detachment 104 was dissolved on the completion of its projects in March 1944. However, work continued in Detachments 101 and 102 for the remainder of the war.[42]

By February 14, 1944, only 125 Jewish laborers remained in Detachment 100, all of them at the Voinești work site along the Siret River, where they were finishing the previous year's canal-digging project.[43] The commander's mid-February report to the General Staff estimated that the detachment's two remaining projects were 96 and 98 percent complete. Further north along the Siret River, Detachment 101 faced a more difficult situation than its southern counterpart. In February 1944, the stretch of the Siret on which Detachment 101 was working burst out of its bank due to heavy precipitation and snowmelt, requiring the repair of fifteen meters of the river embankment and the addition of twenty-five meters to the excavation project. The repairs necessitated by the flooding also added to the expected costs faced by the detachment.[44] On March 9, the detachment filed a report that estimated a total cost of 66.4 million lei for the remaining work, plus the maintenance of the 1,980 Jewish workers who remained at the detachment's four work sites along the Siret River between Ciușlea and Nămăloasa.[45] The detachment's work sites in 1944 were located at Domnești (Company I), Doaga (Company II), Ciușlea (Company III), and Nămăloasa (Company IV). All four were working to reinforce the banks of the river in order to protect the fortifications at their locations.[46]

Conditions in Detachment 101 were poor even prior to the Soviet offensive in the spring of 1944. A February 7 report based on an inspection of the detachment by the chief of the Jewish Office of the General Staff, Lieutenant Colonel Ion Boldur-Lățescu, noted that the kitchen of Company I was dirty and that the food was of poor quality—most days, the workers' rations consisted of only potato soup. Similar conditions were reported in Company II. Boldur-Lățescu also visited one of the detachment's work sites along with another officer named Lieutenant Georgian. They observed that of the 135 men listed in the detachment, only 115 were present at the work site and, of those, only 72 were working, with the remaining 43 having been dispatched on various types of business, during which they were unsupervised. Boldur-Lățescu criticized this practice in a subsequent report, stating that the detachment lacked adequate oversight of its workers. Boldur-Lățescu also documented a claim by the workers in Company II that they had no opportunity or place in which to bathe, presenting a health hazard.[47]

Andrei Voinea experienced similarly unpleasant conditions in Detachment 102. On Voinea's transfer from Timișul de Sud to Păuliș in early 1944, the detachment commander assigned Voinea and his comrades numbers in place of their names, telling them, "Animals don't have names, why should you have names?" Voinea recalls that he and the eight hundred other workers at Păuliș-Suraia were quartered in the stables and stalls of local Banat-Swabian farmers. As in some of the road detachments, the men in Detachment 102 were forced to work for ten hours a day, above the limit set by the General Staff. However, he stated that, aside from the detachment commander, most of the military personnel in Detachment 102 were kind to the workers, as they were grateful to be serving with the labor detachment rather than at the front. Detachment 102 was dissolved on August 20, 1944, the date on which the Soviets launched the Second Iași-Chișinău Offensive. When news of the rapid Soviet breakthrough arrived, the officers in the detachment correctly concluded that the war was lost, and chose to release the workers, making Detachment 102 the last of the fortification detachments created by Order No. 965.555 to be dissolved.[48]

Although the cases of the road and fortification detachments in eastern Romania demonstrate that disorganization at the detachment level was not necessarily correlated with distance from the front, order and conditions in the detachments deteriorated over the last months of the war irrespective of geography. Even in early 1944, conditions were poor in many detachments, particularly those that had been working throughout the winter, as well as those composed of recently repatriated Jews from Transnistria. The increasingly indiscriminate mobilization of Jews for forced labor by late spring only made these problems worse.

On May 27, the Fourth Army Command reported that Jews in eastern Romania had been sent to work without medical examinations, and that many sick and elderly people had been sent out to work. The author noted that while the military situation required that the Romanian people work in defense of the country, such "inhumane" labor amounted to "torture" and did not benefit the country. The report concluded that Jews who were not capable of working should be replaced by Jews working in nonmanual labor who were physically fit.[49] Two days later, another report documented the "tragic situation" of Jewish laborers in Moldavia and the parts of Bessarabia that remained under Romanian control, who had been sent to work without regard for age or fitness. In addition, the commanders there had been ignoring previously established work regulations, and neither the military authorities nor the local Jewish communities had the funds to help them. As a result of the poor conditions, the productivity in these detachments was very low, and the workers were harshly punished or forced to work all night by the commanders as a result.[50]

Rates of absence from work also increased dramatically by the summer of 1944. In its summary report on forced labor in June, the Fourth Army Command recorded that of the 11,005 man-days of labor that were expected that month in Company 2 of Roads Battalion 6, 4,000 had been performed, while the other 7,005 had been lost to absences for medical reasons or because the workers had been sent to attempt to find supplies. Nonetheless, the commander of Battalion 6, Major Ştefanescu, reported an absence rate for the entire battalion of only 4 percent, suggesting that the figures in his report were falsified. The exceptional number of absences in Company 2 was much higher than those reported in other companies—only 3,223 of 18,486 man-days had been lost to absence in the Doaga detachment of Battalion 6—but the fact that so many of those absences (more than half) were due to men trying to obtain basic supplies suggests that a serious breakdown in logistics had occurred.[51] The July 1944 report on the same battalion, prepared by the commandant, Major Ştefanescu, noted continued problems with desertion and the need for punishments to prevent them. He also reported that many of the men in the detachment did not have adequate clothing.[52]

The situation in the detachments became particularly dire in the last days of the Antonescu regime. An August 15 report on a labor detachment in Turcoaia, in Tulcea County, indicated that Jews who were working in a quarry did not have shoes, leaving their feet cut open and constantly bleeding. The laborers' food was poor—they received only a thin potato soup for breakfast and small portions of potatoes, beans, and mămăligă, which was sometimes substituted with half a loaf of bread. Two hundred fifty men were crammed into a barrack built to hold half that number, and they worked from four in the morning until nine in the evening, with no opportunities to bathe. Their clothes were badly worn and as many as half of the men were sick, with many in need of hospitalization. The men could not possibly reach their daily collective quota of seventy-seven wheelbarrows of rock brought down the mountain per day, yet the commander of the detachment, Second Lieutenant Garibaldi, beat the men every evening for falling short of their goal. Many of the men had been working for close to three years with scarcely any leave and were on the verge of collapse.[53]

Though many of the local Jewish communities had reached the end of their resources, the Central Jewish Office continued to carry out relief operations for the Jews in the detachments, with the average monthly expenditure on aid to the detachments remaining fairly constant at between 120,000 and 150,000 lei per month in the early months of 1944.[54] The Central Jewish Office also remained in charge of collecting exemption taxes and obtaining money for those exemptions when individual Jews could not pay. Such situations became more common in 1944 as the rates of "taxation" were dramatically increased. For example, Ilie Brăileanu of Focşani complained to the Central Jewish Office that he had been forced to pay an "exaggerated" exemption tax to continue working as a furrier and could no longer afford the tax (though the General Staff eventually approved his request for a lower rate).[55] In the case of Nachmias Moscu, who worked at the

Fr. Boehm firm in Bucharest, the cost of his exemption increased from 60,000 lei in 1943 to 300,000 lei in 1944 (against an annual salary of 380,000 lei).[56] Despite the rapid inflation experienced in Romania late in the war, a fivefold increase in the cost of exemptions put them well beyond the means of many Jews, requiring more frequent intervention by the Jewish community.

While the labor detachments were often in isolated areas, the laborers and soldiers were not completely cut off from the outside world and information about the state of the war. Testimonies from Jewish laborers who were still working in the late spring and summer of 1944 indicate that the soldiers guarding the detachments were well aware of the situation at the front and were resigned to the country's fate. Andrei Voinea recalled that the soldiers in his detachment were grateful that they were there rather than at the front. On August 20, 1944, he and the other eight hundred men in his detachment at Păuliș were released in anticipation of the imminent defeat of the Romanian army at the front.[57] Earlier that same day, the Second and Third Ukrainian Fronts of the Red Army launched the Second Iași-Chișinău Offensive against the German Sixth and Eighth Armies and Romanian Third and Fourth Armies, attacking the Axis along a broad front, which their depleted forces could not hope to cover. The Soviets quickly broke through the German and Romanian defensive lines, encircling nearly the entire Sixth Army and a substantial portion of the Eighth. The remaining German and Romanian forces retreated in chaos. Within two days, the German-Romanian front had collapsed almost entirely.[58]

On August 23, a diverse group of opposition figures—the National Peasant leader, Iuliu Maniu; the National Liberal leader, Dinu Brătianu; the Social Democratic leader, Titel Petrescu; the Communists Lucrețiu Pătrășcanu and Emil Bodnăraș; the commander of the Romanian Fourth Army, General Constantin Sănătescu; and King Mihai—launched the coup d'état they had begun planning in coordination with the Allies months before, once it became clear that Antonescu would not agree to a separate peace on the Allies' nonnegotiable terms of unconditional surrender. The king brought Ion and Mihai Antonescu to his palace to meet with him regarding an armistice. When the *conducător* yet again refused to surrender, the king informed him that he was dismissed from his post as prime minister. As the prime minister and his deputy departed, they were arrested by the palace guard. Sănătescu was appointed as the new prime minister, ending Antonescu's nearly four-year rule.[59]

After the coup, Romania's armed forces aligned themselves with the Allies and joined the fight against the Axis. Though the Germans moved quickly to seize important oil production, transportation, and military sites, the combined operations of the Soviet and Romanian forces were able to overcome them. In September 1944, the Romanian Fourth Army and Soviet Twenty-Seventh Army dealt crushing defeats to the German-Hungarian forces at Turda and Păuliș, where the fortifications built based on Antonescu's paranoia toward Hungary were utilized by the Romanians and Soviets to repulse Axis counterattacks. By the end of September, Axis forces had been swept from Romanian territory.[60]

The new government and military leadership quickly repealed much of the antisemitic legislation of the Antonescu regime, including the forced labor obligation for Jews. On August 23, 19,447 Jews were working in external detachments, with another 12,016 in local detachments, for a total of 31,463 laborers.[61] Though many of the detachments were quickly disbanded by their commanders after they received news of the August 23 coup (if not before), some Jews, particularly in more isolated locations, remained at forced labor for many days after Antonescu was ousted. On August 30, the new chief of the General Staff, Lieutenant General Nicolae Rădescu, ordered the dissolution of all Jewish labor detachments, including civil defense detachments. Furthermore, when possible, Jewish workers were to be granted free rail transport back to their homes.[62] On September 2, the new minister of national defense, Major General Ioan Mihail Racoviță, followed up Rădescu's order with his own command that all forced labor of Jews was to cease immediately.[63] An additional General Staff order on September 11 stated that an administration for the liquidation of the labor detachments would be formed by the end of September to ensure the return of Jews to their homes and Romanian soldiers to the appropriate units.[64]

Despite the orders of the new government to rectify the situation of Jewish laborers, many of them faced difficulty getting home from their isolated labor detachments. Andrei Voinea recalled that after the detachment commander released the workers on August 20, they were unsure what to do or where to go. His detachment's location was eventually overrun by Soviet troops, and a sympathetic Jewish Red Army soldier gave the members of his detachment passes for unrestricted travel throughout the country. However, while he was free to leave, Voinea still did not have a way to get home and walked some distance down the train tracks before he was eventually able to board a train.[65] Many other Jews were unable to make use of the government's promise of free rail transport because they were too far from major rail lines. As a result, large numbers of Jews displaced by forced labor were only able to return to their homes after weeks of travel by foot.

After the war, the new General Staff's Recruitment Office issued a report on the results of the exclusion of the Jews from the military under the previous regime. It concluded that the exclusion of Jews was "ineffective" and prevented them from participating in the defense of their country, which both denied them a fundamental right as citizens and put an additional burden on non-Jewish Romanians. Because the exclusions created by the previous regime "did not have good results," the new General Staff decided to abolish Decree-Law No. 3984, restoring the right of Romanian Jews to serve in the military, attend officer school, and receive commissions (although nonethnic Romanians were not to make up more than 25 percent of officer school cadets). Jewish officers excluded from the military by the December 1940 law were returned to the service (or reserves) with full restoration of rank and the recruitment of new Jewish soldiers was to resume immediately.[66] Emil Bodnăraș issued a personal appeal to the patriotism of the Jews of Bucharest after the fall of the Antonescu regime and encouraged them to "give [their] arms, [their] means, and all of [their] souls to fight for the extermination of our enemies" by joining new volunteer civil defense battalions in the capital, well before the military allowed Jews to return to active duty.[67]

An additional residual issue from forced labor that the new General Staff had to address was back pay for Jewish laborers. Although nonpayment of wages was a common problem throughout the war, it had been particularly prevalent in 1943 and 1944. Former forced laborer Janos Weinberger recalled that he had not been paid at any point for his work constructing an airfield near Brăila (which was never completed), which he began in the winter of 1943.[68] Wilhelm Filderman, once again the leader of the Jewish community after the dissolution of the Central Jewish Office, led the campaign to recover lost wages for former forced laborers, with mixed success. On December 15, he petitioned the military for the repayment of wages to laborers, noting that many were in "very difficult situations" and that between March and August, they had worked in or near active combat zones.[69]

Filderman scored at least one victory with a petition to the Iași recruitment center, which agreed on January 17, 1945 to pay seventy lei per day to workers who had been working in detachments under direct army control. Pay for workers in other detachments, as well as private enterprises and government institutions, was coordinated with the Council of Ministers.[70] Colonel Gheorghe Zamfirescu confirmed to Filderman in a letter on January 29 that these payments would be made.[71] Filderman's efforts were part of a larger campaign by the Jewish community leadership to support former forced laborers. However, many would never receive their back pay nor any reparations for the disruption of their careers, separation from their families, and, in many cases, serious injuries or permanent disabilities. The families of the forced laborers who were killed also rarely received any compensation from the state.[72]

The laborers also received little satisfaction through the punishment of detachments commanders and officers. Many of those who had participated in the persecution of Jewish laborers never faced justice for their actions. The major war criminals and Holocaust perpetrators were tried in the People's Tribunals in Bucharest (for crimes committed within the wartime borders of Romania) and Cluj (for crimes committed in Hungarian-occupied northern Transylvania) in 1945 and 1946. Ion Antonescu, Mihai Antonescu, Gheorghe Alexianu (the governor of Transnistria), and Constantin "Piki" Vasiliu (head of the gendarmerie) were convicted of war crimes and executed by a firing squad on June 1, 1946. Many lower-ranking perpetrators were sentenced to prison terms, but most were amnestied between 1958 and 1962.[73]

Few Romanian personnel were ever brought to trial for crimes related to forced labor. The commandant of one of the labor groups at the Târgu Jiu internment camp, Lieutenant Trepaduș, who had gained notoriety by tying exhausted, starving laborers from the camp to tree trunks and leaving them to hang by the ropes until they cut into the victim's skin, was tried and sentenced to a short prison term.[74] A few military officials and commanders of local labor detachments were also punished. Major Ștefan Moldoveanu, the former chief of the Jewish Office of the Vaslui Territorial Command, was sentenced to a prison term after multiple Jews reported that he whipped them for alleged desertion. One witness, Iancu Imberg, asserted that Moldoveanu had personally whipped "hundreds of Jews" and that he had received twenty-five lashes from Moldoveanu before being court-martialed for absences from work. Moldoveanu was sentenced to a short prison term in 1945.[75] Colonel Mircea Elefterescu, who had overseen Jews working for the prefect of police of Bucharest, was brought to trial in 1951. One of the witnesses against him, Isidor Grumberg, testified that "there was not a day in which Colonel Mircea Elefterescu did not curse us, did not make us miserable, did not beat us."[76] Elefterescu also received a brief prison term and was required to forfeit some of his personal assets (more than 55,000 lei and a gold watch).[77]

However, Moldoveanu and Elefterescu were the exceptions, not the rule. Even those who were tried for their roles in the forced labor system rarely faced serious punishment. For example, the commandant of Labor Battalion 120, Captain Constantin Clinceanu, was tried by the Bucharest People's Tribunal but was acquitted.[78] Others escaped potential punishment altogether by fleeing from the communist authorities. Bica Bercovici said that an officer from the Doaga camp, Sergeant Codrescu, who had been "very vicious" toward the men there, was able to escape to South America after the war.[79] The lack of legal recognition and restitution for the former forced laborers' suffering compounded the serious financial, physical, and emotional damage that forced labor had done to the Romanian Jews and their families. Most returned to families they had not seen for most of three years, their lives in disarray, with little chance of improving their living situation since they had lost their jobs and, in many cases, their property had been expropriated. Efforts by the Jewish community leadership to obtain restitution for the laborers in the form of back pay for their work were only partially successful, and even those who did receive money generally found it insufficient to rebuild their lives. Most forced laborers, like the majority of Romanian Holocaust survivors, left Romania for Israel or the West in the years following the war.[80]

Notes

1. David A. Glantz, *Red Storm over the Balkans: The Failed Soviet Invasion of Romania, Spring 1944* (Lawrence: University Press of Kansas, 2007), 62–70.
2. Ibid., 367.
3. Jay A. Stout, *Fortress Ploesti: The Campaign to Destroy Hitler's Oil* (Philadelphia: Casemate Publishers, 2003), 190.
4. USHMMA, RG-25.003M, reel 208, file 3723, 188.
5. Trașcă, *"Chestiunea evreiască,"* document 427, 845.
6. USHMMA, RG-25.003M, reel 208, file 3723, 89.
7. Ibid., 223.
8. Ibid., 91.
9. Ibid., 94–96.
10. Ibid., 105.
11. Bărbulescu et al., *Muncă obligatorie*, document 192, 450–451.
12. USHMMA, RG-25.003M, reel 291, file 4597, 8.
13. Bărbulescu et al., *Munca obligatorie*, document 200, 461.
14. USHMMA, RG-25.003M, reel 291, file 4597, 1–8.
15. Bărbulescu et al., *Munca obligatorie*, document 192, 458.
16. Trașcă, *"Chestiunea evreiască,"* document 440, 868–869.
17. Ibid., document 444, 875.
18. Jean Ancel, ed., *Documents Concerning the Fate of Romanian Jewry during the Holocaust*, vol. 8 (New York: Beate Klarsfeld Foundation, 1986), document 8, 8.
19. Bărbulescu et al., *Munca obligatorie*, document 225, 496.
20. Trașcă, *"Chestiunea evreiască,"* document 435, 860.
21. Ibid., document 435, 861.
22. Bărbulescu et al., *Munca obligatorie*, document 206, 470.
23. Ibid., document 222, 493.
24. USHMMA, RG-25.003M, reel 274, file 4577, 290.
25. USHMMA, RG-25.003M, reel 67, file 7763, 38–39.
26. USHMMA, RG-25.003M, reel 274, file 4577, 288–303.
27. Ibid., 1003.
28. USHMMA, RG-25.003M, reel 66, file 7761, 40–41.
29. USHMMA, RG-25.011, folder 13, Fond Batalion 3 Drumuri, file 236, 185–187.
30. Ibid., 232–233.
31. Ibid., 203.
32. USHMMA, RG-25.011, folder 13, Fond Batalion 3 Drumuri, file 232, 333.
33. Ibid., 383.
34. USHMMA, RG-25.011, folder 13, Fond Batalion 3 Drumuri, file 233, 28.
35. Ibid., 303.
36. USHMMA, RG-25.003M, reel 67, file 7762, 10.
37. USHMMA, RG-25.003M, reel 66, file 7761, 172–176.
38. Bron, interview 43924.
39. USHMMA, RG-25.003M, reel 67, file 7762, 53.
40. Bron, interview 43924.
41. Ibid.

42. USHMMA, RG-25.003M, reel 110, file 4223, 3.
43. USHMMA, RG-25.003M, reel 109, file 4219, 99.
44. USHMMA, RG-25.003M, reel 105, file 4192, 42.
45. Ibid., 44.
46. Ibid., 150–152.
47. Ibid., 173–175.
48. Voinea, *Sanduhr aus Steinen*, 80.
49. Trașcă, *"Chestiunea evreiască,"* document 436, 862.
50. Ancel, *Documents*, vol. 8, document 62, 63.
51. USHMMA, RG-25.003M, reel 67, file 7762, 12 and 32–35.
52. Ibid., 10.
53. Ancel, *Documents*, vol. 8, document 119, 138.
54. USHMMA, RG-25.021M, reel 8, file 152, 1–9, 14–20, and 54–60.
55. USHMMA, RG-25.003M, reel 274, file 4577, 556–557.
56. USHMMA, RG-25.021M, reel 13, file 341, 21.
57. Voinea, *Sanduhr aus Steinen*, 80.
58. Axworthy, Crăciunoiu, and Scafeș, *Third Axis, Fourth Ally*, 181–183.
59. Deletant, *Hitler's Forgotten Ally*, 240–242.
60. Axworthy, Crăciunoiu, and Scafeș, *Third Axis, Fourth Ally*, 197–202.
61. USHMMA, RG-25.003M, reel 272, file 2575, 342.
62. Trașcă, *"Chestiunea evreiască,"* document 447, 883.
63. USHMMA, RG-25.003M, reel 274, file 4575, 368.
64. Ibid., 365.
65. Voinea, *Sanduhr aus Steinen*, 81–83.
66. Trașcă, *"Chestiunea evreiască,"* document 446, 880–882.
67. USHMMA, RG-25.021M, reel 11, file 457, 4–5.
68. Janos Weinberger, interview 6274, Visual History Archive. USC Shoah Foundation, accessed online at the United States Holocaust Memorial Museum on February 5, 2015, http://vhaonline.usc.edu/viewingPage?testimonyID=8520&returnIndex=0.
69. USHMMA, RG-25.003M, reel 194, file 3706, 42.
70. Ibid., 38–39.
71. Ibid., 44.
72. USHMMA, RG-25.021M, reel 4, file 75, 634.
73. Ioanid, *Holocaust in Romania*, 287.
74. Ion Butnaru, *The Silent Holocaust: Romania and Its Jews* (Westport, CT: Greenwood Press, 1992), 99–100.
75. USHMMA, RG-25.004M, Selected Records from the Romanian Information Service, reel 6, file 7632, 4–24.
76. USHMMA, RG-25.004M, reel 28, file 24337, 45.
77. Ibid., 145.
78. Creangă, "Balta/120 Labor Battalion," 600.
79. Bercovici, interview 50196.
80. Howard M. Sachar, *Israel and Europe: An Appraisal in History* (New York: Alfred A. Knopf, 1999), 59–60.

Conclusion

JEWISH FORCED LABOR in Romania represents a unique case within the larger phenomenon of forced labor in Europe during the Holocaust. While it shared some features with the forced labor systems in other countries, particularly that in Hungary, the outcomes for the forced laborers in Romania were very different. Although forced labor was an integral part of the Antonescu regime's antisemitic policy, it never became a tool for mass murder, despite Romania's extensive participation in the genocide of Jews in Bessarabia, Bukovina, and Transnistria. The fact that forced labor was not part of the Final Solution in Romania was a product of its role in satisfying the economic needs of the Romanian state and military, as well as the fact that Romanian Jews were never sent to serve as forced laborers at the front. Also vital in this respect was Antonescu's decision not to deport the Jews of the Old Kingdom, since the vast majority of forced laborers would not have been spared. Their survival under a regime that so eagerly participated in mass murder elsewhere is an example of the divergence between the outcomes for Jews inside the Romanian Old Kingdom and outside of it and illustrates the wide variety of Jewish experiences in Romania during the Antonescu era.

Forced labor was introduced on December 5, 1940, by the Law on the Military Status of the Jews, which excluded Jews from the Romanian military and replaced their compulsory military service with "work in the community interest" and special taxes.[1] This law was part of the larger process of Romanianization—the systematic exclusion of Jews from Romanian social and economic life—which was the central feature of Antonescu's prewar Jewish policy. It followed legislation that mandated the termination of Jewish employees of Romanian firms and other discriminatory measures. In this context, forced labor served both an ideological purpose and an economic one. From an ideological perspective, it removed a group of people whom Antonescu viewed as "unreliable" from the Romanian military—the same reason the Hungarian Jewish labor service system was created. From an economic standpoint, it ensured that people who had been excluded from both the military and their jobs would still make a contribution to the Romanian economy and any future war effort through their labor. Antonescu later stated that forced labor and special military taxes were necessary because they prevented Jews from becoming—in his words—"parasites," who neither fought for Romania nor contributed to the war effort on the home front. Both of these goals guided policymaking related to forced labor, which sought to maximize the economic benefits obtained from the Jews' labor while also conforming to the ideological constraints created by Antonescu's Jewish policy.[2]

For most of the war, forced labor was organized by the Romanian General Staff to meet the needs of the military and state institutions, in keeping with its original purpose as a replacement for compulsory military service. Jews were sent to work on projects that would benefit the war effort either directly (such as building and repairing fortifications) or indirectly (such as the construction of railways and roads for both civilian and military use). The mobilization of Jewish laborers in August 1941, conducted in coordination with the Ministry of Internal Affairs, was disastrous. After several days of chaos, the General Staff seized control of the mobilization and deployment of laborers. The General Staff initially worked in cooperation with the Ministry of Labor and other interested parties, including the state railway and road agencies, to make improvements to the system; however, the General Staff gradually consolidated power over forced labor policy. It attempted several rounds of reforms to the forced labor system to streamline the recruitment of laborers and increase the productivity of the labor detachments. Antonescu was content to allow the General Staff to set forced labor policy as it saw fit, since it was intended primarily as a substitute for active duty military service and a source of labor for projects of military importance. However, he remained involved in an advisory role, often providing general "guidelines" for the General Staff's policies and intervening when the results of forced labor were not to his satisfaction.[3]

The General Staff's efforts to improve the forced labor system required it to maintain a delicate balance between economic and ideological interests. This balancing act was most apparent in its policies toward Jewish workers who were still needed by Romanian businesses and industries. Although Antonescu's government passed legislation requiring businesses to replace their Jewish employees with non-Jewish ethnic Romanians, many employers were unable to replace the skilled workers they depended on. As a result, the General Staff had to grant "exemptions" from forced labor to thousands of Jewish workers—a tacit acknowledgement of a critical flaw in the premise of the regime's Jewish policy, which demanded the complete exclusion of these workers for the benefit of non-Jewish Romanians. These exemptions were a valuable commodity, and an extensive network of bribery developed around them.

The system of organized bribery became a more or less official policy after Antonescu's corrupt commissar for Jewish affairs, Radu Lecca, was given power over them in the spring of 1942. Lecca handed out thousands of additional exemptions to those who could pay, undermining the General Staff's efforts to recruit more Jewish laborers and shifting the burden of forced labor onto poorer Jews who could not afford the exemption "fees."[4] However, these exemptions were (to some extent) a mitigating factor, since they allowed those who could afford them to avoid forced labor. Lecca claimed credit for his supposedly humanitarian actions in his postwar memoirs, although the real purpose of his actions was clearly to enrich himself and the other beneficiaries of his large network of systemic corruption.

Although the General Staff sought to maximize the number of laborers available and the productivity of their labor, they did so with the understanding that forced labor was only considered a temporary solution in Antonescu's Jewish policy. As an internal memorandum from November 1941 indicates, it was viewed as a transitional phase between Romanianization and the planned radical solution to the Jewish question—the complete removal of Jews from Romania.[5] Forced labor was primarily a way to extract some economic value from the Romanian Jews before they were expelled from the country. While removing the Jews from Romania had long been a goal of antisemitic politicians, it was only after the war began that doing so became a realistic option, either by expelling the Jews "to the east" or, after the Wannsee Conference in January 1942, by deporting them to their deaths in the Nazi extermination camps. Forced labor was not part of either of these plans but rather an intermediate phase that would precede them. Unlike in Nazi Germany, forced labor in Romania was not viewed as an impediment to the elimination of the Jews because it would end when the deportations began. Thus, while it was not part of the plans for mass murder, it would also not protect Jews from deportation as it had in Hungary; only a few "economically necessary" Jews would be allowed to remain, and those only temporarily.[6]

However, after months of planning and negotiations, Antonescu ultimately decided not to deport the Jews of the Old Kingdom and southern Transylvania. After the fall of 1942, the mass murder of the Romanian Jews became politically undesirable for Antonescu's government—once the war turned against the Axis, Antonescu came to view them as a valuable bargaining chip to use in negotiating a potential separate peace with the Allies. As a result, the vast majority of the Jews living within the prewar borders of Romania survived the war.[7] After Antonescu rejected the German plan, the preferred method for removing Jews from Romania shifted from deportation and extermination to emigration, and forced labor became a permanent part of his government's Jewish policy by default.

Although economic interest and the existence of alternative plans for the so-called solution to the Jewish question had protected the laborers from mass murder up to that point, they were still threatened by a proposal to send Jews to work at the front line in early 1943. The Hungarians had sent Jews to the front the year before, with disastrous results: tens of thousands of Jews were killed outright or abandoned to die after the Hungarian defeat in January 1943.[8] However, the Romanian General Staff ultimately rejected this idea, citing both the difficulty of preventing desertion and the unfavorable reaction such a policy might draw from abroad. As a result, Jewish laborers continued to be deployed almost exclusively within or near the borders of the Romanian Old Kingdom, where the vast majority of Jews survived. This decision—which was made for practical and political rather than humanitarian reasons—was essential to the survival of most of Romania's Jewish laborers.[9]

Despite the General Staff's efforts to improve the productivity of the system, forced labor never yielded the desired results on a consistent basis. Although some detachments were able to achieve their assigned goals, most fell well short of the General Staff's expectations. The poor productivity of forced labor reflected both the inherent flaws of compulsory labor in general and the shortcomings of the Romanian system in particular. Many of the Jews who were sent to forced labor were simply not suited to the type of work they were expected to do—a problem Antonescu pointed out as early as the fall of 1941.[10] White-collar workers were asked to do heavy manual labor for which they had neither the requisite skills nor physical fitness. Furthermore, they had little motivation to work hard, as they received minimal pay and the disciplinary measures that were designed to improve effort through intimidation were inconsistently enforced. The Romanian personnel who were responsible for the productivity of forced labor were often just as disinterested as the workers, and they were a frequent scapegoat for the General Staff in negative reports on forced labor.[11] However, even the detachment commanders who did their jobs diligently were often hamstrung by poor logistics, which plagued the forced labor system for its entire duration. Supplies needed for successful completion of the assigned work, such as building materials and tools, were often unavailable. Projects were beset by budget shortfalls, and the laborers rarely had adequate housing, clothing, food, or medical care. As a result, both the productivity of the labor detachments and the laborers' welfare suffered.

The testimonies and memoirs of survivors reflect diverse experiences with forced labor. Although almost all of them described the work as exhausting (and often dangerous) and the living conditions as difficult, their recollections about their treatment by the Romanian officers and soldiers assigned to guard them were more varied. In many cases, the officers and soldiers treated the laborers harshly, meting out corporal punishment for minor infractions and subjecting them to frequent verbal abuse.[12] Other survivors recalled the personnel in their detachment as disinterested in their jobs, allowing workers to slack off or even desert without consequence.[13] However, a minority of survivors recalled that their detachment's commanders or guards treated them decently; some of them were simply happy not to be sent to the front, while others did so out of respect for the workers' professional qualifications or personal decency.[14] While the location of the labor detachment and the type of work the laborers were assigned to do were important in dictating the nature of their experiences, the most important determinant was their interactions with Romanian personnel, who had the capacity to either exacerbate or mitigate the laborers' suffering through their attitudes and actions. Unfortunately, negative interactions were more common than positive interactions, adding to the misery produced by the grueling work and uncomfortable living conditions.

It is difficult to ascertain the number of people who were killed or injured while working in the Romanian forced labor system due to incomplete statistical information and poor record-keeping practices. Official statistics compiled by the General Staff in a report from March 28, 1946, give a death toll of 36. Adding the 88 known deaths of deportees from the September 1942 transports yields a death toll of 124.[15] However, the General Staff's figures were based on incomplete reports that covered only part of the forced labor system's existence (mostly from late 1942 to early 1944) and a small number of detachments, and it is almost certain that their statistics significantly understate the death toll. The inadequacy of the centralized records and diffuse detachment reports—as well as the scarcity of such reports for 1941 and most of 1942—makes it difficult to extrapolate an estimate from this figure, and any such effort requires significant assumptions. However, based on the sampling of surviving records and corroborating testimony from Jewish laborers, it is likely that the true death toll (including the deportees to Transnistria) was probably between 500 and 1,000, with about 5,000 to 10,000 illnesses and injuries (some of which were serious and resulted in permanent disability).[16]

This estimate is significantly lower than the number of forced laborers killed in Germany and Hungary, reflecting the differences in the purpose of forced labor, where forced labor was used, and the relationship between forced labor and mass murder in each country. The fact that the number of probable deaths is lower than in Germany or Hungary does not, of course, discount to any extent the tragedy of these deaths nor the cruelty of the forced labor system and the suffering of the survivors. Most of the injuries and deaths of Romanian Jewish laborers were the direct result of the negligence of Romanian personnel, and in many cases this negligence was no doubt underscored by antisemitism and a disregard for the humanity of the workers. Survivor testimonies indicate that many officers and soldiers expressed openly antisemitic attitudes and were flippant with regard to basic safety and needs like food and medical care. A small number of reports also indicate workers being shot for attempting to escape, which was legally permitted for much of the war. Nonetheless, Antonescu's view of forced labor as a transitional policy and his unusual decision to de-escalate the persecution of Romania's Jews just as the persecution of Jews in other parts of Europe accelerated prevented forced labor from becoming a tool of mass murder or a part of the extermination process, unlike forced labor in other countries. The fact that most of the forced laborers survived in the same country where so many other Jews were killed demonstrates both the contradictions in the Antonescu regime's policy toward the Jews and the diversity of Jewish experiences during the Holocaust in Romania.

Notes

1. Benjamin, *Legislația antievreiască*, document 25, 95.
2. USHMMA, RG-25.002M, reel 18, file 483-41, 62.
3. Bărbulescu et al., *Munca obligatorie*, document 66, 218–219.
4. USHMMA, RG-25.003M, reel 181, file 3001, 369–370.
5. USHMMA, RG-25.003M, reel 144, file 2410, 12–13.
6. Friling et al., *Final Report*, 171.
7. Ibid., 249.
8. Rozett, *Conscripted Slaves*, 62.
9. USHMMA, RG-25.003M, reel 185, file 3274, 10–11.
10. USHMMA, RG-25.002M, reel 18, file 483-41, 59.
11. For example, USHMMA, RG-25.003M, reel 108, file 4201, 247.
12. For example, Andrei V., interview from Projekt Zwangsarbeit 1939–1945, za280, audio interview.
13. For example, Louis Beno N., interview from Projekt Zwangsarbeit 1939–1945, za279, video interview.
14. For example, Endre Altmann, interview 11613.
15. Trașcă, *"Chestiunea evreiască,"* document 453, 894–899.
16. This rough estimate was reached by multiplying out the numbers of deaths from available detachment reports across the total number of detachments and extrapolating from those figures to cover the duration of the forced labor system. This method obviously relies on broad assumptions, and this figure must therefore be regarded as only a very general estimate—a slight refinement of the "thousands" of laborers killed and injured cited in Chioveanu, "Muncă forțata," 91. The absence of a complete, centralized source of statistical data on the fates of the laborers precludes a more precise estimate at present. Nonetheless, this figure is illustrative in comparison with the numbers of forced laborers who died in other countries.

Bibliography

Unpublished Archival Collections

Central National Historical Archives / Arhivele Naționale Istorice Centrale (ANIC). Bucharest, Romania.
Fond Preșidentele Consiliului de Miniștrii, Cabinetul Militar (PCM CM).
United States Holocaust Memorial Museum Archives (USHMMA). Washington, DC.
RG-25.002M, Romanian State Archives Records.
RG-25.003M, Selected Records from the Romanian Ministry of Defense, 1940–1945.
RG-25.004M, Romanian Information Service Records.
RG-25.011, Romanian Forced Labor Camps, 1942–1943.
RG-25.013M, President of the Council of Ministers, Military Cabinet. Fond 764.
RG-25.016M, Centrala Evreilor, 1941–1944.
RG-25.021M, Records Relating to the Holocaust in Romania.
RG-31.006M, Czernowitz Oblast Archives Records.

Published Archival Documents

Ancel, Jean. *Documents Concerning the Fate of Romanian Jewry during the Holocaust*. 12 vols. New York: Beate Klarsfeld Foundation, 1986.
Bărbulescu, Ana, Alexandru Climescu, Laura Degeratu, and Alexandru Florian, eds. *Munca obligatorie a evreilor din România: Documente*. Bucharest: Editura institutul național pentru studierea holocaustului din România "Elie Wiesel," 2013.
Benjamin, Lya, ed. *Evreii din România între anii 1940–1944*. Vol. 1, *Legislația antievreiască*. Bucharest: Editura Hasefer, 1993.
———. *Evreii din România între anii 1940–1944*. Vol. 2, *Problema evreiască*. Bucharest: Editura Hasefer, 1993.
Carp, Matatias. *Cartea neagră: suferintele evreilor din România, in timpul dictaturei fasciste, 1940–1944*. 3 vols. Bucharest: Ateliere grafice Socec, 1946–1948.
Trașcă, Ottmar, ed. *"Chestiunea evreiască" în documente militare române, 1941–1944*. Iași: Institutul European, 2010.

Memoirs and Published Testimonies

Filderman, Wilhelm. *Memoirs and Diaries*. Edited by Jean Ancel. 2 vols. Jerusalem: Yad Vashem, 2004 and 2015.
Gerbel, Fred. *Sâmbătă se deportează: reportagii din vremea prigoanei*. Bucharest: Holicom, 1946.
Lecca, Radu. *Eu i-am salvat pe evrei din România*. Bucharest: Editura Roza Vânturilor, 1994.
Palty, Sonia. *Evrei, treceți Nistrul!* Cluj-Napoca: Editura Dacia, 1992.
Șafran, Alexandru. *Resisting the Storm: Romania, 1940–1947, Memoirs*. Jerusalem: Yad Vashem, 1987.

Sebastian, Mihail. *Journal, 1935-1944: The Fascist Years*. Chicago: Ivan R. Dee, 2000.
Voinea, Andrei. *Sanduhr aus Steinen: jüdische Zwangsarbeiter in Rumänien 1940-1944*. Konstanz: Hartung-Gorre, 2000.

Recorded Oral Testimonies

Projekt Zwangsarbeit 1939-1945. https://www.zwangsarbeit-archiv.de/.
United States Holocaust Memorial Museum Archives. Washington, DC.
    RG-50.030, United States Holocaust Memorial Museum Oral History Collection.
USC Shoah Foundation Visual History Archive. http://vhaonline.usc.edu/.

Secondary Sources

Achim, Viorel. *Munca forțată în Transnistria: "Organizarea muncii" evreilor și romilor, decembrie 1942-martie 1944*. Târgoviște: Editura Cetatea de Scaun, 2015.
Ancel, Jean. *The Economic Destruction of European Jewry*. Jerusalem: Yad Vashem, 2007.
———. "The German-Romanian Relationship and the Final Solution." *Holocaust and Genocide Studies* 19, no. 2 (2005): 252–275.
———. *The History of the Holocaust in Romania*. Jerusalem: Yad Vashem, 2011.
Axworthy, Mark W., Cristian Crăciunoiu, and Cornel Scafeș. *Third Axis, Fourth Ally: Romanian Armed Forces in the European War, 1941–1945*. London: Arms and Armour, 1995.
Balta, Sebastian. *Rumänien und die Großmächte in der Ära Antonescu, 1940–1944*. Stuttgart: Franz Steiner, 2005.
Bărbulescu, Ana. "Muncă obligatorie în România anul 1941: ideologie vs. randament economic." *Holocaust: Studii și cercetări* 1, no. 2 (2009): 59–70.
Beevor, Anthony. *Stalingrad: The Fateful Siege: 1942–1943*. New York: Penguin Books, 1998.
Benjamin, Lya. "Politica antievreiască a regimului Antonescu 1940–1944 (Cu referire la evreii din Vechiul Regat și sudul Transilvaniei)." *Holocaust: Studii și cercetări* 2, no. 1/3 (2010): 9–35.
Bozdorghină, Horia. *Antisemitismul lui A.C. Cuza în politică românească*. Bucharest: Editura institutul național pentru studierea holocaustului din România "Elie Wiesel," 2012.
Braham, Randolph L. *The Hungarian Labor Service System: 1939–1945*. Boulder, CO: Eastern European Monographs, 1977.
Browning, Christopher. *Nazi Policy, Jewish Workers, German Killers*. Cambridge: Cambridge University Press, 2000.
Butnaru, Ion C. *The Silent Holocaust: Romania and Its Jews*. Westport, CT: Greenwood Press, 1992.
Chioveanu, Mihai. "Death Delivered, Death Postponed: Romania and the Continent-Wide Holocaust." *Studia Hebraica* 8 (2008): 136–169.
———. "The Dynamics of Mass Murder: Grasping the Twisted Decision-Making Process behind the Romanian Holocaust." *Sfera Politicii* 20, no. 2 (2012): 25–35.
———. "Muncă forțată în holocaustul din România." *Sfera Politicii* 20, no. 5 (2012): 82–92.
Clark, Roland. *Holy Legionary Youth: Fascist Activism in Interwar Romania*. Cornell: Cornell University Press, 2015.
Climescu, Alexandru. "Sanctions and Interdictions Applicable to the Jews Subjected to the Mandatory Labor Regime in Romania." *Holocaust: Studii și cercetări* 4, no. 1 (2012): 65–76.

Deletant, Dennis. *Hitler's Forgotten Ally: Ion Antonescu and His Regime, Romania 1940–1944.* London: Palgrave Macmillan, 2006.
Eaton, Henry. *The Origins and Onset of the Romanian Holocaust.* Detroit: Wayne State University Press, 2013.
Friling, Tuvia, Lya Benjamin, Radu Ioanid, Mihail E. Ionescu, and Elie Wiesel, eds. *Final Report of the International Commission on the Holocaust in Romania.* Iași: Polirom, 2005.
Glantz, David. *Red Storm over the Balkans: The Failed Soviet Invasion of Romania, Spring 1944.* Lawrence: University Press of Kansas, 2007.
Glass, Hildrun. *Deutschland und die Verfolgung der Juden im rumänischen Machtbereich 1940–1944.* Munich: R. Oldenbourg, 2014.
Gruner, Wolf. *Jewish Forced Labor under the Nazis: Economic Needs and Racial Aims, 1938–1945.* Cambridge: Cambridge University Press, 2006.
Heinen, Armin. *Rumänien, der Holocaust und die Logik der Gewalt.* Munich: R. Oldenbourg, 2007.
Hitchins, Keith. *Rumania, 1866–1947.* Oxford: Oxford University Press, 1994.
Iancu, Carol. *Evreii din România, 1866–1919: De la excludere la emancipare.* 2nd ed. Bucharest: Editura Hasefer, 2006.
Ioanid, Radu. *The Holocaust in Romania: The Destruction of the Jews and Gypsies under the Antonescu Regime, 1940–1944.* Chicago: Ivan R. Dee, 2000.
———. *The Iași Pogrom, June–July 1941: A Photo Documentary from the Holocaust in Romania.* Bloomington: Indiana University Press, 2017.
Ionescu, Ștefan Cristian. *Jewish Resistance to "Romanianization," 1940–1944.* London: Palgrave Macmillan, 2015.
Maier, Dieter. *Arbeitseinsatz und Deportation: Die Mitwirkung der Arbeitsverwaltung bei der nationalsozialistischen Judenverfolgung in den Jahren 1938–1945.* Berlin: Edition Hentrich, 1994.
Megargee, Geoffrey P., Joseph R. White, and Mel Hecker, eds. *The United States Holocaust Memorial Museum Encyclopedia of Camps and Ghettos.* Vol. 3. Bloomington: Indiana University Press, 2018.
Rozett, Robert. *Conscripted Slaves: Hungarian Jewish Forced Laborers on the Eastern Front.* Jerusalem: Yad Vashem, 2014.
Sachar, Howard M. *Israel and Europe: An Appraisal in History.* New York: Alfred A. Knopf, 1999.
Shapiro, Paul. *The Kishinev Ghetto, 1941–1942: A Documentary History of the Holocaust in Romania's Contested Borderlands.* Tuscaloosa: University of Alabama Press, 2015.
Solonari, Vladimir. "A Conspiracy to Murder: Explaining the Dynamics of Romanian 'Policy' towards Jews in Transnistria." *Journal of Genocide Research* 19, no. 1 (2017).
———. *Purifying the Nation: Population Exchange and Ethnic Cleansing in Nazi-Allied Romania.* Baltimore: Johns Hopkins University Press, 2009.
Stout, Jay A. *Fortress Ploesti: The Campaign to Destroy Hitler's Oil.* Philadelphia: Casemate Publishers, 2003.

Index

Abrud, 112
Acmecetca concentration camp, 53, 128
Adjud, 93, 139
Aerial Regiment III, 135
Alexandrovca concentration camp, 89–90
Alexianu, Gheorghe, 72, 147
All for the Fatherland Party, 13
Altmann, Endre, 42, 45
Ananiev, 128
Angelescu, T. V., 120
Antonescu, Ion: 26, 28, 30, 38, 40, 41, 47–49, 52, 58, 62, 64, 67, 68, 69, 70, 79, 84, 86, 88, 102, 107, 114, 115, 117, 120, 126, 137, 138; execution of, 147; government of, 1, 7, 20, 43, 45, 47, 85, 93, 95, 129, 133, 134, 144–146; ideology of, 29, 34; Jewish policy of, 4–8, 11, 17–19, 22, 24, 27, 53, 64, 72, 75–76, 87, 90–92, 94, 100–101, 105, 106, 127–128, 151–153, 155; rise to power of, 16–17
Antonescu, Maria, 79, 84, 86
Antonescu, Mihai, 6, 28, 33, 47–48, 84, 86, 91–94, 96, 145, 147
APACA (Atelierul Publice Autonome de Confecții de Armatei), 134
Apostolide (Captain), 85
Arad, 42, 81, 92, 121, 124, 125, 128, 138
Arad County, 91, 120
Arad-Pecica canal, 121
Ardeleanu, Constantin, 103
Arhip, Ion, 77
Association of Christian Students, 59
Auschwitz concentration camp, 4
Averescu, Alexandru, 17

Bacău, 103, 117, 121, 139
Baia, 81, 135, 139
Bălan, Nicolae, 92
Baldovinești, 137
Balta, 76
Balta-Rădulești, 121

Bălți, 66, 114, 115, 133
Banila, 52
Bârlad, 79, 137, 139
Bercovici, Bica, 41, 60–61, 148
Bercu, Matilda, 135
Belzec extermination camp, 6, 91, 93
Benvenisti, Mișu, 92, 126
Berezeni-Falciu, 117, 139
Bergher, Arcadie Andrei, 127
Berlin, 3, 91, 93
Bicaz, 139
Bodnăraș, Emil, 145, 147
Bogdanovca concentration camp, 53, 89–90, 128
Boldur-Lățescu, Ion, 142
Botoșani, 120, 128, 133, 136, 139–140. *See also* Uman-Botoșani Offensive
Brăila, 141, 147
Brăila County, 120
Brăileanu, Ilie, 144
Brașov, 61, 80
Brătianu, Dinu, 13, 145
Brociner, Haskal, 41, 43, 64
Bron, Natan, 66–67, 78, 141
Bucharest, 6, 27, 36, 37, 41, 45, 53, 64, 66, 69, 75, 102, 126, 133, 147, 148; deportations from, 88–90, 128; forced labor in, 23, 32, 35, 46–47, 61, 63, 67, 79, 81–82, 127, 134–135, 137, 145; pogrom, 20, 53
Budu, Constantin, 111–113
Bumbești, 38
Burah, Diamant, 135
Busuioceanu, Mircea, 83–84

CFR (Căile Ferate Române), 35, 58, 66, 71, 93, 135; labor detachments of, 32, 33, 37–38, 41, 42, 44–45, 46, 65, 67, 76, 77–78, 80, 81, 82, 103, 110–113, 116, 117, 118, 119
Călărași internment camp, 28–29, 61
Călărași-Lăpușna, 114–115

161

Călinescu, Armand, 13
Călinești, 83
Câmpina, 134
Cânepiști, 44
Caracal internment camp, 29
Caragea, Viorel, 63
Caransebeș, 111
Carol II, 12–14, 16–17, 18
Carp, Matatias, 89
Cartianu, Gheorghe, 40
Central Commission for the Review of the Jews, 63–65, 67, 70, 77, 84–85, 109
Central Jewish Office, 64, 70, 84–86, 92, 109, 126–127, 144, 147
Central Romanianization Office, 63, 84, 109
Cerbu, Iulius, 103–104
Cernăuți, 22, 52, 104, 128, 136
CFR Detachment 12, 78, 80, 85
CFR Detachment 16, 80
CFR Detachment 17, 78
CFR Detachment 18, 78
CFR Detachment 49, 111–113, 118
CFR Detachment 58, 46
CFR Detachment 59, 46
CFR Detachment 66, 42
CFR Detachment 106/107, 111–113, 118
Chamber of Commerce, 36, 63
Chamber of Labor, 36, 37, 63, 104, 105
Chernivtsi. See Cernăuți
Chiriac (Lieutenant), 123
Chirinaco, 128
Chișinău, 22, 52, 66, 114; Iași-Chișinău Offensives, 133, 136–137, 143, 145
Cincu, Dumitru, 124
Ciobănița internment camp, 30
Ciudei, 52
Ciușlea, 121, 142
Clinceanu, Constantin, 148
Cocrasca, 128
Codreanu, Corneliu Zelea, 12, 13, 16, 17
Codrescu (Sergeant), 148
Cohen, Baruch, 43
Command of the Eastern Areas, 102
Communist Party of Romania, 145
Constanța, 30–31, 46, 141
Corbu, 121
Cornești, 86, 114

Costin, Paul, 45
Cotroceni, 23, 32, 35, 43, 76, 79, 114, 135
Cotu Lung, 120, 121
Council of Ministers, 8, 17, 18, 33, 35, 47, 68, 80, 86, 93, 94, 109, 147
Council of Patronage, 79, 84, 86
Covaliovca, 128
Craiova, 45, 61; Treaty of, 19
Craiova internment camp, 29
Crant (Ministry of Labor official), 63
Cristea, Miron, 13
Criștian, Nicolae, 105
Cuza, Alexandru C., 5, 11–13, 17–18, 59
Czernowitz. See Cernăuți

Dadilov labor camp, 41, 43
Dâmbovița Gendarmerie Legion, 40
David, Rita, 83
Davidescu, Radu, 48, 67, 107
Dealul Spirei, 82
Detachment 1016, 137
Deva, 41, 138
Diaconescu, Teodor, 78, 80
Doaga, 121, 123, 142, 144
Doaga labor camp, 23, 26, 27, 29, 41, 148
Dolj internment camp, 34
Domanovca concentration camp, 53, 90, 128
Domnești, 142
Dorohoi, 136
Dragalina-Tutova, 117, 139
Duca, Ion, 12
Dudești, 42
Dulfu (engineer), 63, 84
Dumitrescu, Ilie, 85
Dumitrescu, Nicolae, 139

Edineți, 52
Eichmann, Adolf, 91–93
Einsatzgruppe D, 22, 52
Elefterescu, Mircea, 148
exemptions from forced labor, 37, 45, 47, 50, 51, 53, 77, 83–86, 88, 92, 103, 104, 106, 109, 126, 135, 144–145; bribery to obtain, 1, 33, 64, 67, 84, 152; medical, 76, 107, 108, 138; review of, 59, 62–63, 65, 70, 75, 137
external labor detachments, 23, 31–32, 35, 67, 70–71, 78, 90, 96, 101–103, 105–106, 136,

146; conditions in, 40, 110–126, 139–143; corporal punishment in, 77; desertion from, 81; exemption from, 41

Făgăraş, 41, 42
Falciu, 138, 139
Făleşti, 115, 116, 118, 119
Fălticeni, 122
Farkas, William, 1, 41, 103
Feig, Allen, 41
Fifth Pioneers Regiment, 27, 120
Fifth Territorial Command, 67
Filaret, 82
Filderman, Wilhelm, 12, 17, 31, 64, 85, 92, 100, 126, 147
Final Solution, 2–3, 5, 6–7, 8, 53, 75, 90–93, 151
Floreanu, Marcel, 79
Floreşti-Soroca, 85
Focşani, 78, 118, 120, 144
Fourth Army Command, 135, 136, 138, 139, 140, 143
Fourth Pioneers Regiment, 120
Fourth Territorial Command, 77, 80, 104
Fraţescu, Vasile, 79
Froimescu, Efraim, 92

Gagiu, Mircea, 140
Gai-Ier Canal, 122
Galantar, Bernard, 103
Galaţi, 103, 119, 120, 121
Garibaldi (Second Lieutenant), 144
Gaz Metan, 103
General Directorate of Police, 83
General Directorate of Roads, 32, 35, 65, 114
General Headquarters, 8, 30, 32, 43–44, 47, 49–50
General Inspectorate of Labor Camps and Detachments, 50, 58–60, 65, 69, 70, 83, 84
General Instructions for the Use of Forced Labor (1942), 69–70, 72, 75, 76, 77, 78, 79, 82, 96, 100, 116, 119, 128, 138
General Instructions on the Application of the Regulations on the Law on the Military Status of the Jews (1941), 34–35, 59, 66
General Staff, 17, 20, 22, 26–27, 32, 33, 35, 37–38, 39, 40, 41–42, 45, 47, 48, 49, 53, 58,

62, 63–64, 65, 66, 68, 70, 71, 72, 75, 79, 80, 81, 83, 89, 100, 101–103, 104, 105, 106, 107, 108–109, 110, 112, 114, 118, 119, 122, 123, 124, 126, 127, 128, 129, 133, 135, 138, 141, 143, 144, 147, 152–153, 154, 155; Jewish Office of, 85, 86, 95, 138, 142; orders of, 8, 34, 36, 50–51, 59, 67, 69, 76–77, 78, 82, 88, 90, 120, 121, 134, 136, 140, 146; Recruitment Office of, 46, 146
Georgian (Lieutenant), 142
Gerbel, Fred, 33
German Eighth Army, 133, 145
German Eleventh Army, 22, 52
German forced labor system, 2–3, 49, 155
German Fourth Panzer Army, 94
German Military Mission (Deutsche Heeresmission), 47
German Sixth Army, 94–95, 145
Gestapo, 62
Ghelerter, Isaac, 118
Ghidighici quarry, 66–67, 78, 80, 115, 116, 117, 141
Gigurtu, Ion, 14, 16
Gingold, Nandor, 64, 85, 92
Giurgiu, 41
Giurgiu internment camp, 29, 38, 54n20
Glogojeanu, Ioan, 53
Goga, Octavian, 5, 12–13, 17
Goldberger, Max, 43, 79
Goldfain, Bercu, 61
Goldstein, Artur, 138
Golta, 89, 128
Göring, Hermann, 2
Grigorovici, Ion, 123–124, 126
Grinăuţi, 115, 116, 118, 119
Grisaru, Solomon, 135
Grumberg, Isidor, 148

Haimovici, Uşer, 83
Hârşova, 141
Haţeg, 79
Heleştieni-Valea Humăriei, 122, 123
Herscovici, Leon, 45, 81
Herşcu, Butun, 135
Heydrich, Reinhard, 3
Himmler, Heinrich, 2–3, 65
Hitler, Adolf, 5, 14, 16, 18, 22, 52, 93
Hunedoara, 138

Hunedoara County, 39
Hungarian labor service system, 3–4, 101, 102, 151, 153, 155
Hungarian Second Army, 4, 95, 101
Huşi, 66, 137, 141

Iacobici, Iosif, 21, 33
Ialomiţa internment camp, 29, 34, 38
Iaşi, 11, 29, 59, 66, 69, 80, 104, 107, 114, 115, 128, 133, 134, 136, 138, 139, 140, 147; Iaşi-Chişinău Offensives, 133, 136–137, 143, 145; pogrom, 28, 53, 61; University of, 87
Iaşi County, 141
Imberg, Iancu, 148
internment camps, 26, 27, 28, 29–31, 34, 38–40, 45, 46, 51, 148
Ionescu, Augustin, 30
Ionescu, Nicolae, 79–80
Iosipovici, Iosip, 135
Iron Guard, 12, 13, 16, 17–18, 26, 27, 44, 60; rebellion, 20

Jewish Labor Detachment 100, 120–121, 124–126, 142
Jewish Labor Detachment 101, 120–123, 126, 142
Jewish Labor Detachment 102, 81, 120–121, 123–126, 138, 142–143
Jewish Labor Detachment 103, 120, 122–124, 126, 142
Jewish Labor Detachment 104, 120, 122–126, 142
Jewish Statute, 14–16, 18, 19

Kaner, Nathan, 138
Killinger, Manfred Freiherr von, 91, 94
Kishinev. *See* Chişinău
Konev, Ivan, 133
Krüger, Friedrich-Wilhelm, 3
Kunţ, Mateiu, 111
Kursk, Battle of, 95

Labor Battalion 120, 76, 102, 128–129, 148
Labor Battalion 1017, 139
Latinu-Vădeni, 42
Law No. 59, 102–103, 106, 113

Law on the Military Status of the Jews (Decree-Law No. 3984), 11, 16, 19–21, 23, 26, 27, 32, 35, 146, 151
Lazăr, Lazăr D., 139
Lecca, Radu, 58, 62–65, 67, 70, 83–85, 86, 91, 92, 93, 101, 109, 126, 152–153
Legion of the Archangel Michael. *See* Iron Guard
Leiba, Iancu, 140
Leizerovici, Haim, 44, 66, 83, 86
Lipner, Pinchas, 79, 80
Livezeni, 38
local labor detachments, 23, 31, 32, 35, 40, 68, 70, 71, 77, 79, 81–83, 95, 101–102, 104, 106, 107, 110, 134, 136, 146
London, 17
Luftwaffe, 19
Lugoj, 27
Lugoj internment camp, 29
Lupovici, Aurel, 42, 67
Lupu, Herşcu, 79
Lupu, Szabo, 83
Lwów (L'viv) Ghetto, 93

Maciu quarry company 5/7, 139–140
Mădârjac, Alex, 83
Maniu, Iuliu, 13, 92, 126, 145
Margulius, David, 106–107
Marinescu, Ion, 47
Marinescu, Nicolae, 63
Matca, 122, 124–125
Mauthausen, 4
Mazarini, Nicolae, 38
Mehedinţi, 44
Mereni internment camp, 30
Mihai I, 16, 145
Mihailovici (officer), 67
Military Cabinet, 48, 67–69, 76
Ministry of Agriculture, 32, 76
Ministry of Culture, 87
Ministry of Finance, 19, 21, 34, 62, 63
Ministry of Industry and Commerce, 63
Ministry of Internal Affairs, 26, 27, 29, 32, 34, 39, 45, 51, 64, 152; Directorate of Public Order of, 136
Ministry of Justice, 109

Ministry of Labor, 18, 22, 34–37, 50, 51, 58, 63, 70, 109, 152
Ministry of National Defense, 15, 18–19, 47, 65, 86, 107, 109, 122; Fortifications Service of, 120, 122
Ministry of Public Works and Communications, 35, 120–121, 122
Ministry of the National Economy, 34–35, 36, 37, 62, 109
Mintia labor camp, 39
Mociulschi, Theodor, 59, 63, 84
Moghilev, 128
Moise, Marcel, 44
Moldoveanu, Ştefan, 148
Moscu, Nachmias, 144
Moţca-Soci, 122
Mucichescu, Tunari, 83

Nămaloasa, 123, 142
National Agrarian Party, 12
National Christian Defense League, 12
National Christian Party, 13
National Christian Union, 12
National Labor Council, 22
National Legionary State, 16–18, 60, 62
National Liberal Party, 12–13, 145
National Peasant Party, 12–13, 92, 145
Neamţ County, 32, 67
Nedeleanu, Louis Beno, 44, 82–83
Nicolaescu, Ioan, 123
Noua Suliţă, 52
Nuremberg Laws, 14

Oberquartiermeister Rumänien, 46
Oceacov concentration camp, 72
Odessa, 53, 89
Ohlendorf, Otto, 52
Olaru (soldier), 83
Olteanu (Sergeant), 111
Olteniţei Garden, 82
Orăşeni, 93
Orezeanu, T. C., 42, 65, 93
Orhei, 111
Osmancea internment camp, 30–31
Ostbahn, 93
Ostrogozhsk, 4, 95, 101

Palty, Sonia, 89–90, 128
Panaitescu, Traian, 33, 77–78, 80
Pantazi, Constantin, 33, 35
Paris, 17
Pârliţa-Ungheni, 114–119
Paşcani, 33, 81, 120
Pătrăşcanu, Lucreţiu, 145
Păuliş-Suraia, 142–143, 145
Păuliş-Utviniş canal, 122
Paulus, Friedrich, 95
People's Party, 17
People's Tribunals, 147–148
Petrescu, Titel, 145
Petrovici, Ion, 87
Piatra Neamţ, 139
Pipera, 135
Ploieşti, 19, 27, 30, 31, 77, 80, 134
Podu Iloaiei, 28–29, 133
Popescu, Eugen, 51–52, 94
Popescu, Gheorghe, 83–84
Popescu, Ion "Jack," 30
Prahova County, 27, 30, 31
Predeal, 107
Prezan, Constantin, 16–17
Pulca (lawyer), 64
Putna, 115, 117
Putna County, 138

Racoviţă, Ioan Mihail, 146
Rădescu, Nicolae, 146
railroad construction detachments. *See* CFR
Râmnicu Vâlcea, 83
Rath, M., 31
Rauch, Aristide, 28
Red Army, 4, 66, 95, 100–101, 117, 129, 133–134, 136, 141, 145, 146
Reich Labor Office, 2
Reich Main Security Office, 53, 90
Richter, Gustav, 6, 53, 90–91, 92–93
Reşiţa, 111
Reven, Strul, 135
Ribbentrop, Joachim von, 93
road construction detachments. *See* General Directorate of Roads
Roads Battalion 1, 79–80, 106–107, 139, 141
Roads Battalion 2, 139, 141

Roads Battalion 3, 78, 80, 85, 114–119, 136, 139–140
Roads Battalion 4, 139, 141
Roads Battalion 5, 139
Roads Battalion 6, 140, 144
Roads Battalion 8, 83, 85, 136, 139, 141
Roceric, Ioan, 63
Roman, 114, 117, 122, 128, 136, 139–140
Romanați internment camp, 29, 34
Romanian army, 8, 84, 94–95, 105, 145
Romanian Fourth Army, 22, 52, 94–95, 145
Romanian Gendarmerie, 52, 147
Romanianization, 5, 7, 11–12, 13, 14, 17–18, 20, 47, 87, 88, 101, 127, 151, 153
Romanian Orthodox Church, 92
Romanian Third Army, 22, 94–95, 145
Roșcovan (doctor), 66
Rosenfeld, Paul, 41
Rotenberg, Iosif, 103

Sächter, Solomon, 103
Șafran, Alexandru, 85, 92, 126
Sănătescu, Constantin, 133, 145
Sânpaul, 122
Schindler, Oskar, 2
Schottek, Martin, 42, 81
Schwab, Hugo, 77
Schwefelberg, Arnold, 92
Scobâlțeni, 29
Sculeni, 52
Sebastian, Mihail, 27, 61
Second Pioneers Brigade, 123
Second Territorial Command, 83, 105
Second Ukrainian Front, 133, 145
Secureni, 89
Segal, Carol, 80
Senior War College, 46
Serbanești-Bacău, 140
Seventh Pioneers Regiment, 120, 125
Severin County, 111
Sibiu, 42
Sighișoara, 41
Siguranța. *See* Special Intelligence Service
Sima, Horia, 16–17
Simca, Solomon, 31
Simileasca-Buzău, 141

Sipoteni, 115
Siria, 120
Slivina concentration camp, 72, 128
Sloim, David, 135
Smilovici, Iosub, 135
Sniatyn, 93
Social Democratic Party, 145
Soviet Fifth Tank Army, 94
Soviet Fifty-First Army, 94
Soviet prisoners of war, 28, 41, 111, 114
Soviet Sixty-Fifth Army, 94
Soviet Twenty-First Army, 94
Soviet Twenty-Seventh Army, 145
Spânu, Radu, 78, 114, 117–119, 139–140
Special Intelligence Service, 28, 62
SS, 2, 3
Stalingrad, 4, 94–95, 113; Battle of, 95
Stănescu, Marin, 27
Ștefanescu (Major), 144
Șteflea, Ilie, 63–64, 68, 83–84
Stoenescu, Nicolae, 33, 48
Storojineț, 52
Storper, Arthur, 47
Straja-Neamț, 139
Strunga-Găureana, 122, 123
Suceava, 127
Suldanești, 66
Sulimovici, Lazar, 31
Supreme General Headquarters. *See* General Headquarters
Supreme General Staff. *See* General Staff

Târgoviște, 27, 40, 134
Târgu Frumos, 133, 139
Târgu Jiu internment camp, 26, 27–28, 29, 34, 38, 49, 148
Târgu Neamț, 89, 120, 122
Tătărescu, Gheorghe, 12, 14
Tecuci, 137, 139
Teiș-Târgoviște internment camp, 30, 31, 34, 40, 46
Theodoru, Mihail, 45, 61
Third Ukrainian Front, 145
Tifești quarry, 121
Timișești-Păstrăveni, 122
Timișoara, 92, 105, 111, 127

Timiș-Torontal County, 91, 111
Timișul de Sud, 142
Tiraspol, 89, 135
Toma, Constantin, 140
Tomașuiu (Captain), 42
Transnistria Governorate, 7, 53, 147; camps and ghettos in, 85, 96n4; deportations to, 6, 68–69, 72, 75–77, 88–91, 93–95, 100, 101, 102, 107, 126, 155; massacres in, 52, 151; repatriations from, 128–129, 135–136, 143
Trepaduș (Lieutenant), 38, 148
Țucărman, Iancu, 29
Tudor Mușetescu Theater, 46
Tulcea County, 144
Turcoaia, 144
Turda, 41, 42, 92, 113, 145
Turda County, 91
Turnu Severin internment camp, 29

Uman-Botoșani Offensive, 136
Union of Romanian Jews, 12
Urziceni, 79

Valea Homorodului, 80, 82, 85, 103
Valea Ozanei, 123–124
Vârciorog, 44
Vasiliu, Constantin "Piki," 52, 147
Vaslui, 137, 148
Vinnytsia, 93
Vitcu (Colonel), 81
Vlașca internment camp, 34, 54n20
Voinea, Andrei, 44, 111–113, 142–143, 145, 146
Voinești, 120, 121, 142
Volansk, Iosef, 135
Vulcănescu, Mircea, 48–49

Wainstein, Froica, 89
Water Service, 120
Wehrmacht, 2–3, 19, 46–47
Weinberger, Janos, 147

Zamfirescu (engineer), 83
Zamfirescu, Gheorghe, 107, 147
Zisserman, Victor, 46
Zlătescu, Gheorghe, 29

DALLAS MICHELBACHER is an Applied Researcher at the United States Holocaust Memorial Museum in Washington, DC.

www.ingramcontent.com/pod-product-compliance
Lightning Source LLC
Chambersburg PA
CBHW020416230426
43663CB00007BA/1187